AMERICAN
TIME BOMB

AMERICAN TIME BOMB

ATTICA, SAM MELVILLE, AND A SON'S SEARCH FOR ANSWERS

JOSHUA MELVILLE

CHICAGO
REVIEW
PRESS

Published by Chicago Review Press Incorporated
814 North Franklin Street
Chicago, Illinois 60610
ISBN 978-1-64160-545-8

Library of Congress Control Number: 2021940061

Typesetting: Nord Compo

Printed in the United States of America
5 4 3 2 1

Virtually all of existence in amerika today is a political confrontation.

—Sam Melville, January 20, 1971

CONTENTS

Part I: Chrysalis

Part II: The State Is Our Enemy

Part III: Mother Right

Part IV: White Man's Rules

Author's Note

COMPOSITES
AND ALTERATIONS OF FACT

MY HIGH SCHOOL DRAMA TEACHER, Anthony Abeson, gave my class his definition of art:

> Art is a lie that tells the truth.

Everything you see in a movie, on a TV show, or on stage is fake. Oak doors that appear to be heavy are usually made of cardboard. The illusion of weight—the slam, the lock turning, the hinges squeaking—are all created by sound effects and the actions of characters crafted by gifted actors, writers, directors, and editors. Reality in virtually any medium is a lie. Yet, the good ones resonate. This is the lie that tells the truth.

I never fully appreciated what this meant before I started writing *American Time Bomb*. To tell my father's story, I spent many years collecting "facts." My father impressed upon people a sense of personal ownership of himself. As a result, most of his friends, coconspirators, and fellow inmates of Attica, whom I'd encountered, insisted they knew the "real Sam Melville." Upon further research, it turned out that each one had constructed a half history, often clinging to idolized or demonized versions of the man. The net result was that I had many facts but many more half-truths.

With my acquisition of thousands of FBI documents and court transcripts and my personal archive of interviews with movement organizers, I have attempted to synthesize everyone's truth into one cohesive re-creation of an extremely dualistic man, the historic events in which he played a key role, and the truth about his alleged murder.

Most dialogue in this work was invented but inspired by my notes and taped conversations, established facts, and previous oral histories. On occasion, to fill in gaps and make the story more accessible, I added a few speculative scenes I believe occurred based on known facts. Some will argue that this version of events is my *half-truth*. And this would be fair. To maintain transparency and to help readers who wish to go deeper and develop their own truths, the endnotes document the sources for the dialogue and facts.

For the few sources still alive, I fact-checked with each one who agreed to be a part of my process. To help readers, in the backmatter I have included a list of named figures and the many acronyms of political groups. Supporting court transcripts and referenced FBI reports are published with redactions on the Archives tab at www.AmericanTimeBomb.com.

Some characters are composites of more than one individual and are identified by fictional names set in SMALL CAPS on first mention. A more detailed breakdown will follow here.

I will start with the character of "Diane Eisner"; she is an amalgam of two real women with whom my father was involved after he and my mother split up. This character corresponds somewhat to the fictionalized character also called Diane in Jane Alpert's memoir *Growing Up Underground*.

"Gilbert Bernstein," and "Lester Barns," are altered names for two East Village activists who became my father's collaborators. They were never charged with the crimes depicted herein, so I have substantially altered their personas as well as their names.

"Ivan Lopez," another of my father's collaborators, is a composite inspired by the two anonymized characters "Bobo" and "Roberto" in *Growing Up Underground*, and a Puerto Rican radical, Carlos Feliciano, whom my father knew in prison and whom the FBI connected to bombings credited to Movimiento Independentista Revolucionario en Armas (Armed Revolutionary Independence Movement), or MIRA.

Regarding H. Rap Brown, although I discussed his actions as depicted herein with people who are close to Mr. Brown, I could not interview him directly, because he is serving life in a supermax facility. Therefore, I am obliged to disclose that actions allegedly taken by Brown, including implications of connections to bombings in Wisconsin and Chicago, are based on allegations from memoirs and oral histories of others and events alleged in FBI reports.

On the law enforcement side, the actions of Special Agent "Joe Anderson" composites actions performed by several real-life FBI agents who worked my father's case, including John Robinson and the well-known agents known as "the three Joes"—Joe Sullivan, Joe Corless, and Joseph MacFarlane—as well as agents Terry Roberts and George Twaddle.

Wesley Swearingen is the real-life FBI bomb expert who initially profiled my father. However, I time-shifted our conversations and composited some of them with material from an agent I identify as "Henry Byers," my father's interrogator, whom I spoke with in 2015, and another FBI source who requested to remain anonymous.

Finally, Ed Cunningham in part IV is a real Attica guard, but his role composites several guards who were taken as hostages during the four-day event that has been called the bloodiest confrontation between Americans since the Civil War.

Regarding Attica inmate leaders themselves, most every past book or movie about Attica avoided specifying which inmates led the uprising and what they did. And so fifty years' worth of dramatic recreations, oral histories, and documentaries have scant mention of incriminating felonies performed by the inmate leaders, like making about three hundred Molotov cocktails and a rocket launcher (attributed to my father), electrifying the blockades, digging the L-shaped trench visible in many Attica photos, inmates murdering several other inmates, and finally forcing hostages onto the open roof at knifepoint, a threat that ended the negotiations and triggered the assault. In my view, it is debatable, after this much time, as to whether these obfuscations were worth compromising accuracy or the lives lost, by both prisoners and guards, in protest of mass incarceration.

History should pardon past authors and filmmakers. They have kept Attica relevant and rendered the pursuit of objective facts an ongoing one. In their defense, most every inmate leader had died by the time most of their projects began. By contrast, I spoke with Attica leaders themselves during my weeklong visit in 1991—specifically, Herb Blyden, Frank Smith, Akil Al-Jundi, Jomo Omowale, and Jerry Rosenberg. They and other participants felt they owed the son of the man who helped define their place in history a more complete vision of Attica than the sanitized one they swore to under oath. To honor their sacrifice, I felt it important to be honest about their contributions as well as my father's, whether they were noble, justified, or sometimes quite shortsighted.

It has been decades since my father attacked his government. Why should anyone care today? In 1968, the election of President Nixon sparked a violent polarization of right and left. Within two years, the counterculture's steeping anger inspired my father and other educated pacifists to destroy buildings and ravage prisons for the next decade. The obvious parallels to the recent rise of right-wing populism and the reactions by so-called antifa factions awakened me to the notion that my father's story, as well as my investigation of his life and death, might offer today's activists a long-view perspective on our culture's near-term future.

So I would like to thank every reader for taking an interest in my journey. I hope it brings resolution, if even in some small way, to those whose parents, siblings, and friends chose revolution over Little League. To that end, please keep in mind that *American Time Bomb* is a candid look at people on both sides of the law, all viewing the world through complex moral prisms. There are no clear heroes in these pages.

Including me.

PREFACE

ON THE MORNING OF SEPTEMBER 20, 1971, radical defense attorney William Kunstler had a difficult choice. That day there would be almost two dozen funerals for inmates of Attica killed during the assault to take back the prison. Kunstler, whose name had been in the *New York Times* nearly every day for representing the inmates, could deliver a eulogy for only one. He chose my father, Sam Melville.

Days earlier, members of the Weather Underground, incensed by what they felt was my father's state-sanctioned murder, had set off a bomb in the office of the New York prison commissioner. Rumors spread that their next action would be to steal my father's remains and burn them on Governor Rockefeller's lawn. To prevent this, on the day of his memorial, a van carrying a battalion of Black Panthers pulled up to the small church in the East Village. At the request of my mother, militant organizers coordinated an effort to have Panthers guard my father's body. The request met with little resistance. No one in their community needed reminding that my father was something of a modern-day abolitionist; like John Brown, he was a White man who crossed the ethnic divide to help forge the most effective "slave revolt" in modern US history. Authorities must have agreed; while the names of Attica victims were being withheld for weeks, Rockefeller's proxies told the *Times* on the same day of the retaking that "Mad Bomber Melville" was no longer a threat to the good people of New York. All these events would inspire civil rights icon Martin Sostre to write, "Sam Melville was the only real political prisoner at Attica."

As a child, however, I knew none of this.

For almost two years following my father's death, I'd been under the impression that he was simply living "on a faraway reservation," doing volunteer work. That was the cover story he and my mother had agreed to tell me, which he represented faithfully when he wrote to me from prison. Almost two years after his death, when I was eleven, Mom showed me his picture plastered across the front page of the *New York Times*. It was then I learned that the man I'd always called Dad was known to the rest of the world as the Mad Bomber, one of the most notorious domestic bombers of the twentieth century, and an engineer of over a dozen targeted attacks against racism and US imperialism in the summer of 1969. That day, Mom also showed me *Letters from Attica*, an anthology of his prison letters, posthumously published in 1972. Quotes from my father's letters had found their way into articles on Attica, books on the '60s, and even interpretive dance pieces.

I was angry and cried for much of that afternoon. I felt that my father had been stolen from me. Then I opened *Letters from Attica* and learned there were others who shared my grief. Activists, lawyers, and lovers. We were now a unique sort of family. I would spend the next twenty years connecting with some and learning everything I could about a man I called Dad but whom the general public knew only as a terrorist.

When I asked Mom why he had done these things, my mother downplayed his historical relevance, claiming that he was just another hippie caught up in the times. So I was puzzled over the decades as to why my father's name appeared in dozens of books and was sometimes central to entire chapters about the era. In 2010 one historian labeled him "the essential blueprint for every radical organization throughout the 1970s."

In my midtwenties, I began a mission to learn how the man who taught me to respect all life transformed into someone who would bomb skyscrapers. I discovered that beneath my father's politics, base emotions were at work: bitterness toward his parents, guilt for his abandonment of me, and the appeal of the free-spirited counterculture. This led me to ask several uncomfortable questions that this book addresses. Was my iconic father a *true believer* or a deadbeat dad who found a fashionable outlet for his rage? Can there be redemption for a movement that accepts violence as a rational solution, on any level? Was his death avoidable, were it not for law enforcement turning reasonable dissent into tragic confrontation?

At the crossroads between one urge to follow in his footsteps and another to settle down with a family of my own, I became like Hamlet, inventing conversations with my father's ghost. When his spirit would appear, I'd ask, "Was it worth giving up your son to change a world stuck in its ways? In my future, should I hold bombs or babies?"

This book is his reply.

This is how I imagine it.

He's crouched down, clutching a bottle bomb, arm cocked, waiting for the uniforms to become visible on the catwalks. But the bomb never leaves his hand.

As inmates run for cover, the odor of gunpowder, blood and agony spreading, a loud pop from the shotgun of a faceless policeman is the last thing he hears. He never sees the shooter. Doesn't know his name. He feels only a sharp pain in his chest. Then he is on his back, staring at the cold gray sky, feeling warmth soaking through his shirt.

Looking down from above, a boy appears. He barely recognizes me from old photos. Are you an angel, he might be thinking, or the devil come to take me?

We had only a few years together. Now, in death, we will have a great deal of catching up to do.

A bullet ends his life and begins our relationship.

—from my journal, age thirteen

Introduction

MY GIANT

"THE MORE YOU CAN DO WITHOUT, the freer you are," my father said to my pouting lips. He was consoling me about the queen I just lost in another of our taxing chess games. At age six, I'd seen how he applied this principle to every aspect of his minimalist life. What I could not know is that soon he would apply it to me, his only child.

To understand Sam Melville's fatalistic style of tough love, one must begin the story with my parents' courtship in 1958. When I interviewed their friends from the Bronx, they said that, aside from the cliché that opposites attract, few felt my mother and father would last beyond the infatuation stage. My mother, twenty-two-year-old Ruth Kalmus, was fetching and sharp. She held a degree in education and was eager to transcend the immigrant docility of her mother's "old country." She studied luxury homes in style magazines, planning to own one herself someday. My father, Sam Grossman (his original name) was twenty-four, a strapping six-foot-two, broad-shouldered maverick. His eyes of two different colors, one blue and one hazel green, projected his jaundiced view of American decadence. In place of higher education, he studied the dictionary.

Tiring of boorish suitors, my mother saw potential in the neighborhood politico who used a precise vocabulary and a Martin guitar to become a tastemaker to the "red-diaper babies" in their blue-collar quarter. These were the children of devout members of the Communist Party of the United States. In the spring of 1958, she devised a counterintuitive strategy to distract him from their neighborhood's Marxist minions. She began dressing more fashionably than the bohemian gals with whom Sam held court—more like a city girl, with

1

heavier makeup, and expressing conservative values that mocked his progressive ones—specifically, "I'm saving myself for marriage."

They wed within a year and moved across the river to the land that promised limestone finials: Manhattan's Upper West Side. My father cared less about its lavish buildings and more that the district had redefined itself as the cradle of counterculture. By 1960, the Jewish doctors and lawyers who pioneered the area in the 1930s had been replaced by artists and progressive teachers orbiting Columbia University.

My mother brought stability to their tiny one-bedroom on Eighty-First Street by teaching sixth-grade English at a Harlem public school. With her eye ever upward, she carried business cards promoting herself as an interior decorator. She attracted only the occasional client, and my father would smile endearingly at her "bourgeois hobby."

Sam's dream was to become an outspoken Marxist orchestral conductor. He worked the classical section at Sam Goody record store and took courses in music theory, guitar, and voice at City College. After class, he planted

Ruth, 1967. *Author's collection*

roots in multiple chess clubs, dank storefronts crowded with (mostly Russian) deep thinkers who believed the way your opponent played the game revealed more about a man than he could tell you himself. Nights were spent in Riverside Park, where he shot hoops on courts controlled by "the Negroes." His skills earned him an early pick, but what earned him their respect was his readiness to confront racist, harassing cops as he defended their right to play after sunset.

Mom was charmed by his romantic approach to life, his intellect, his masculine courage, and accepted these as a compromise to the fact that her husband was not an "earner." Rather than pricey bungalows in the Catskills, their summer weekends were spent camping on the Appalachian Trail with Sam's Communist friends from the old neighborhood. The group's debates consumed as many hours as pipes and cigarettes, while my mother read in their tent, avoiding the bugs and bombast. She knew that when Sam was talked out he would serenade her by fingerpicking Bach on his Martin, followed by tender affection.

Life, at the dawn of Camelot, was good.

Sam and his pipe, carefree a year before fatherhood, 1961. *Author's collection*

In July 1961, my mother announced she was pregnant. Shortly thereafter, my father yielded to the first of what would become a series of existential changes. He said to her, "I guess I'd rather have my son think of me as a successful engineer than a starving musician."

In the weeks that followed, his guitar strings began to atrophy. He traded his conducting and choir classes for a three-month course in plumbing design at the Polytechnic Institute of Brooklyn. With his night-school degree in hand, he used his charisma to land an entry-level drafting position at the prominent engineering and design firm of Syska Hennessy. To a firm rife with Irish partners, the lone Jewish supervisor advocated that Sam was the perfect fit to interphase with the "European developers" renovating the Upper West Side. My father accepted his role.

From a corner pay phone, he called Mom with the good news. She, in turn, dialed her mother, giddy that her red-diaper rebel would now be a white-collar professional. Everything my mother knew about life taught her that this was right. However, an hour after Sam was supposed to be home, she stared at his dinner growing cold. "Sam had never been even five minutes late for anything," Mom claimed each time she told me this story. She called the people who knew Sam best.

By the time his old neighborhood friends schlepped from the Bronx, all three TV news channels carried a story about a bomb drill in Midtown. (Civil Defense alerts, to prep for a Soviet attack, were almost nonexistent by 1961, and, to the initiated, something of an amusing relic of the duck-and-cover days of the 1950s.) Sam's friends tried to calm my mother, surmising that Sam was in an air-raid shelter. "He'll be home when they give the all-clear sign," one said. But four hours later, she began to envision something more dire. When the phone finally rang, she grabbed the receiver in desperation. Her husband was in a holding cell.

Sometime after 10 PM, the front door swung open. "Did I miss the girl popping out of the cake?" Sam joked with a wide smile. My mother said nothing, which said everything. She stormed into the kitchen for a smoke while Sam faced his Bronx friends and sped past the minutiae of the job interview to focus on the part he knew they'd remained to hear: the arrest.

"As I left the building I came upon that ridiculous billboard for *My Fair Lady*, still bragging about its Tony awards from three years ago." (Their parents complained that Broadway had corrupted *Pygmalion* by reducing every innuendo of Marxism to a peppy dance number.) "Shaw must be turning in his grave," Sam said, and painted a picture of nine-to-fivers scurrying in a purposeful ballet toward the fallout plaque below the billboard. He pivoted from the crowds and started home. Half a block into his protest, he was stopped by uniforms putting up barricades. When they insisted he should proceed to a shelter, my father pushed back with sarcasm—"The Russians aren't really coming, y'know"—and was arrested.

The Bronx friends raised their glasses, and for a few moments Sam felt like the tastemaker he once was. But, after he said good night to his comrades, my mother brought him down to earth with a scowl. "It's not just *your* liberty you're risking anymore," she said, with one hand rubbing her bulging womb and the other flicking her cigarette.

Sam beamed at her tummy. "Still think it's a boy?"

"If it is, are you gonna take him to Party meetings with angry old men?"

My father was envisioning a son with whom he could bond over basketball and chess. "I promise," he reassured, enfolding his muscular arms around her. "This will be the last time you'll hear about my being in trouble."

Sam, Ruth, and Jocko, 1962. *Author's collection*

Two years into motherhood, routine would chip away at romance. Between nursing me, housework, and decorating their spacious new four-bedroom apartment on Ninety-First Street, my mother couldn't care less about Sam's physical demands or kowtowing to her pseudointellectual in-laws, who would appear in her living room every other month for a home-cooked dinner. Sam's father, Bill Grossman, was an officer in the Communist Labor Party. He talked incessantly about the scam of the two-party system that robbed the working man of a real choice. Helene, Bill's second wife, was a child, almost twenty years younger than Bill and only five years older than Ruth. She stuffed envelopes for the Party mailers and exhausted Mom with hot news of hip artists like Andy Warhol, forgetting that Ruth was a decorator and already quite familiar with them. One September night in 1963, tired of cooking, my mother ordered Chinese, with Sam's permission.

Bill entered their apartment with his requisite critique of my mother's choice of fire-engine red wall-to-wall carpeting. "Ruth . . . such extravagance."

"Yes, well, at least it's red," she replied, forcing a smile.

The next dig was of Sam's discerning purchase of the latest phonograph system with stereo sound. "Two speakers, to fill all two thousand square feet of this palace," Bill snarked. Sam thought about giving Bill a lesson in responsibility: *decadent* was what Party members call someone who prioritizes family over protests. Bill was an absentee father to Sam most weekends, organizing labor strikes. But Sam had sacrificed his dream of a music career for the stability and high pay offered by Syska Hennessy. His reward was the company assigning him its biggest job, the Lincoln Center renovation, which encompassed the Metropolitan Opera House and Avery Fisher Hall. He considered trying to impress his father by mentioning that the project would put him in daily contact with some of the city's most important architects. But he knew this would only lead to a debate on capitalism, and he had promised Ruth that tonight he would not debate. Instead he thanked Bill vapidly and spun (once again) the choice by explaining that the large apartment was affordable only through the socialist principle of rent control. But as Bill strolled past a closet where three-piece suits had replaced Sam's chinos, he flashed Sam a narrowed eye.

After dinner, while Mom and Helene stretched the baby fat of my cheeks, Bill signaled to Sam that they go to the study for their tradition of pipes and politics. Sam sprang from the table. He had so few opportunities for informed discourse these days. However, tonight, what Bill told my father deeply disturbed him.

When they emerged from the study, Sam was masking disdain with deep draws on the stem of his Meerschaum. He curtly ushered Bill and Helene out with a hasty good night and pressed his ear against the door, listening for the descent of the elevator. When its sound faded, he faced Ruth with a look of disgust. "I'm changing our name. I mean, like, tomorrow."

"Why? What happened?"

"Do you have a favorite?"

"How about *Melville*, after Herman Melville?" She was pleased to discard the immigrant branding of *Grossman*. She knew Sam would take to her suggestion too. Melville was the author of *Moby Dick*, deemed by many Marxists as the quintessential reproach to capitalism. The doomed whaling ship *Pequod* was a metaphor for the American factory system, its workers brought to their untimely deaths by Ahab, a mad captain of industry.

Of course, as Sam's friends from the Bronx pointed out, the book was also about the vengeance of an old sea dog bent against a powerful animal who'd maimed him in his youth—much as Sam's father had done to him.

Sam did not see the connection.

While the Syska office saw Sam's transition as a mere name change on his tax forms, Ruth's first sign of trouble was in the laundry. Sam had stopped wearing underwear. "It's a middle-class hang-up," he told her. To avoid her continued pressure to talk about his acting out due to his anger at Bill, Sam moved the radio to the study, where he could absorb political talk radio on WBAI, the noncommercial, listener-supported radio station. Its programming, largely a mixture of political news and opinion from a leftist perspective, became his companion while drafting plans for the upgrading of Brooklyn Borough Hall. It was understood that he was not to be disturbed.

Soon a cold draft began to replace their conversations. His withdrawal eventually sent my mother snooping through his study. *Maybe he's cheating*, she thought. What she found made her wish it were that simple: a folder wedged behind the daybed, hidden the way an alcoholic would hide a bottle. It was filled with many articles about Fidel Castro's recent revolution in Cuba, the

IRA's struggles in Ireland, and revolts in China and—of all places—Canada. Some French Canadian freedom fighters, called the FLQ (Front de libération du Québec), wanted Quebec to secede. They had set off bombs in the financial district. *Canadian terrorists?* she thought. *Canadians are so polite.* Ruth wondered how long it would be before Sam broke his word about staying out of trouble.

Confronting him was a nonstarter. He was coming home after his dinner was wrapped in foil and the cacophony of vacuum cleaners and an inquisitive three-year-old were dormant. He would walk through the apartment's many rooms, feeling their size and lamenting his overhead. Through the bedroom window, he could see his river view with New Jersey's lights sparkling on the black ripples of the Hudson. And the finale—Ruth, passed out in their bed, my tiny body nested into her armpit and a tawdry celebrity bio on her bosom: Brando, Monroe, and others, as if the decadent lives of Hollywood's depraved might have been my bedtime story.

Within days, my father began grooming me for better things. Starting with his favorite children's story, *The Emperor's New Clothes*, Dad would annotate the fairy tale with his own political subtext. Mom would comment from her armchair, "Do you really think Joshua understands that the naked emperor is a metaphor for President Johnson? He's only three."

Dad hated the name Joshua—and even more when Mom used it strategically. He had conceded to her insistence for the large apartment in the doorman building, the fancy furniture, and imported red carpet. His line in the sand was to call me not by the bougie biblical name she insisted upon but by his own agnostic moniker. "I prefer that Jocko understand the evils of government power, not what costar Marlon Brando slept with."

I loved it when he stood up for me and called me Jocko. He was my giant. When we walked the streets, my little legs couldn't keep up, so he'd put me on his shoulders. Seven feet above the ground, the wind would sweep across my smiling face. We never wore jackets, even in winter. To resist the cold was part of the fun. But Mom would frown when we returned. "He's going to catch cold." On weekends, he would present to me a heavy machine called a Wollensak, a reel-to-reel tape recorder with vacuum tubes. He would teach me a song, sometimes one he wrote just for me, and we would sing it in harmony, rehearsing over and over with him on guitar. Sometimes it was wrestling. Dad held my small body high in the air and then zoomed me toward the sprawling red carpet like a crashing airplane. Then he tumbled onto his back as if I'd pinned him in an intricate countermove. I would laugh, "Again, Daddy!"

He was a one-man amusement park, and I was the only one in line for the ride.

Until Mom interjected, "Why are you teaching him to be violent?"

"It's not violence to defend yourself."

"But you let him beat you. You're five times his size."

"I want Jocko to know that he should never be afraid, no matter how big the opponent. I want him to get used to winning and like the feel of it."

"One more, Daddy," I insisted, drawing him back to me, and I bellowed, "Religion is opium for the misses." And my giant raised me high above his head like a trophy. "Jocko may be drafted into Vietnam. Did you know that casualties have risen to thirteen hundred?"

Mom tipped her ash. The longest war of her generation, World War II, had lasted only seven years. "Do you really believe a skirmish in some third-world country will go on for over a decade?" How could she have known that Vietnam would go on for nearly twenty years, drafting tens of thousands of men, many of whom were under nineteen? She pressed, "Would you have made the same argument when we went into Germany in '42?"

"In '42, we were fighting fascism. Today, *we* are the fascists," he responded calmly. "Perhaps you should spend more time reading the news instead of gossip."

Soon Mom began to think that what seemed like a doting father might actually be a husband pulling away.

The next day, she summarized his dominance to two single girlfriends. They insisted, "Men are optional these days, Ruth. It sounds like you're just scared to be alone." And so, after days of contemplation, my mother made a choice that took considerable courage for a woman in 1965. She told Sam she was going to go back to work and asked him to leave the apartment.

"What about Jocko?"

"My mother will watch him during the day."

"Your mother will come from the Bronx every day to watch a three-year-old?"

"Yes. I'm not happy with what you're teaching him. And I think if I'm happier without you, Josh will be too."

She had spent days preparing for a debate, but instead, Sam rose quietly, packed a small gym bag, and glided out the door, no different than if he were stepping out for a carton of milk.

And with a whisper, their six-year marriage was over.

———————

Eight years later, the world had changed. Men had landed on the moon, America had ended its war with Vietnam, a president was being pressured to resign, and then came that Saturday.

On a spring morning of 1973, I was building a model starship *Enterprise*. My eleven-year-old dream was *to boldly go where no man had gone before.* Suddenly, Mom's scowling face poked through my door as if I were in trouble. But it felt different. "Come," she commanded.

I followed her into the living room with its Kandinsky prints and its sea of red carpet I had walked on since I could walk. She and Tim, my stepfather of recent years, were perched straight-backed on the sofa. She lit up a Marlboro. "Josh, this is about your father."

"You mean Sam?" I asked, since Tim was sitting right next to her.

"Yes, Sam. He's dead."

I wasn't sure I'd heard her correctly. "When?"

"A while now," she said, realizing that it had taken her almost two years to fulfill my school psychologist's recommendation that I be told *immediately*.

I blinked. "How?"

Mom nudged Tim with a mix of anger and sadness. He rose silently, like an obedient butler, left the room, and returned with an oversized black folder, placing it in front of me with no explanation. The dog-eared corners of yellowed newspapers peeked past its edges like a warlock's book of secrets. I lifted the cover, and my childhood ended.

THE BOMBINGS: EVIDENCE INDICATES IT'S ONE MAN

The 1969 *New York Post* headline screamed at me. I pulled out another clipping. This one was almost two years old, from September 1971.

MAD BOMBER MELVILLE KILLED AT ATTICA

It claimed my father was shot dead while throwing bombs at hostages in a prison uprising. There were dozens of clippings. Curated by Mom. Waiting for this day. "What is all this?" I asked, still dry-eyed. "I thought he was helping Indians on a reservation."

"There was a riot," Mom said. "A big riot in the prison where he was, and he was killed."

"Why was he in jail?"

She took a long drag on her cigarette and served the reduction she'd rehearsed all morning. "He was misled by crazed hippies who blew up buildings to protest the war."

This sounded familiar. Not that long ago, my school was evacuated. Teachers said it was for a fire drill, but the hip seniors whispered that it was because of the Weathermen, hippies who blew up buildings and police precincts to protest US participation in the Vietnam War. I looked at Dad's picture in the paper. He looked like a trapped animal. "Did anyone die?"

"No. No one was killed. He was careful. He only destroyed property."

That was a relief. I had also heard that many Weathermen were never arrested because they were hiding, in a cave, or underground, or something like that.

"How did they catch him?"

"He was betrayed by a friend—an undercover cop." She drew my attention to the photo next to my father's in the *New York Times*. It was of a goofy-looking man whose name I could not sound out: Demmerle. The paper said the informant had a young son about my age.

"Why didn't he just stay in his cell when the riot happened?" my cracking voice asked. Mom could see I was bargaining with the finality of it all. But her answer only made the image of his death worse. "He was dragged out of his cell. He didn't want to be in the riot."

Her responses started to sound similar:

He was misled by hippies.

He was betrayed by a friend.

He was dragged to his death.

Dad was always the victim.

Mom rose abruptly and addressed Tim: "Get the tape thing." He left the room, and Mom walked to the curio cabinet to remove a book. "You should see this too." She placed it in front of my growing pile of Dad's demise. There was a picture of him on the book's jacket, smiling and smoking a pipe. *This was the man I remembered.* But why was he on a book?

Letters from Attica anthologized his prison writings: letters to friends, essays about prison conditions, and his prison newsletter, the *Iced Pig*. There was a foreword by a famous lawyer whose name I recognized, even at age eleven: William Kunstler. He claimed to have delivered my father's eulogy at a funeral where Black Panthers guarded my father's body.

After the foreword was a profile of my father by the pretty accomplice whose picture was also in the papers next to his. Her name was Jane; Mom said she was his girlfriend. Jane dedicated her profile "For Jocko Melville." Only Dad called me Jocko. *Who the hell was she?* I tried to read her words, but they were confusing. So I skipped to the letters, but I didn't recognize any names of the people to whom his letters were addressed. *Would they now know me by Dad's private name?* Then a letter he had written to me from what I thought was the Indian reservation caught my breath. The entire thing, right in this book.

> *April 15, 1970*
> *Jocko,*
> *By the time you read this you will be 8 years old.*
> *That's getting pretty close to being a young man already. I'm sorry I can't send you a present from here but they don't have anything suitable for you. I hope you will consider the gift from Mommy as being from me too—unless it's one of those new pollution toys that give off smoke or something. In that case I don't want any part of it.*

I flipped through the pages and found another:

> *June 24, 1970*
> *Dear Jocko,*
> *In your last letter you asked what kind of job I have. Well, I am a temporarily retired social reformer. If you don't understand that perhaps Mommy can tell you, but she is not a specialist, you must remember, and she might explain it differently than I would. Until recently I was part of a demolition company but we went out of business. In the immediate future I think I'll be making license plates just to get some ready cash and perhaps some useful experience.*

I remembered this letter and how it seemed like an odd answer to my question. Now I saw that my father was trying to be funny. Was this a laughing matter, or did he know I would eventually see the irony? Maybe Dad was trying to teach me that humor is the best way of dealing with pain.

Then, toward the back, I found our last communication.

March 18, 1971

My Jocko,

I know it's been a long time since I wrote and I have certainly neglected you. But I do not like to write letters. I have to work very hard at relating to your life now. The small boy I remember is not you anymore—nor am I the same person I once was. Your mother tells me beautiful things about you and what you are doing and I am very glad and happy for you. But to participate so remotely in your life is not easy.

Really, to think of you, I want to be with you and part of your existence—share your experiences, and see you grow and change. That's the only real excitement and meaning between people no matter if they are father and son or whatever. I read your mother's words and wonder is she just saying things that don't have a reality—it's hard to imagine you thinking about me at all now. Soon perhaps, your mother will tell you some things about me and then I will not have to feel so dishonest when I try to write to you.

About your opening move in our chess game: P–Q4 is a very aggressive beginning. Well, all right, let's see if you know this response: I move P–KN3.

Keep working and studying and growing.

I love you much.

Dad

I never got a response to my next move. Shortly after that, the chess board vanished, and my desk was only for homework. Tears began to well, and looking at his picture I began to recall his unusual scent: sandalwood mixed with sage, like the aftermath of a campfire. My next thoughts morphed the deep red living-room carpet into burning wood, as the memory of our last time together came into focus. We were in the forest on the Appalachian Trail in 1968. I was six.

"Jocko, not leaves. Leaves make smoke."

"But they're easy to make the fire with," I said.

Dad turned and squatted down to my level. "If the rangers see the smoke, they'll make us go back to the campsite. Why don't you gather some kindling?"

I looked at the uneven ground where we would be sleeping. "But what about the sign back there?" I meant the No Trespassing plaque we passed.

My father took a deep breath. "Property is one person convincing you that they own the very thing you need." He smiled at my confused face. He knew it would be years until I understood—years he would be absent.

After I had returned with kindling, his hazel eye connected with mine as his blue eye, vacant and distracted, seemed to droop like his smile. "You know Daddy loves you. Don't you?"

"Sure . . ."

"Soon, I'll be going away for a while. And . . . well . . . I just want you to know that no matter what happens—no matter what—I'll always love you. You understand that?"

"Where are you going?"

"To do some work for Native Americans on a reservation."

"What are Native Americans?"

"Indians, but we should not call them that."

"Can I visit?"

The fire was dying, and Dad began to feed it with the small sticks I had gathered. "Help me get this going. Remember how I showed you?"

"No *leafs.*"

"Right, but blow from the bottom, like this . . ." And he did so.

Maybe he thought all social reformers had to deliver these ominous good-byes to their children. Or explorers or astronauts, who might never return. Today, with the shards of my father laid out on the very spot where we once wrestled and the scent of a campfire in my memory, I realized that his letters were more than just mail-order parenting. They were life lessons for after he was gone.

"Josh? Are you OK?" Mom's voice brought me back to the present. She started her next cigarette watching my first tear slide down my cheek. "Do you have any questions?"

Too many, I thought, and mainly, *Where do I go from here? And how should I honor my giant?*

Tim reentered the room, carrying "the tape thing," Dad's heavy Wollensak. By 1973, it had been rendered obsolete by portable cassette players. But I loved this big old machine. Dad had taught me how to thread it with a reel of quarter-inch recording tape. I did so, and in a moment my father was alive, and we were singing. But eventually the flutter of the take-up reel triggered the flood of tears I had been holding in. And I realized . . .

He was gone.

I had lost him.

But it felt like he was stolen.

The day began with a child building a starship. By morning's end, I had entered a growing class in America: children of incarcerated fathers. They tend not to do well in life. They are five times more likely never to finish school and seven times more likely never to marry. They often end up angry and in prison themselves, gravitating toward the grift or tending to follow in their father's footsteps. The FBI knows this. They stay close.

At age eleven, I already had their attention.

PART I

CHRYSALIS

1 | A WEATHERMAN APPEARS IN MY LIVING ROOM

LIKE MANY BOYS WITHOUT A FATHER, I began a collection of father figures. In 1974, when I was twelve, a man named Robin would become the most significant. "I'm Richard," he said, "but everyone calls me Robin. It's a real honor to meet you."

Robin Palmer was a forty-four-year-old ex-Weatherman who looked like a Woodstock version of Popeye: a stout, toned body bulged through a fitted T-shirt and frayed denim cutoff jeans. "I thought you should have this," he said, his broad smile of perfect teeth connecting to the corners of thick muttonchop sideburns. I looked down at his calloused hands—the rough hands of a seaman. They presented what looked like a Bible but was actually a leather-bound edition of *Moby Dick*. "This was Sam's favorite book, uh huh."

I would learn, years later, that Robin picked it up at a used bookstore.

After the United States withdrew from Vietnam, the movement receded, and Weathermen who considered my father a hero occasionally appeared at our apartment. "I'm so sorry about your dad," Robin said. "You should be very proud to be his son." Many were venerated in the deep-left New York political scene. It was given that I was to hold them in high esteem, so I wanted to trust what Robin told me that day in his Jack Kerouac pentameter, "I know some cats think they got the scoop . . . that Sam was murdered. But that's all willy-nilly bunk."

"I only know that he died at Attica."

"We were squatting in the dirt when the shooting stopped. He looked at me and said, 'Well, at least we tried.' And he started to stand up. And I told him to keep down. I said, 'Sam, stay down. Stay down.' But man, he just stood up. He just stood up. I know. Then I heard a shot. He fell back and looked like he went to sleep, right there in my arms—just like in the movies."

It sounded like a movie: contrived, rehearsed. But at age twelve, to challenge an adult was unthinkable. Instead, I just nodded and asked, "Why were you in Attica?"

"Well, I was in with your Dad. Sam and I were in the group that did the bombings."

"Did you know the friend who turned him in?"

Robin hesitated. "I was arrested about a year later with a different group."

This was confusing. If they were in the same group, why had he not been caught with my father? Like the others? Later, I asked Mom why she wanted me to meet Robin. She said it was because of my repeated requests for a deeper connection to Sam. Her best effort was to allow an ex-Weatherman and ex-con, who had no children of his own, to take her child to the chess clubs that he and Dad had frequented. But Robin's surrogacy was short lived. One afternoon he took me to an event at a church in Greenwich Village. I learned, years later, it was a fundraiser for two of their coconspirators who were still fugitives. Being twelve, all I could perceive was that the colorful activists in attendance knew who I was. "Your father was a hero," several repeated. "You should feel very proud."

I heard those same words several times that day, and each time I looked down and suppressed a slight twitch. Mother told me, time and again, that these people had seduced my father with hippie sorcery. Taken him from me. I wanted to respond, *How am I supposed to feel about a man who hoped to save the world but abandoned his only child to do it?* Instead, bashfully, I replied with "Thank you."

When I told Mom about the church fundraiser, she yelled at Robin. "If you people are intent on raising money in the name of Sam Melville, instead of financing fugitives, why not start with the child support he never gave me?" She'd had it up to her neck with bake sales in Dad's name, adding that Robin had a great deal of nerve exploiting me. With the FBI still frequenting her office, she assumed someone was always watching. "I'm trying to keep Josh out of this."

Robin Palmer as I met him in 1974. *Courtesy of the Whiting family*

Within a few months, Mom unlisted our number and moved my stepfather Tim and me from our elegant two-thousand-square-foot, four-bedroom apartment with crown moldings. Tim, Mom, and I would now live in a charmless two-bedroom in one of the low-income Section 8 buildings on Roosevelt Island: a two-mile outcropping of Fordham gneiss under the Fifty-Ninth Street Bridge with no subway access. Pre-1975 maps of New York labeled it Welfare Island, from the years when it held a prison and an asylum. But by 1977 the island had been renovated into an ultramodern community with buildings that looked like stacked cement Jenga pieces, and, for panache, an aerial tramway transported its residents like cattle to their corporate prairies in Manhattan. This was the new escape for the middle class being squeezed out of New York's most desirable borough. Gone for us was the Upper West Side with its vibrant coffee shops buzzing with literati. Roosevelt Island had one bar/restaurant where locals told sad tales of their failed ventures.

No matter. The move was safe. And even though Mom felt it was a significant step down the social ladder she had worked her whole life to climb, we had a fresh start—free of radicals. What she didn't know was what no change of venue could prevent: that now, at age fourteen, my father's prison letters were part of my subconscious.

> *Dear Jocko,*
>
> *I feel that the study and care of the environment is a very important subject to all people. Do you talk about the environment in school or with mommy or your friends? If not, you should. The air you breathe in New York City is polluted because of gasoline engines in automobiles and buses and all the many factories like Con Ed that send smoke up in the air. If your schoolteachers are not teaching you anything about pollution then you must begin to ask them questions about it. Ask mommy and talk about it with your friends . . . and what I told you about eating meat is also important. The animals you eat are part of the environment. You must think of them as your fellow creatures to share the earth with. I know mommy and nana have told you meat is very healthy and you must eat it, but fat content is responsible for much heart disease and other diseases that can be very bad for the body and the mind.*

I kept him alive by debating the environment, food, politics, or anything, really. Since I was the last pick in every sport I attempted, debating became *my* sport. I exhausted my opponents and enjoyed the process. I preferred the word *Socratic* to describe my demeanor; teachers chose the word *disruptive*. I mimicked Dad's sarcasm whenever I could not connect with the course material. And I rarely connected. If I couldn't joke about the lesson, I'd debate its merits—relentlessly. I changed schools almost every year.

The first episode occurred at age twelve, shortly after I started hanging out with Robin. I was at the pricey and progressive New Lincoln School, where we called instructors by their first names. There, my homeroom teacher became fed up when I asked, "Steve, why doesn't the cafeteria serve a vegetarian option? Killing cows is not good for growing children. . . . And why are we learning about the stock market and World War II? We should be talking about the illegality of Vietnam and capitalist exploitation." Despite his sympathy to my points, Steve put my desk by the wall, far away from all other students. I often buried my face in my folded arms, feigning a nap while tears dripped down my nose into a puddle on my desk.

Mom thought that if a progressive environment didn't work, a conservative one might. In a 180-degree move, when I was thirteen, she switched me to the Browning School for boys on East Sixty-Second Street. It was a jacket-and-tie training ground for Park Avenue preppies. Its notable alumni included oil baron John D. Rockefeller, whose son Nelson Rockefeller was the governor of New York, the man who ordered the Attica assault. Mom told me, "Don't mention your father." She added that I should not challenge the teachers, whom we had to address not by their first names, as we did at New Lincoln, but as "Sir."

Oddly enough I had more in common with the one Black student at the school than the White kids that came from privilege. I came from a broken home and my mother had to work two jobs to afford Browning's tuition. I had an allowance, not a trust fund, and I could not contribute to conversations about weekends in the Hamptons.

Then came the whammy. Although Dad's headline-making death at Attica was starting to fade from the public memory, that year some ex-Weathermen regrouped and called themselves something like the Sam Melville Group. They claimed responsibility for bombing multiple skyscrapers, and my father's name once again was in the spotlight. One can imagine how parents felt about sending their child to a pricey private school with the son of the man who blew up the very institutions that had made them rich.

The year after we moved to Roosevelt Island, when I was fourteen, the Browning School's dean suggested that I might be happier elsewhere for high school. In yet another reversal, Mom persuaded me to audition for the ultra-progressive New York High School of Performing Arts. It was a school for kids who didn't fit in elsewhere. It flaunted this fact. Dancers went to class in leotards, musicians jammed in the hallways, thespians acted out scenes in the lunchroom. Academic grades were weighted against those in your specialized department of drama, dance, or music. On the Performing Arts application, I was asked, "Why do you want to study acting in high school?" I liked debating, so I thought, *I want to be a lawyer. Lawyers were powerful. They held the fate of my father.* So, I wrote in the blank that I wanted to be a lawyer and that lawyers need acting training.

I was accepted.

The school was in the heart of the theater district. A few blocks north was 30 Rockefeller Plaza, home of NBC's new hip comedy show *Saturday Night Live*. It was also where eight years earlier, in 1969, a bomb built by my father ripped out the elevators and collapsed two floors of the offices of Standard Oil—the Rockefeller family business. Days after the explosion, the *Daily News* printed the bomber's communique:

> The Vietnam War is only the most obvious evidence of the way this country's power destroys people. The giant corporations of America have now spread themselves all over the world, forcing entire foreign economies into total dependence on American money and goods. From the inside, black people have been fighting a revolution for years. And finally, from the heart of the empire, white Americans too are striking blows for liberation.

Most days after class, my friends and I were getting high in the plaza across from the RCA building. As artists we all hated Rockefeller, the ultimate icon of capitalism, and we rarely talked about our own parents. I don't think any of us even knew what each other's fathers did for a living, unless they were famous. So, in a highly diverse, antiestablishment school like Performing Arts, and considering what my dad did to Rockefeller, I thought bragging about him for once would yield some social equity.

How wrong I was.

You could hear your watch ticking through the city traffic when I said, "My dad blew up Rockefeller's office in '69." Most were probably thinking that they wanted to work in 30 Rock one day, since it contained NBC's television studios.

I realized then that my relationship with my father was a private thing and, unlike other kids with famous fathers, not one I could brag about.

When I missed him the most, I would get out the big, bulky Wollensak, thread up a reel of quarter-inch tape, and listen to him playing guitar and singing magnificently. At age seventeen, when my grandmother offered to buy me an instrument for my birthday, I chose a Martin guitar. I taught myself to play using songbooks and practiced, as Dad had, for hours each day, singing rebellious folk songs I'd written in rebellious moods, wondering if this would make him proud. I formed few close relationships and was reduced to being thought of as an argumentative oddball, attractive only to rebellious and often aimless peers. Many years later, when I obtained my FBI file, I saw what a profiler wrote about me in 1979: "Subject is most likely to develop anti-social tendencies."

Like his father.

Sam Melville on Jones Beach, June 1965. Photo taken by my mother. *Author's collection*

Me with my guitar, age nineteen. *Author's collection*

While doing whatever tasks I could to connect with my father's sprit, Tim, my flesh-and-blood stepfather, stepped out for coffee one night and didn't return. A few months later, I learned he'd moved to Austin, Texas, with a younger girlfriend, to paint and write plays. "You have to just forget about me, Josh," he told me when he called long distance. I never saw him again.

Tim's contract with my mother was similar to Dad's in the beginning of their marriage: Mom made the money and Tim provided support and companionship. But Tim gave up on his dream of being Tennessee Williams when Mom insisted he start driving a cab to contribute, just as she pressured Dad to give up music to become a plumbing designer. Mom was good at getting men to live down to their potential. This made father number two gone.

So filmmaking became my next escape. It created the same private world as music had and indulged my love of science fiction—stories about far-off places at future times. Mom bought me a Super 8 camera, and I spent weekends with friends filming us doing crazy skits and reenacting scenes from our favorite movies.

After high school, the "it" place to study film was UCLA, where I heard Spielberg and Lucas got their start. They were gods to me because of their recent releases, *Close Encounters of the Third Kind* and *Star Wars*. But to keep me close to home, Mom said she would only pay for a local college, like the School of Visual Arts. Surely the proletariat version of UCLA, the school was in a renovated warehouse in the artsy East Village, near where Dad lived after my parents' split. Being downtown with its vestiges of the counterculture still visible somehow in my mind meant being closer to him, and in an odd way created balance for being financially dependent on my mother. I assigned the school my own nickname: University on the Corner of Lexington Avenue, or UCLA.

Coincidentally, only four blocks away, on a November night in 1969, my father was arrested by a twenty-man team of FBI agents in front of the Regiment Armory. He was carrying a duffel bag full of dynamite. I started at the faux-UCLA in 1980 and passed the spot of his arrest daily, each time with imagined versions.

The school's professors were only slightly older than the students. Teachers and students often hung out socially, and many had radical sentiments. And so, although I had forgotten all about '60s fossils like Robin Palmer, it was at "UCLA" that the second of Dad's familiars appeared. Under the pretext that anything can be considered research for a writer, my screenwriting professor brought in a middle-aged belly dancer to give a lecture. She had black hair down to the base of her back, light-brown skin, and facial features that suggested mixed ethnic origin. She introduced herself as DIANE EISNER. After twirling in circles, discarding a series of shawls, and discussing the meaning of each, Diane talked about her participation in the Weather Underground and named "modern revolutionaries," including Che Guevara and Fidel Castro—but at the top of her list was Sam Melville.

Although no one in the room recognized the name or knew she had just lionized my father, my back arched and my nostrils flared. I had to raise my hand. I just had to. "Why him?"

"I feel that Sam Melville embodied the '60s in America. He was the blueprint that turned a movement into a revolution."

My father, a blueprint for a revolution? This was a far cry from being "led astray by crazed hippies."

When class was over, I approached her and confessed, "I'm Sam Melville's son."

She looked at me with wide eyes until she realized I was telling the truth. Then she wrapped her arms around my body so firmly I had trouble breathing. Face pressed to my chest, she said, "I'm so sorry" and added the uncomfortable words I'd heard since I was a child: "He was a hero. You should be proud."

Later, over dinner, she talked about the East Village scene in the '60s and how Dad had inspired the movement to reach new levels. She wrote down her number and added her full name: Diane Eisner.

"I told your father I loved him very deeply. But he broke my heart."

"How did he do that?"

"Well, he was a sort of man-about-town to a younger girl like me, and he wasn't very faithful."

As she spoke, I connected dots in the timeline between the caring giant I remember and the man New Yorkers knew as the Mad Bomber, realizing that Diane might be the missing link in his transition. "Do you have any insight into why he became violent?" I asked.

"Violent? Your father was *never* violent. He was the gentlest man I have ever known."

"Well, radical."

"Oh. I see. It was around the time of Columbia."

I had no idea what she meant by "Columbia." I wanted to know how he got involved with the "crazed hippies" Mom ranted about and how he was caught. "Do you know anything about the friend who turned him in? Demmerle?" I still couldn't pronounce his name.

"Your father was too trusting—" she began, and then abandoned her comment. "Listen, I don't want to tell you anything negative."

"You sound like my mother," I smiled. "She said she would always try to be positive about Sam because she says every boy needs to feel his father loves him."

"No. I was talking about your *mother*. She was what pushed him. I don't want to say anything negative about *her*."

Now I was really listening.

2 | THE COLUMBIA GATEWAY DRUG

IN 1966 DIANE EISNER WAS A SENSUAL, twenty-seven-year-old, biracial activist who taught psychology at City College. She lived near the Columbia University campus and came to Riverside Park regularly, sometimes just to look at the Hudson but mostly to inhale the musk of the basketball courts. She partied with several players on and off but took special note of the thirty-one-year-old Ashkenazi who stood out when he argued with racist cops trying to break up their game.

Sam noticed her as well, reading on a bench. The constellation of freckles on each of her light brown cheeks would periodically peek up at him from the edge of her book. After a few glances, he approached and extended the ball. "Would you like to play?" She swooned at the tart aroma of sweat on rubber. Up close she could see that his eyes were two different colors, and one was lazy, clearly blind and vacant. She learned from the other players that he had a child and an ex. Some said that he left her because she was a bougie racist. This added to his appeal. "I would love to play," Diane smiled, trying not to lose herself in his glistening muscles, "But you would have to teach me."

When the sun set over the Jersey Palisades, Diane would march a line of Black and Latino ballplayers past her doorman's disapproving eyes. Aside from her spaghetti, the fare served in her apartment was pot and politics. Sam excelled at politics, but pot was something he'd only heard about. Diane was happy to tutor him in the substance and in trade he romanced her with songs and poems. Diane's parents were both university professors of African studies. Coming from some privilege, she was generous with her possessions,

29

particularly her '62 Volkswagen Beetle, the keys to which she would gladly loan to any brother who seemed cool.

One night after the ballplayers had left, she gazed at Sam as he finger-picked "Greensleeves." She pressed her full-figured body against his strong back, wrapped her arms around his broad shoulders, and produced an open palm with keys. "My bed is more comfortable than the cots at the Y."

The next day Sam transferred what few possessions he took from Ruth's into Diane's closet. The words "living together" were never uttered, nor were terms for fidelity. In later times, this would be called *friends with benefits*. In 1966, it was called *free love*.

———————

After a day of drafting plans at Syska, he'd meet Diane, and they'd wander up Broadway, where she'd point out the new activist groups meeting in Upper West Side cafés. They reminded Sam of his Bronx days, when he and his friends sang to the effervescence of angry youth, which was slipping away from him with each birthday.

One night in mid-1966, she stopped Sam in front of three block-printed letters drawn with soap on a dented steel door: SDS. Through the window, he could see a fog of cigarette smoke engulfing a young crowd focused on a single lecturer. "Who's speaking?" Sam asked the young woman at the entry. She was barely twenty, aglow with eagerness and wearing no bra. "It's a reading from Tom Hayden's *Port Huron Statement*." Hayden was the president of Students for a Democratic Society, and the words my father heard coming from inside were from this manifesto: "With nuclear energy, whole cities can easily be powered. Yet the dominant nation-states seem more likely to unleash destruction greater than what occurred in all wars of human history." They entered the smoky cave, and what he heard next would become his gateway into activism. "The new left should rally support and strengthen itself by looking to universities. But it should ally with outside groups and build an assault upon the loci of power," proclaimed the reader.

The new left, Sam thought. The idea teased him.

In less than one minute, Hayden's words had summarized everything Sam felt was wrong with his father's Progressive Labor Movement: not enough action and endless talk from overly intellectual old men. SDS was about young people getting involved—and not just men.

The following month, in November, Diane's spacious pad was chosen as the location for an SDS briefing. Their agenda was the concern about the growing gentrification of Morningside Heights by the expanding Columbia University campus. Columbia had been buying up tenements and converting them into new classrooms and housing for professors. This meant evicting locals, many of whom were poor people of color. SDS, which had been aggressively setting up chapters at campuses around the country, was determined to activate the Morningside community.

By 6 PM, the apartment was crowded with activists from the Upper West Side, the East Village, and Queens. Long hair and beads would have made distinguishing men from women a challenge to many over thirty. With one exception: George Demmerle, age thirty-two, wearing a factory smock stained with grease. His dim, sleepy gaze was the perfect camouflage for the cunning wannabe FBI informant who was hoping to rile the room into subversive acts he could then report. He scanned potential targets helping themselves to celery sticks, brushed aside his wavy brown bangs, and brooded with entitlement. "I'm here for the meeting."

"Can I get your name for my contact list?" Diane asked.

"I don't sign lists. How do I know this ain't a fed front?"

She respected his privacy and welcomed him.

About an hour into the meeting, Sam called to say he was running late. Disappointed, Diane kept looking at the door as the session progressed. A knock at one point caused the room to hush as if it might be narcs. Instead, Robin Palmer entered with his smiling muttonchop sideburns. Beside him was his twenty-five-year-old partner, Sharon Krebs.

Sharon was a successful organizer for several demonstrations that had made the front pages of the underground press. Charismatic and outspoken, she dressed to show off her sharp curves and had a crow's nest of blonde hair that might benefit from a brush, if you could figure out where to begin. She'd recently left a successful husband, who was also an activist. A month later she moved in with Robin, who was ten years her senior. They were seen most places together.

Sharon took center stage, pulled a Kool from her lips, and, with a forceful exhale, announced she expected everyone to donate money for what she called

FUNY, which stood for the Free University of New York. "We're gonna dismantle the fascist, imperialist lies about this so-called democracy, throw down the real shit about Korea and Vietnam, and assemble a think tank for the next American revolution." The building she had leased was a derelict warehouse in the East Village on Fourteenth Street between Second and Third Avenues.

Donations flowed, including sums from two undercover cops who had infiltrated SDS. Meanwhile, Demmerle refused to give anything. Instead he got into a loud debate with Robin, whom he recognized from a "fag protest group" he had a brief engagement with two years back, called the Veterans and Reservists Against the Vietnam War. Demmerle spat an abrasive tone to catch the attention of all: "I had to bail on the V&R. Their stance on America's illegal invasion of Vietnam is way too soft. V&R is ex-military, f' Christ's sake. They got guns. They should use them!" He shouted that what the movement needed was soldiers, not a bougie free school. Robin went on the defense, "Oh, yeah, man, the V&R is yesterday. I'm down with a new group, the Crazies. We're into staged protests with a storyline and no street permits from the Man. 'Guerrilla theater,' we call it. FUNY is our incubator."

Demmerle squinted skeptically. "Sounds more like a masturbator." He was only interested in FUNY and the Crazies if they were about armed revolution. They exchanged numbers.

Sam missed the entire meeting. The next morning, determined to bring him into the movement, Diane escorted Sam to the Columbia University campus, where a rally was in progress to protest President Johnson's recent order to increase the number of US "peacekeeping" troops in South Vietnam. The *Times* claimed there was to be an escalation from 75,000 to 125,000 soldiers and that Johnson was more than doubling the number of men drafted, from 17,000 to 35,000 *per month*. Most draftees came from impoverished areas where college deferment was out of reach.

White, Black, and Hispanic Columbia students took turns standing on the large sundial at the center of the campus, preaching against the war, as well as against the Morningside Heights takeover that displaced the Black community. It was a carousel of youth, anger, and sexual energy, as they sang, gave speeches, and danced, some half-naked.

Sam was mesmerized. "Man, these kids are amazing."

These were not the long-bearded curmudgeons of his father's labor movement. Nor were they the preachy intellectuals of SDS. They personified the early days of Castro as he renounced his career as a corporate lawyer to become a leader of a revolution that defined modern Communism. "They really figured it out," Sam shouted into Diane's ear.

"Figured what out?"

"Marriage. Family. Debt. That the American Dream is a steaming pile of shit. They figured it out before they got sucked in and trapped."

He was ready to commit, he told Diane. She assumed he meant to living with her and eagerly lent him the keys to her Bug so he could finally retrieve his things from Ruth's: his clothes, books on Russian literature, classical LP collection, and turntable. However, while en route, a delivery truck stopped short and sent the Bug crashing. Doctors said Sam was lucky to be alive. Only his arm and jaw were fractured. Recovering in the hospital, he decreed the things left at Ruth's superfluous. "The more you can do without, the freer you are," he repeated to Diane from an ICU bed.

Doctors assured her that some nihilism was normal after such a trauma and that he should get counseling. Lawyers visited him in the ICU and were enthusiastic that the accident would yield thousands in damages. Sam shook his head cynically at the idea of both. He had no intention of paying fifteen dollars an hour for a shrink. He was more interested in whether he would be fit enough to participate in the next MOBE rally in Washington, sure to attract thousands in a march down Pennsylvania Avenue. MOBE, a street name for National Mobilization Committee to End the War in Vietnam, was a nonviolent protest group. It had become known for ultralarge rallies. Diane was happy that Sam was being activated but began to suspect that the "commitment" he spoke of was not for her.

In March 1967, still sporting a wire frame on his jaw and wearing only overalls and a T-shirt, Sam carried his guitar across the crema of snow covering the Columbia campus. He nodded at the occasional female grad students who listened to him sing on the majestic steps of the campus library. His destination was the mathematics building, where the Columbia student madrigal group was rehearsing. He was chosen to be their musical director and, after tedious days at Syska, was finally doing something creative, even if it was only semiprofessional.

Sam entered the rehearsal to find it had been preempted by national SDS leader Tom Hayden. He had news of SDS's discovery of a secret memo stating that the Columbia board of directors had approved CIA recruitment efforts on campus for the spring 1967 term. The room was outraged.

Sam wedged himself next to Diane as a Columbia activist took the floor and preached to the room, "We need to show all Columbia students that goals can be achieved through political radicalism, not through liberal talk." (This was Marc Rudd, who would, four years from now, become a Weather Underground organizer.) He called for each of them to be outside tomorrow to stop the CIA from entering the campus.

"Right on," shouted a forceful female voice behind Sam. "The CIA is a criminal organization. It not only has no right to recruit. It has no right to exist!" Applause spread.

Sam smiled and looked back to see the shouting sideburns of Robin Palmer. Next to Robin was an equally impassioned woman with a nest of blonde hair: Sharon Krebs, who added to Robin's screed, "Remember Iran in '53? Guatemala in '54? It's not just a question of Vietnam. It's a question of the pig's whole immoral, imperialistic foreign policy."

When the meeting broke, Diane introduced Sam to Robin and his intense, chain-smoking girlfriend. Sam was happy to meet someone else over thirty in the New Left. He asked Robin how long it took to grow out his muttonchops, and together they mused on whether the look would suit him. His connection with Sharon was more chemical.

The four of them spent the evening at Prezy's Hamburger Joint, where Sam studied Sharon's sensuous lips forming subversive syllables. She claimed that at tomorrow's confrontation they should all expect to be arrested. Sam tried to impress her. He had already been arrested five years ago in 1961, he said. Robin laughed. "Shit, man, tomorrow will make my fifth arrest *this year*."

At 9 AM the next day, when CIA recruiters arrived at Columbia's iron gates, they were shocked to encounter a line of protestors outside Dodge Hall, chanting, "CIA must go! CIA must go!" The demonstration made headlines and embarrassed one of America's premier Ivy League universities. The New Left had drawn first blood.

While Sam, Robin, Sharon, and Diane were shouting at the CIA, ten blocks south, Mom waited impatiently in front of our building. Gripping my five-year-old hand, she looked sadly at the frown that dragged my chin to my chest.

"When is he coming?" I asked her. She stopped reminding me about "Daddy's day" after that; between December 1966 and March 1968, I'd see less than two dozen. They often required rescheduling. To make up for this, Dad promised Ruth that he would attend any event she planned for my sixth birthday in mid-April of 1968. But this promise, like many, would fall prey to the movement. The assassination of the Reverend Martin Luther King Jr. on April 4 spurred protests and an angry national mood that continued for weeks and threatened to cast a somber shadow over the day of my party scheduled for Saturday, April 20.

That week Sam and Diane met Mom and me in Riverside Park to renegotiate the date of the party. Mom folded her arms as she had during their marriage, with a cigarette pinched in the fingers of a lazily upturned hand, and told me to go sit on a bench while the grown-ups talked. "It's always going to be something, Sam. Isn't it?" Her fuming penetrated. "It was the MOBE thingamajig in Washington last April, a protest at Columbia the April before. Politics isn't going to get any less eventful."

He tried to explain the significance of the timing of King's murder. King had hated violence and had stayed uncomfortably quiet about the US military assault in Vietnam for years and then was killed one year to the day after his public denunciation of the war at a church only a few blocks from Columbia. The same month as King's murder, Muhammad Ali, the heavyweight boxing champion, made headlines when he refused to report for military service. The past year had seen milestones in the antiwar movement, as resentment for America's involvement in Vietnam spread outside the States. Twenty thousand Buddhists protested in Southeast Asia. One committed suicide by setting himself on fire in front of news cameras. Amid the notable events, the one Sam most pointedly explained was a proclamation by Fidel Castro to liberate technical literature, music, and books into the public domain. All intellectual property now belonged to the Cuban people.

Mom lit a second cigarette. "Well, Sam, I'm sure Cuban musicians and writers will rejoice that their work has been *liberated* from royalty payments. And apparently history is made each year on Josh's birthday."

Now Diane chose to get involved. She rattled off achievements by SDS and Sam's contributions at recent meetings. Diane had no idea what Mom was like when challenged. But Dad did. To abort the looming cat fight, he interjected with a compromise: "OK, OK! How about I take Jocko to the movies next week?"

Mom shook her head. "He likes space sci-fi stuff," she said flatly, looking back at me as I pretended to study the ground.

Diane interjected, "*2001: A Space Odyssey*?" (It had been released the day before King's assassination.)

"That's a drug movie, thank you. This is a *family* matter. And you are *not* family," she stabbed, thinking Dad was pushing some progressive point by bringing his *shvartsa* hippie slut to this fight. Then, looking at Diane's nose, Mom found her answer: "There's the space movie with the monkeys."

"*Planet of the Apes*?" My father cringed as Diane bit down hard on her cheeks. But he saw my eyes widen when I heard the title.

And Mom smiled in victory. "Yes. That one. The planet with the apes."

A week later, growing rancor among Columbia students caused several activist groups to unite and organize a mass protest that got out of hand. Poor Black people were being evicted so the school could demolish their homes and build a gym that would exclude the local Harlem kids. Students stormed the dean's office, barricaded several buildings, and shut down the university.

About a mile south, Dad and Diane sat in the dark, bored to death while I was sandwiched between them, watching a big-screen display of an American astronaut being hunted by talking gorillas. It was so cool. "It's a madhouse!" Charlton Heston screamed when the apes locked him in a cage, "A madhouse!" Suddenly the screen dimmed, the theater lights brightened, and the manager addressed us. "We are letting you know about the Columbia situation in case you have folks that might be affected."

Sam imagined the pageantry: young voices, fists in the air, and an ocean of signs and slogans. The revolution was starting—while we watched a stupid movie.

He pivoted to me. "If we go now, I'll take you to *two* movies next week."

I pouted, recalling similar offers.

Diane scurried past us—"I'll meet you there"—leaving my father to count the minutes until the closing credits.

He dropped me back at Mom's an hour or so later and met up with Robin on 110th Street. Together, they wove through the gathering mob until they reached the main administration building. Sam and Robin scaled the limestone facade and climbed into the second-story window, where students were occupying the dean's office like a palace coup. One yelled through his bullhorn out the window to waiting TV cameras: "We will free Columbia of the company men and profiteers and cake-eaters who control its future and direct its participation in the death industries! Our weapon is our solidarity!"

Soon the media junkets trained their TV cameras on the campus entrance to film the well-known Black activist H. Rap Brown. Brown was the leader of the Student Nonviolent Coordinating Committee. SNCC played a leading role in the 1963 March on Washington, but by early 1967, its liberal backers denounced the group after Brown took control from Stokely Carmichael and shifted the agenda from a nonviolent omniracial action group to one that focused on more aggressive Black militancy. Brown replaced the *N* in the SNCC acronym: *Nonviolent* became *National*. Today, he arrived at the Columbia gates with a brigade of intimidating Black demonstrators.

At Brown's side was renowned White radical attorney William Kunstler, standing out like a full moon on a country night. Surrounded by SNCC activists, Kunstler declared that Black students had a legal right to occupy the entire campus. The word of the famous movement attorney was all the permission protesters needed. Brown gave the go signal, and students of all colors began to ravage Earl Hall, the Mathematics Building, and Low Library, toppling vending machines and garbage cans to block the doors.

News of the takeover reached the FBI's office at 54 East Fifty-Sixth Street. The Bureau marshaled dozens of undercover agents, issued fake *Time* magazine press credentials, and released them a few blocks away. Mixed in the group was a recently recruited FBI informant looking to earn his bones, George Demmerle. A bit undersized compared with most men, Demmerle compensated by being the loudest agitator in a crowd. "Tear it down, motherfuckers. Tear it down," he yelled, and the thirty-four-year-old added the popular youth mantra: "Never trust anyone over thirty!"

Protests and speeches went on for days. Finally, Columbia's provost called in police at 5:30 AM on April 30 to clear the students from the buildings. Sam was at the head of a group that confronted the advancing uniforms. Standing near him was the man who in three years would become his biographer, thirty-three-year-old John Cohen, a bright, outspoken intellectual with a mane of dirty-blond hair and John Lennon glasses. John was shocked to see Sam unexpectedly hurl a wastepaper basket at cops with Herculean confidence and then lead a group of protestors winding through the narrow gap between buildings. Cohen recognized Sam from a Peace and Freedom Party meeting a month back, where Sam had offended the coalition by insisting that their talk about change would accomplish nothing. "The Communist Labor Party talked for decades," Sam challenged the room. "The only way to make change is with *action*." Now John saw that Sam lived his philosophy. He yelled over the sirens to his new hero, "I'm starting a committee to stop the Morningside Park gentrification! I want you to run it with me!"

"I'll give it a couple of meetings," Sam shouted back. "Then we have to actually *do something serious*, or I'm out!"

John and Sam's first coauthored action was the following week: a fifty-person occupation of a building owned by the university on 114th Street. Police, still patrolling the Columbia area in large numbers from the takeover the week before, responded by sealing off both ends of the block and chasing protestors inside, cornering Sam and others in the basement. They used their nightsticks to beat him, tie him up, and lock him alone in a storage closet for over an hour while they hunted down John.

In that hour, a beast grabbed hold of my father.

Bound. Gagged. It felt like rape. And to my father that meant war.

In the holding cell he and John shared that night—the first of several—they formed a bond to destroy the establishment by any means necessary. The next day they were charged with criminal trespass, arraigned, and fingerprinted.

It was the start of their FBI files.

3 | HOOVER'S "BLACK PROBLEM"

THIRTY-ONE-YEAR-OLD JOE ANDERSON, a dark haired, fast-talking special agent, resided within the FBI's elite subclass called the Intelligence Division. In 1968, one month after the Columbia takeover, he was assigned to a three-hundred-agent team tasked with reorganizing files on "known subversives." They would henceforth be coded as the "167 Files."

The first 167s would concentrate on activists connected to what FBI director J. Edgar Hoover openly called "the Black problem." Anderson shook his head sadly, thinking, *The old man is really out of touch.* He labeled BPP: BLACK PANTHER PARTY on one bay of filing cabinets and on another bay SNCC: STUDENT NONVIOLENT COORDINATING COMMITTEE. The thickest file in SNCC belonged to H. Rap Brown, who would need his own drawer soon. A third bay was labeled THE NATION OF ISLAM.

Next came the more Anglican groups who sympathized with Black nationalism. One was the Veterans and Reservists Against the Vietnam War. Others were SDS and the beatniks, who were 1950s counterculturists, some of whom had transitioned into antiwar groups.

Somewhere in these thousands of dossiers were Sam Melville, Diane Eisner, and John Cohen. Anderson would attach no significance to their recently created files, nor the existing records belonging to Robin Palmer and Sharon Krebs. He knew only that somewhere in the countless ceiling-high stacks, throughout the New York Field Office, was the name that would furnish his promotion to special agent in charge (SAC). This had become his sole focus after Hoover issued a new mission statement a year back:

> Our Nation is undergoing an era of disruption and violence caused to a large extent by various individuals generally connected with the New Left. Some of these activists urge revolution in America and call for the defeat of the United States in Vietnam. They continually and falsely allege police brutality and do not hesitate to utilize unlawful acts to further their so-called "causes." The New Left has on many occasions viciously and scurrilously attacked the Director and the Bureau in an attempt to hamper our investigation of it and to drive us off the college campuses. With this in mind, it is our recommendation that a new Counterintelligence Program be designed to neutralize the New Left and the Key Activists.

To make the Counterintelligence Program (COINTELPRO) a success, younger agents felt a new breed of confidential informant was necessary. They pushed back on the old man's standard for CIs being "college educated and from good homes." This was the climate that permitted factotum George Demmerle to gain the trust of the nation's most elite law enforcement agency.

Born into a broken family during the Great Depression, Demmerle as a child was shuffled through multiple foster homes. Constant rotation formed a man who, by age thirty-four, appeared distracted and forever searching for purpose in the long draw on his cigarette. He hated his greasy tool-and-die job. The men he worked with were old and grumpy. He saw himself growing more like them each day. Since 1964 the FBI had paid him five dollars here and there for each name he gathered at rallies, protests, and meetings. However, he was anxious to go bigger, get involved with targeted ops, and become a full-time confidential informant.

On each visit, Demmerle presented his ticket out of obscurity: a small leatherette address book with people he had met at the V&R, SDS, and other groups. "These kids are not the usual working-class misanthropes," he would pitch. "They're privileged and a growing threat to national security."

Interviewing agents scribbled lazy notes. They had plenty of CIs, they told the factory worker. None bought his theory: that the same suburban slackers they had gone to prep school with were developing into a mob that would overthrow the government. The fact that Demmerle had once been a member of the ultraconservative fringe group the John Birch Society, which had ties to the Ku Klux Klan, did not help. What did this racist lowlife know about the values of decent Americans?

On Demmerle's fifth visit in early 1967, Anderson drew the short straw. Unlike other agents in the Intelligence Division, Anderson had no FBI legacy. He related to Demmerle's ambition. Thumbing through his address book, Anderson recognized names he had recently seen in files related to Hoover's "Black problem." He rose, locked Demmerle in the interrogation room, and jogged up two flights of stairs to appeal to his boss's sense of FBI tradition. "Sir, in the 1930s, when the Communist Labor Party was the concern, we recruited reds. To disable the Ku Klux Klan in the '50s, we recruited good ol' boys. And last year, to defuse the Black messiah we expected to rise out of the Nation of Islam, we recruited darkies."

"What's your point?" growled his assistant director, biting off the tip of a fresh cigar.

"Sir, now the hippies are the problem." He laid out a thick yet recently created file about a quirky, growing group of activists, the Youth International Party, or Yippies. The file claimed its members were mostly White and educated. Earlier that year, the Yippies had assembled almost a thousand people around the Pentagon to "exorcise the evil within," and attempted to levitate the building—by chanting. Anderson got serious: "Sir, Yippies use humor to incite and encourage young, educated men to quit school or actively sabotage corporate culture by 'dropping out.'"

"Dropping out?" *Dropping out* was jargon coined by Timothy Leary ("Tune in, turn on, and drop out").

"Yes, sir. You damage the establishment by putting your efforts toward revolutionary action, and"—Anderson parodied a hippie drawl—"you deprive the Man of the ability to exploit you."

"Fascinating. But not an FBI problem." The cigar puffed.

The stubborn cloud of smoke growing around Anderson's head came from the mouth of forty-three-year-old Assistant Director John Malone, an old-school Hoover loyalist notoriously averse to modern methods of criminology. This quality—along with his unusually large forehead—earned him the nickname spoken behind his back by more than a few of the twelve hundred agents in the New York Field Office: Cement Head.

"Sir, this George guy's book puts him in the vortex of a Yippie subfaction called the REVOLUTIONARY CONTINGENT. And I have reliable intelligence that the group is planning on throwing Molotov cocktails through windows of army induction centers."

Bombing induction centers was a federal threat that Malone dared not take lightly.

The two agents stormed into the interrogation room, and Malone got in Demmerle's lethargic face. "And you can get us more names?"

"Yup," Demmerle insisted, and he presented the same theory he had been trying to sell them since 1964. "The Blacks are not your real problem. They're underfunded. But these White kids from the suburbs. . . . You can see a pattern starting as they move from an all-talk protest group who sit in and talk shit, to a more militant group." His proof of concept was Robin Palmer, whom he had met at the V&R. Anderson backed this up. He pulled Robin's file, which claimed that he was discharged from the navy in 1960, after which he taught high school English but lost his teaching license after his arrest in a police raid on a porn factory where he had been employed as an "actor." However, his family background would never have predicted this. Robin's father, Ephraim Laurence Palmer, served as president of the National Science Teachers Association, was the director of the Audubon Society from 1946 to 1950, and edited the *Cornell Rural School Leaflet* for thirty-four years. Robin's mother, Katherine, was a director of the Paleontological Research Institution in New York and a Tertiary paleontologist; she was recognized for her doctoral study on Veneracean lamellibranches. "But these days," Demmerle smirked, "the prodigal son is leading a guerrilla street theater group called the Crazies, which rallies at a subversive hippie school, FUNY."

"Funny?" asked Malone, "What's funny about that?"

"Nothing, sir," Anderson translated. "FUNY is a sort of radical academy."

By this point, in early '67, FUNY was becoming a serious counterculture concern, attracting legit professors fired from accredited universities because of their extreme liberal indoctrination of their students. Early FUNY courses included "Latin America Dictators," "Theory and Practice of Social Movements," and "Russian Literature," taught by Sharon Krebs herself. But in the past two months, FUNY had begun to offer classes taught by "known subversives" and with far more concerning course titles: "How to Fire a Rifle," "Sabotage at the Office," and "Revolution 101." Anderson insisted, "We have

CIs all over it, but we can't penetrate with Ivy League squares. To go deep, we need people from the street." Malone generally offered new CIs Dewar's, but that day in 1967 he did not even offer Demmerle coffee. Instead, the assistant director chewed on his thick cigar, cringing as he agreed to put a blue-collar hobgoblin on the payroll. As penance, he jammed his finger into Anderson's chest and barked, "Only fifty dollars a week, and you *personally* will be his control agent."

During his first year, Demmerle's undercover work uncovered little. He frequented classes at FUNY, which had morphed into a larger organization called Alternate U. He exploited his dim-witted resting face by volunteering for the antagonist roles in street-theater protests organized by Robin and the Crazies: he played a hapless chicken named Lyndon [Johnson] who got decapitated and also played a beggar named Henry [Kissinger] who faked the assassination of a live pig and got thrown into the Hudson River for a "kosher baptism." He tried to escalate the Crazies and other students at Alternate U from discussions about protests into plots to destroy a bridge or subway. No one took him seriously. Some said he talked more a like Hollywood movie version of a hippie than an authentic one. To up his game, he began advertising, boldly and often, that he possessed dynamite and blasting caps stolen from army trucks.

One day, Demmerle showed up in Washington Square Park wearing a cop's riot helmet painted bright pink. When he modeled it in Anderson's office the day before, Demmerle claimed he was perfecting a public image that was contrived to lure in the most dangerous subversives. He stood in the center of the fountain in Washington Square Park and shouted, "The helmet is my crown, and from now I will only respond to 'Prince Crazie.'" He would settle for "Crazy George" on more than one occasion, however. Anderson was starting to regret his bet.

Then, in 1968, the intelligence Demmerle gathered by watching Rap Brown and his SNCC battalion at the Columbia takeover inspired a surprisingly elegant op. "The key to gaining credibility with the White groups is through the Black militants. Let me organize a fundraiser for Huey Newton to pay his legal bills. And *you* sponsor it." Newton, a cofounder of the Black Panther Party, was awaiting trial for murdering a police officer. Anderson laughed, "You want the Bureau to finance the defense of a subversive killer? A subversive *cop* killer?"

"You bet," Demmerle explained. "We get undercovers to pledge the money. Then I'm in like Flynn."

FBI undercover agents helped the event "raise" about $4,000, and, as Demmerle predicted, the founder of the Black Panther Party, Bobby Seale, showed his gratitude by making Demmerle the defense captain for the party's sister organization, the Young Patriots, a militant group fighting Black poverty.

It got better from there.

News that Crazy George was now a Black Panther executive reached Yippie leader Abbie Hoffman. He cornered Demmerle in front of the Second Avenue Deli the next week. "We need your kind of initiative," Hoffman insisted, and he offered him a post in the upper echelon of the Yippies—if he passed the initiation.

In his memoir, Hoffman lamented that one of his biggest missteps was that he believed LSD acted like truth serum. For Demmerle's initiation, during July 1968, Hoffman had Crazy George follow him around the Village while perpetually tripping on LSD. However, faking the effects of acid proved easy when your proctor was also under its influence. One afternoon Demmerle met Hoffman in Veselka, the sixty-year-old Ukrainian greasy spoon on Ninth Street and Second Avenue. It was a nest for subversive liaisons and Beat poets nursing a single cup of coffee for hours. Over the cacophony of European dialects of its proprietors, Demmerle slammed a box of clock parts and a pound of artist's clay on the table where Hoffman was enjoying his pierogi. "This is army surplus C-4, motherfucker," Demmerle claimed. He wanted to host a bombmaking class at the Yippie storefront next door. "You *are* crazy, George," Hoffman smiled.

Hoffman rejected the proposal, but as a reward for his passion he made Demmerle his "bodyguard" for the mass demonstration he and his Yippie cofounder, Jerry Rubin, were organizing for next month's Democratic National Convention in Chicago. They planned to repeat a guerrilla theater stunt they saw Demmerle do with the Crazies in July, where Demmerle faked the executing of a live potbellied pig. This time Rubin planned to nominate the pig, named Pigasus, as the presidential nominee. "I know you're tight with the Crazies. I want all of them there. Can you make it happen?"

"I'm not Prince Crazy for nothin'."

Robin Palmer holds Pigasus at a New York Crazies Guerrilla Theater event. Behind him in a bowler hat is FBI undercover agent George Demmerle. Other agents are also in the crowd. *Courtesy of Roz Payne / Roz Payne Sixties Archive (https://rozsixties.unl.edu)*

When Demmerle reported that Hoffman and Rubin intended to disrupt the convention, Anderson gave specific instructions to what had, by July 1968, grown into an elite core of hippie CIs: "You are to provoke Chicago demonstrators into destroying property." He promised a raise to $250 a week to each CI arrested for inciting the crowd.

At the August rally in Chicago, Rubin and several Crazies, Demmerle and Robin among them, were arrested and charged with disorderly conduct as they tried to nominate the pig. Released the next day, the same group of about two hundred demonstrators joined Hoffman, Tom Hayden, and hundreds of others in Lincoln Park. As police overreacted with nightsticks and tear gas against mostly peaceful demonstrators, Demmerle handed his cohort Robin Palmer several bricks he pulled off a decaying retaining wall and yelled, "On the count of three, we go."

Robin did not need the count. Cocking his muscular, navy-trained arm, Robin threw his brick at an advancing CPD patrol car, smashing its windshield. They were wrangled by police in the mass arrests, along with almost two dozen protesters that the FBI claimed to have planned a riot. Twenty-four hours later, the district attorney released all but a small handful of "conspirators." The DA kept Abbie Hoffman, Jerry Rubin, Tom Hayden, and Bobby Seale. The papers gave them a name that history would remember: the Chicago Eight. (Seale's trial was eventually severed, lowering the final number to seven.)

It was a defining moment for Demmerle. After that day, he was both a trusted informant at the FBI and a sidekick of the country's number one subversive, Abbie Hoffman.

The next week, Demmerle told his wife he was leaving her and their five-year-old son to go "under deep cover." He needed to move out of their one-bedroom in Queens to a studio apartment on Third Street, three blocks from the Yippie headquarters. Around the corner was another studio apartment that in a few months would become the dynamite stash for the man who would ultimately define Demmerle's place in history: New York's City's soon-to-be Mad Bomber, Sam Melville.

On an early morning in May 1968, Sam rubbed sleep from his eyes as he staggered into a strange woman's Lower East Side tenement bathroom. The radio was tuned to WBAI, where Yippie leader Jerry Rubin was delivering a sermon for the youth of America:

> The prison uniform for men in America is the white shirt, tie, and sports coat or suit. The prison uniform for women is girdles, bras, stockings, high heels, and a painted and perfumed mask. That uniform symbolizes the fact that you owe your soul to business America; the necktie around your neck is like a hangman's rope around your neck. The uniform means you're working for someone else. The rebellion begins on your face. Long hair, beard, no bras, and freaky quills represent a break from prison America.

Sam listened while he washed his face. His reflection in the chipped mirror showed the same chrysalis as America's youth. His thinning hair had reached his shoulders. His cheeks had not met a razor in months. He wore sandals and overalls these days to Syska meetings and had no idea what had happened to the three-piece suits he wore to negotiations just two years ago. Likewise, the Upper West Side and SDS had become overrun with what seemed to Sam like overly didactic intellectuals. Activist groups clung to bougie, official-sounding terms in their names like "coalition" and "committee." In contrast, the groups downtown bore names that advertised their lust for revolution: the Motherfuckers; MOBE; the Black Panthers; the Crazies; and of course, the Yippies—all of whom composed the bleeding edge of the New Left.

Sam finished up in the bathroom, thinking that tonight he would broach the subject with Diane about moving downtown. Before leaving, he ran his hand over the naked curves of the sleeping protestor he met at the previous night's rally. She had invited him over after recognizing him from TV news as he the man arrested with the SNCC leader Rap Brown at the Columbia takeover. She stirred to kiss him goodbye. He promised to call her sometime.

At 7 AM, he started his morning bike ride to Syska. Cycling around the southern tip of Manhattan, he passed the recent groundbreaking for the 110-story World Trade Center. Sam remembered two years back when he was sitting in on the bid-planning meeting at Syska and laughed out loud. "It will make a great target for the Soviets someday," he joked to the room.

When he arrived at the Syska office, drawings for a shopping mall in the Union of South Africa lay sprawled on his desk. They called for segregated bathrooms in keeping with the country's apartheid laws. Sam was weeks late in finishing the plumbing schematic. Sweating in his bike pants, he walked down the hall to his boss's office to confess that he didn't believe that sewage considers the color of a man's skin.

His boss knew what this meant. "We'll be sorry to lose you," said the man who had advocated for his hire seven years ago. "Where are you going?" He hoped it was not to a competitor.

Sam dripped sweat on his desk, "I'm moving downtown."

This was a relief. In 1968, "moving downtown" was urban code.

It meant Sam was *dropping out.*

4 | FROM WALL STREET TO BLEECKER STREET

IN 1981, AT AGE NINETEEN, instead of dropping out I was buying in. When my name came up on the waiting list for a Section 8 apartment on Roosevelt Island, I was stoked to have a place of my own before all my peers. Mom was not pleased when she found out I had filed an application without consulting her. We had gradually grown apart in the three years since Tim left, and she used whatever leverage she could to keep me close. "I'm not helping you pay for an apartment."

"I'll get a roommate and a job," I said like a consolation, but the truth was I could not wait to start working. "UCLA" was feeling like a caucus of privileged anarchists. I was seriously considering not returning next semester. Mom offered to give me a few bucks for food and guitar strings—just enough to keep me dependent—if I stayed in school. I promised I would give it one more year. However, her lectures were getting longer. To keep my independence, as predicted by my FBI profiler, my attraction turned toward the grift. Over the summer break of 1982, I discovered how much it could pay. I discovered telemarketing.

I first sold magazine subscriptions. Then I graduated to numismatics, the fancy term for rare coins, except these coins had been dipped in a tarnishing solution to make them look old.

I ran into a buddy who was doing phone sales for a Wall Street investment firm. I had only been selling part time at this point and had only sold low-ticket items. He wanted to recruit me. "But I don't know shit about investing," I retorted. He smiled. "No one there does. Yet the motto in the office is 'Another day, another *K*.'"

I began opening accounts at the firm's less-than-glamorous boiler room on Fifth Avenue, inspiring farmers to look at our brochure. "Gentlemen," my manager said to the room of trainees, "welcome. Does anyone here know what the difference is between rape and seduction?" We all looked daftly at each other's young, eager faces until he shouted the answer. "Salesmanship!"

I entered this fraternity believing it was only supposed to be a summer job. "Hey, I'm a fuckin' financial wizard sitting in the shadow of the Empire State Building," I said to many a midwestern farmer or doctor. Twirling my shoulder-length curls, I added, "Where the fuck are you? Nowhere, that's right; now shut the fuck up and listen to me." And it was only my first week.

By summer's end, I had taken to the job like a snake to a slither. I had made enough bread to cover my rent for a year, and the managing director learned that I wanted to return to school. I called him "Closer Dan," a portly middle-aged crew cut with an endless symphony of seductive lies. He became my next father figure—yet another criminal.

Closer Dan took me out for rotating-conveyer-belt sushi, and over miso soup began with congratulations. In two months at the firm, I had moved beyond an entry-level canvasser and was already earning $1,500 a week in commissions. I had real talent, he said. "If you stay, I'll move you to the downtown office on Wall Street, where you'll get your Series Seven and start selling the real shit." The downtown office was at 140 Broadway, the Marine Midland Bank building my father bombed in 1969. I had to wonder what Dad would think of my even considering this six-figure offer. As a halfhearted refusal, I came clean about his place in history. It was my way of having Dad be my metaphysical agent. "I hope you can see why I can't really say yes."

Closer Dan just smiled and pulled out a photo of himself from 1971, a portal to his former life of thirty pounds ago, with shoulder-length hair and a tie-dyed T-shirt. His next lines took an express elevator into my subconscious. "Josh, I marched in the antiwar movement, *with* Abbie Hoffman, no less. We lost sixty thousand Americans over roughly twenty years in Vietnam. Do you want to save sixty thousand lives? Just take away everyone's driver's license for *one* year."

In a single snark, Closer Dan had distilled my father's ideology, and indeed the entire antiwar Boomer generation, down to the amber backwash at the bottom of a bourbon glass. How had he been so prepared for my rebuttal? I tried to remember if I shared any family details with him before today. Maybe it was my long hair. Years later, when I got my FBI file through the Freedom of Information Act, I learned that Closer Dan had been visited by G-men. It turned out that when the children of political bombers hit milestones, like a job in a major law firm, hospital, or Wall Street brokerage, the Bureau likes to update its files.

However, Dan didn't need coaching from the FBI to know how to manipulate me. His dispassionate diatribe about the antiwar movement was dialed right into the upwardly mobile mood of Reagan-era New York, once the epicenter of left-wing intellectualism. The 1980s version of free love had become sex with a coke whore.

That afternoon I bought a $700 Armani suit.

The next week I bought another.

Every day, I rode my ten-speed bike to my office, past buildings that Dad had targeted for destruction. Every day, I walked through the same Marine Midland Bank lobby that Dad had cased in 1969 and rode in the same elevator shafts Dad had blown to bits, up to floors he demolished eleven years ago. With my straggly hair and my army-navy satchel as my briefcase, I might've even looked somewhat like him to the low-resolution security cameras that recorded my comings and goings. I fell in love with the trading floor, abuzz with a hundred monitors like the bridge of the starship *Enterprise*, and my desk, with its state-of-the-art lawn-green computer monitor, was like my captain's chair. And forget just making the rent. By faking the role of a financial rainmaker, within a few months I had earned enough to fill my apartment with thousands of dollars' worth of professional music recording equipment—my other starship bridge. I gave my roommate his notice, converted his bedroom into a recording studio, and went into a side business making demos for the neighborhood bands and rap groups. I convinced myself that ripping off middle America by day was a necessary evil to subsidize the creation of art by night. And why not? I had heard that the Weather Underground and Black Panthers had robbed armored trucks to finance their revolution.

I got home at six o'clock each night after a day of hard pitching, twisted the knobs on my recording console for another eight hours, crashed at two in the morning, and got up again at seven. When I got to the office, I beelined to the bathroom to change from my "Have a Nice Day" T-shirt and bike shorts into the Armani suit I had rolled up in my messenger bag, picked up the phone, and began another eight-hour day of lying. The other brokers made fun of the contrast between my suit and my long hair, but there was no way I would cut it. Closer Dan once offered me $500 if I would trim just three inches. Not a fucking chance. This bullshit job was temporary. I was going to get out next month—six months at the most.

When almost a year and a half had flown by, the echoes of Dad's letters from Attica about the decline of capitalism had faded.

> *15 years means i could be eligible for parole in about 5 to 7 years.*
> *I'm not down about it though—the system won't last even that long.*

Those lofty words in a letter to his cohort and biographer, John Cohen, could not have been more misguided, along with these that my father wrote to my mother from Attica a year later:

> *Dear My Divorced Wife,*
> *A recent issue of Time magazine coos seductively that Amerika is "cooling off," that the violent convulsions of '69, '70 have passed and that sober reflection about this country's destiny shows we are a good people who sometimes go astray but generally tread the virtuous path. If you want to believe a man who is often very angry but nevertheless sometimes possesses a remarkable ear, I tell you we are living in the eye of the hurricane. That the violent and irrepressible winds of change are swirling round us throughout a world that will no longer pay the bill of our government's rapine appetite. And that soon the tremors of the last couple of years will be as a sleeping lion lazily swatting a fly with his tail.*

What a fool. Not only was capitalism alive and well, but it was also thriving more than ever. New York had become addicted to the promises of trickle-down economics, embraced by the Me Generation, and Dad's predictions about the system breaking down became like bread crumbs getting kicked into the dirt on the path of my schizophrenic lifestyle. My father's side of my persona spent weekends with avant-garde, free-thinking musicians and budding playwrights. We were smart, liberal, had all the answers, and connected all the conspiracies. Come Monday, that was hammered into submission by my mother's influence, the conservative fist of Wall Street. It trained me to see life in black and white, as a series of winners and losers, with little gray in between. And my father, who died at thirty-seven in prison thinking money was evil, was one of the losers. Meanwhile, I was a master of the universe, making more in a week than all my artsy friends made in a month. I was betraying everything my father died for. But I didn't care. For the first time in my life, I was accepted. On Wall Street, no one cares if your father was a terrorist.

The one thing left out of my Wall Street training was how to deliver bad news. In 1984, a flash-crash of the commodities market cost my clients all their money. Closer Dan sauntered his thick torso over to my desk. "There's only one ethical thing you can do now, Josh. Sell them another package." Dan claimed that if I showed weakness, the clients would blame me for their bad judgment. "Remember, the difference between rape and seduction."

I was trying to forget that bullshit, which he repeated with such pride that it felt like a gut punch to my sense of decency. But I decided to test his pretzel logic by returning the call of a client who had trusted me with a Utah church fund of $40,000. I told him I had good news and bad news. The bad news was that his position was 100 percent insolvent. The good?

"I have another program that will probably earn you double. It will only be another 40K."

His screaming voice forced me to pull off my headset. A broker at the next desk leaned toward me. "Hang up! This guy's going to be trouble." However, Closer Dan was smiling at his protégé from across the room. He knew. He knew even more than I did, that with my profile—a father killed in prison, a disapproving mother, and the side salad of narcissism that came with that package—I was born to fuck this guy.

"Hey, shut up, and listen," I finally interrupted him. "You've tarnished my record. I've never lost a client's money before." Which was just as true as the fact that I had not made anyone money either. "If you were me and you had lost a person's money, wouldn't you want to do anything you could to make it up to them?"

He screamed, "You're damn right, I would."

"Well, if you hang up the phone on me, I can't do a thing for you."

He was silent, as was the entire floor, now listening to this conversation over the training speaker. Closer Dan had taught me that the longer the silence, the higher the likelihood that the prospect will say yes. And no matter how long it took—no matter how long—you never broke that silence, because the first person who spoke next lost.

I stayed the course for almost two minutes, an eternity by phone-sales standards, and he finally broke. "You really think you can do it?"

My commission was seven Gs and a contest prize of two weeks paid vacation in Europe. I decided this was my ticket out of Wall Street. Armed with a Eurail pass, I remembered what Mom told me: that Dad never packed more than he could fit in one backpack and his guitar case. I would do the same. And just the way Dad had been a troubadour on the Columbia campus, I was going to sing in train stations and into the heart of every au pair day-tripping in a six-dollar-a-night youth hostel. I told Closer Dan that I'd be taking extra time beyond the two-week prize. He was unhappy, probably sensing that this might have been my breaking point. He halfheartedly wished me well. As I was leaving the office, he picked up the phone to make a call—in retrospect, it was probably to the FBI.

Maybe it was coincidence, but that day I found a gray ghost waiting for me in the lobby of the Marine Midland building: Robin Palmer. The ten years since I had seen him last had not changed his super-short cutoff jeans, with shards of frayed denim, defying the December cold, or his thick '70s-porn-star sideburns. "How did you find me?" I asked.

"Oh, y'know, I just looked in the phone book."

Well, not exactly. Robin had been checking each yearly edition of the public registry, knowing one day I would get my own listing. When I was a boy, it never occurred to Mom why he had been so persistent in wanting to be in my life. Sitting in front of me now in 1984, Robin made me wonder. He was—and had always been up to that point—the sole agent for the story of Dad's death. That day, I asked him to recount the event.

"Well . . . we were squatting in the dirt, shoulder to shoulder behind a barricade, and when the shooting stopped, he looked at me and said, 'Well, at least we tried.' And he started to stand up. I told him to keep down. I said, 'Stay down, Sam,' y'know, behind the barricade. But he stood up. He just stood up. Then I heard a shot. He fell back and looked like he went to sleep, right there in my arms . . . just like in the movies."

It was almost word-for-word what he had told me as a child. *How many times had he repeated this?*

"What did my father mean by 'Well, at least we tried?'"

"Well, just that . . . uh, we tried to make things better—to end the war, to get rid of Nixon."

I remembered the public anger against Nixon and how hippies compared him to Hitler, but I also knew that in 1971 the former president was about to start his final term. Did my father give up his freedom and then his life to get rid of a president with a four-year shelf life? "And you were right next to him when it happened?" I asked Robin, "Did you see who shot him?"

"No. That guy was far away, man."

"And you didn't get hit?"

"The bullet must've whizzed right by my head. I was really, really lucky."

Robin *was* lucky.

While many inmates in Attica were beaten senseless when the state police retook the prison, Robin made it back to his cell without serious injury. He was granted conditional release soon after, serving less than three years for his crimes, which climaxed in his arrest for the attempted fire-bombing of First National City Bank on December 4, 1970, with his girlfriend, Sharon Krebs.

"Take a ride with me," he said, and we mounted our bikes and pedaled north toward the East Village. Sliding through the slush, I pressed the question that kept taunting me. "Did you know the guy who turned Dad in? The informant. Did you know he was a cop?"

"Well, everybody in the Village knew Crazy George. He was in with a lot of cats. He went by Prince Crazy."

"But did you *know* him?"

"Not really. Only through the movement."

Robin was lucky indeed.

We cut through Washington Square Park, past Bleecker Street, which was a rallying point for so many demonstrations in '69, and arrived at the corner of Second Avenue and Ninth Street. "This is where everything really went down," Robin said to me. "Not in DC, but right here."

I chained my bike to a No Parking sign, but Robin just leaned his against it and walked away, motioning grandly at the common street as if it were a landmark. We were standing by Veselka, the Ukrainian coffee shop I'd been to many times for 2 AM blintzes. Robin claimed that, at the storefront next door, Abbie Hoffman organized the Yippies in 1968. It was now a stereo store displaying the latest trend, the compact disc player.

"In '68 you moved to the East Village to be part of the underground," Robin began his sermon. "Today, you move here to reward your success."

This seemed true. The legendary concert hall, Fillmore East, was just three blocks south. Known as rock promoter Bill Graham's Church of Rock and Roll, on any given night you could see Jimi Hendrix, Jefferson Airplane, Led Zeppelin, John Lennon, or the Grateful Dead, who all played multiple shows from 1968 through 1971. Now, in 1984, it was an AT&T retail outlet, selling pagers and advertising the coming of these weird clunky gray bricks called mobile phones. My artsy friends cringed at the idea, saying, "Only an obsessed capitalist needs to have a phone with them at all times." They hated the Greenwich Village gentrification of the mid-'80s, which gave birth to farms of overpriced renovated tenements and video rental outlets welcoming the growing number of Maclaren strollers and thirtysomethings who grabbed a VHS of *Easy Rider* or *The Big Chill*. Sure, you could still get a copy of leftish magazines, like the *Village Voice* or *Rolling Stone*, but instead of at a street corner kiosk smothered with stickers, they were waiting for you at your concierge. Inside you would find "risqué reporting" on urban redevelopment, or speculation on when Kubrick would make another movie. This East Village housed the *new* New Left—one peg away from the old right.

Robin took a seat at an outdoor table, immune to the chill, and motioned for me to join him. "By '69, it was clear that the democratic process was not adequate to deal with the situation, and things were incestuous. One activist group grew out of another, each getting more extreme."

I wondered, *If the democratic system wasn't adequate to deal with "the situation," what were Robin, my father, and the radicals proposing to replace it with? Anarchy? How would that be any better?* I asked, "And Demmerle? He was a Yippie?"

"Well, Crazy George was a Yippie and a Crazy *and* a few other things. And by '69, fancy protests with floats and flags weren't ending the war. So the next step was to actually blow something up."

"Didn't Sam care that people might get killed?"

"Well . . . but no one *was* killed. And Sam was not a 'mad bomber' like the papers said. He was *sane*, dammit. Probably one of the sanest people in the movement. Your dad once said to me, 'What's the crime of bombing a bank, compared with the crime of starting one?'"

Clever, but Wall Street had made me cynical about organic "movements." I had seen how pricey PR firms seduced whole floors of Stanford financial analysts to become evangelists for crappy stocks. I failed to see why passionate activists would be any less manipulable. "Who paid for all this?"

Robin tilted his head, stumped for the first time. "Who paid for what?"

"A movement doesn't just happen without hacking and backing. Who paid for publicity, for protests, organizers, fliers, concerts at the Fillmore, transportation, permits for protests, lawyers, and bail! Who put up the cash?"

"Well, my dad had a house he put up as my bail whenever I was arrested, if that's what you mean." He clearly had no idea what I was implying. Robin was referring to his boyhood home, which he had inherited when his father died in '79. "When I saw the goddam estate tax that [President Jimmy] Carter brought in, well, that's when I figured it all out. My father already paid those taxes, damn it! So now I support Ronald Reagan. Yep. Voted for him twice. Yeah, that's right," he said to my raised eyebrows. Reagan, a former film star, had captured the Oval Office in 1980 and instantly divided our country ideologically to the point of cultural civil war. Neocons lauded him as a capitalist savior, while the *New York Times* called him a "senile actor."

"But didn't you support Communism in the '60s?" I asked.

"Yeah. At the time I thought, *The enemy of my enemy is my friend.* But there was more truth about Communism in the *Readers Digest* than there was in all the periodicals of the left. Today, the liberals are the enemy, y'see?" Robin had become woke to "the evils of the welfare state," and had transformed from navy man to porn actor to radical to, finally, Republican. "The liberals supported Russia and Communism back then," he said. "But Communism was a lie, y'see?"

What I was starting to see was that my political compass was quite underdeveloped. Either that, or Robin had none.

Robin looked away. It seemed like this meeting was not going the way he'd hoped. Of what was he trying to convince me? "Listen, Josh, many in the New Left came from money and are more bourgeois than they care to admit. Jerry

Rubin, Bill Kunstler, Tom Hayden, Bill Ayers—all of 'em. Oh yeah," Robin insisted, "mainly the White ones. They won't admit it—y'know, publicly—but it's true. If they lived back then like they do today, they would've been called conservatives. Maybe even fundamentalists. They know it."

Seriously? Did the New Left leaders telling students to turn away from capitalism come from cash? And for added irony, most organizers were *over thirty*—the very people they told students not to trust. To me this was comic. Radical organizers were not much different than the "establishment" they were fighting. They just wore sandals instead of Italian wing tips and recited Mao Tse-tung instead of Dale Carnegie. Many, like Robin, had professional parents who could afford bail and top-shelf lawyers to broker reduced charges. When the revolution was over, their families were waiting to help them ease back into the establishment. Meanwhile, my father, from upstate White trash, went into the revolution without a safety net.

Robin swung around to my side of the table. His intense blue eyes were burning into mine. "I sat here many times with your father. I really loved him. And I'd like to help you if I can."

But by now I saw Robin as another one of Dad's privileged enablers, facing the eyes of the child he helped to orphan. *No wonder he and many ex-radicals told me that Sam was a hero and I should be proud.* Maybe they were looking for my forgiveness—or, perhaps, permission to forgive themselves. Did I seem like I needed their pity? "Tell me more about the undercover cop."

"Well, there were UC pigs everywhere. They had them in all the groups."

Another nonanswer. "But I mean, help *you*," Robin stayed on message, "as in, to be a part of your life."

"Sure," I replied. But I didn't really want him in my life. I was tired of his double-talk, and Robin created the impression that my father left me for a transient cause. Then again, maybe Dad was on to something about the system not having but fifteen years left to give. Robin's history coupled with "Greed is Good" T-shirts worn by the yuppies in the Village were living proof of the predictions in Dad's letters. Private, for-profit prisons began that year with "hardened criminals" being manufactured by Reagan's War on Drugs, and in what seemed like a coincidence, in Silicon Valley, a small startup called Cisco Systems applied for its first business license to launch what the *Wall Street Journal* called the Information Age.

But it was really the Surveillance Age, and this was no coincidence. Orwell's dystopia was in anterograde as we moved a step closer to a police state, shaped by a government obsessed with surveillance and snitches and by disparities of wealth pushed to extremes. About 0.007 percent of the US population was imprisoned in 1984. Within the next decade that number would multiply by roughly 1,000 percent. With each new inmate, a solar system of fatherless children like me would be created—except that they would be absent the advantages Mom had worked fifty hours a week to afford her son.

And here was I, a snake on Wall Street, surely part of the problem.

When I returned from Europe in January 1985, I marched into my office and cleaned out my desk. Europe's down-to-earth values showed me that there was more to life than making money, and now I wanted to do something that would make my father proud—even if I was not sure exactly what that was. It sure as shit was not exploiting people's hopes through Wall Street.

Closer Dan saw me through the glass of his corner office and came out of his cave. "It's a shame to lose you. You could sell the devil a lighter," he said, adding that he'd hoped I was not going to work for a competitor.

I shook my head. "Don't worry. I—as you say—I have a talent for persuasion; I should use it for something noble, something that will make a difference. I'm gonna probably move downtown and get into music."

"Music?" he said, "Downtown?" as if I were joining the circus. He authorized the last four-digit paycheck I would see for a good long while. And as I was leaving the front office my final image of Closer Dan was his stern, focused grimace watching me enter the elevator. As the doors closed, he reached for the phone.

5 | "HE LEFT YOU HIS EYES"

WITHIN TWO WEEKS OF LEAVING SYSKA, my father was teaching twenty-nine students how to install air conditioning. The Voorhees Technical Institute was excited to have a former Syska Hennessey designer on their staff for only fifty dollars a week. They didn't bother to vet Sam's credentials or inquire why he was fired, and Sam was excited by the idea of teaching as a platform to practice his oratory, a necessity for a serious revolutionary. He told Diane, "I wish I could chuck the curriculum."

"What would you teach instead?" she asked while making dinner.

"That air ducts are the most vulnerable part of any building and could easily channel an explosion."

She stopped sautéing. "Is that true?"

"As long as the president hates to sweat, even the White House is exposed." Then he pivoted: "Have you thought about the Village?" This was Sam's third time suggesting that they abandon her pricey flat on 108th Street and relocate to the emerging activist epicenter. "SDS, Yippie HQ—they're already there. Everything will be downtown soon." He began to kiss and rub her shoulders. After dinner and sex they searched the classifieds.

The next day, a message from Mom was waiting for him at the Voorhees front desk. There were two parts to it. First, she was hoping he might send a portion of his fifty dollars a week paycheck as child support. She had started a job as a computer programmer, but, on a woman's salary of only eighty dollars a week, she was having trouble paying for my private school. Sam laughed and made a note to change jobs after the move to downtown. This time he would not tell her where he landed. The second part gave him pause: his father, Bill, had died. His funeral was the next day.

Over dinner that night, Diane asked, "You are going to go, aren't you?"

Sam shook his head—"Not a fucking chance"—and went on to explain how Bill had abandoned Sam as a toddler, content to have his alcoholic mother raise him and his two sisters on a waitress's tips. To combat the crushing poverty, she moved from the Bronx to her hometown of Tonawanda and entertained "uncles" in the afternoon. Fed up with her whoring, when Sam was sixteen, he punched one of them and left home. "I dropped out of high school and started working as a pinsetter. I was fine with that, but Mom wrote Bill with a bullshit story that I had run away. He actually drove up from the Bronx. The first thing he noticed when he found me was my eye."

Sam's mother had left him alone when he was six or seven. Upon returning home, she discovered a cinder had hit him in the face. "She was too drunk to drive me to the emergency room or didn't have enough gas. Who knows." As a result Sam was blinded in one eye, which was left distant and a pale shade of blue.

"Are you blaming that on your father? He had a calling with the Party," she rationalized. "You were his sacrifice."

"I know," Sam agreed. "She was impossible, so I didn't blame him for leaving. But I thought, *Now was a chance for him and me to start over*. 'Sam, you finish high school. And the minute you do—the very minute—you come live with me.' I got my GED when I was nineteen and took a bus to his apartment."

By then Bill had moved in a young volunteer, Helene. She was barely twenty-three. Bill was forty. "And she was pregnant," Sam said, like he still couldn't believe it. "I stayed at the Y that night. I lived there until I met Ruth." He began packing his pipe with added aggression. "He and Helene would come to our new apartment for dinner every couple of months, always with little bougie jibes on how Ruth and I were living in a doorman building. Then one night he tells me he's quitting his post at the CLP after twenty years. And why? He wanted the party to double his salary so he can buy a house with a pool in Manhasset. Of course, they laughed at him. Then he hits me with *his* solution: 'So I'm buying a restaurant.' He said it as if he had won a competition. And not just any restaurant."

The restaurant was a Jahn's—known for its gluttonous proportions and its Kitchen Sink, an ice cream sundae large enough to serve eight. "This is the same guy who organized a taxi driver's union with the AFL-CIO. But now he's all, 'The Bronx is not so cheap anymore, Sam. Helene wants a private school for the new baby.' He was a hypocrite and a quitter to me after that. The next week, I changed my name."

Diane looked at the strongest man she'd ever known swimming in a sea of pain he could not confront: "Did you ever think that maybe you're really angry because he abandoned *you* for the party, but he was willing to give the party up for his new baby?"

"Not really," he said, taking a deep draw on his Meerschaum. "Young wives want swimming pools and private schools. What can you do?"

She sighed. "And the restaurant?"

"The pigs kept tabs on former party organizers. They put pressure on banks to keep interest high, and the health department was pinching him every other week. Everyone knew it would eventually crush him."

Diane was seeing a new side of Sam: not a budding activist but an angry boy with a personal stake in punishing his father by quashing all hypocrisy. She rested a comforting hand on his shoulder. "I think if you don't go tomorrow, you'll regret it."

"Not gonna happen."

But to his surprise, the next day, Sam found himself standing over his father's casket, holding back rage and searching for words.

As he headed for the exit, he saw through the window of the funeral parlor his nine-year-old half brother sitting solemnly in the backseat of the Town Car Helene had rented with the last of Bill's credit. Sam had spent many afternoons playing basketball with the child. He wanted to comfort him and to tell him to get out of that house as soon as he was able. But what was the point? Both of Sam's parents were gone. His mother had moved to California with yet another alcoholic boyfriend. They had not spoken in years. Sam had barely spoken to me, his own son, in months. Now the father who taught him to fight the power was dead. It was for the best; he thought, *If you want to change the world, a family is a liability.*

Helene intercepted Sam as he continued toward the door of the parlor. She thought about commenting on his choice to show up wearing overalls and sandals but knew that this would probably be the last time they would speak.

"He left you his eyes," she said instead, presenting Sam with the organ donor paperwork. "He told me that he wanted to help you fix your vision."

Sam barely looked at the envelope. "The more you can do without, the freer you are."

He threw the papers in the trash.

6 | ROGUE

BY MARCH 1985 I HAD FINISHED my two-year stint on Wall Street and started my music career. I produced demos out of my second bedroom for the next year or so until I realized that a kid with no family in the biz cannot bootstrap a career. I needed a mentor. A new father figure. This time one that understood what *I* wanted.

Rogue Recording was one of the best-kept secrets in the New York music scene. Started by former members of the neo-punk band the Velvet Underground, the cozy studio in the Music Building on West Thirty-Eighth Street reflected their counterculture roots and embraced the era when music was recorded with every musician in the same room. Despite its humble appearance (or maybe because of it) major recording artists would book time at Rogue to make demos before heading to bigger studios to finalize their vision. Those big, fancy studios near Times Square had rates that were hundreds per hour and hip assistants who hovered to fetch coffee or blow. Rogue, located in the seedier Garment District, was twenty-five dollars an hour, and you got your own coffee. Sometimes you brought your own toilet paper. My plan was to live off my broker's commissions and home-studio bookings so I could pay my dues as an intern at this hidden gem.

To get the job, I did something that I never thought possible: I played the Sam Melville card. I knew my audience. John Hechtman, the studio manager, was a thirty-seven-year-old, potbellied throwback with thick glasses. My interview with him was in the dungeon-like control room, lit by lava lamps and the equipment's vacuum tubes that glowed like candles in a Buddhist temple.

Hechtman leaned back a bit smugly, clutching a sheet of rolling paper over his Grateful Dead T-shirt, which followed the curve in his belly and caught the overspill of sinsemilla. He thought he would trick this young engineer from the digital age by giving me an old-school analog tape test. "Thread me up a quarter-inch," he said as he pointed to a bulky ten-inch reel-to-reel tape machine.

I smiled. Dad's Wollensak was exactly that. And I had remembered everything he taught me. Hechtman was impressed with my speed and accuracy, barely looking down. He leaned back in his chair, prepping another joint, and decided to get personal: "So, why, with your Wall Street success, do you want to sweep my floor?"

The truth was that I did not have the connections for an assistant's gig at the big studios in Midtown. It felt to me like those jobs went to young men whose dads were record executives or friends of pop stars who booked huge blocks of time. When I explained my theory to Hechtman, he asked me if my father was anyone of note. My answer froze his fingers twisting his half-rolled bone. When I concluded Dad's résumé with Attica, he sprang up, spilling the weed. "Holy shit. You are so *fucking* hired."

"Thank you," I said for the five-dollar-a-day job. "When could I start?"

He pointed toward the rug. "Start by picking that shit up and rolling it."

It did not take long before word of my pedigree spread to the owners. They asked me about my father with giddy curiosity. One said his next-door neighbor was good friends with my father: Robin Palmer. I held a poker face. "Never heard of him."

About a week after I learned Robin now knew where I worked, Hechtman interrupted my floor-sweeping to tell me the FBI had stopped by "for a chat."

At age twenty-three, this was my first indication that I was on their radar, but I never connected it to Robin. "I told them to fuck off," Hechtman said proudly. "Yeah, I told these fuckers that if they wanted information on a Rogue employee, they could call our lawyers!"

Hechtman made me feel protected and accepted. At the time, this was worth far more than money. While my Wall Street peers were turning prematurely gray, conning farmers for two hundred grand a year, I had found a place where I was working with my first positive father figure. And we were twisting knobs for legends.

Later that year the legend du jour was Bob Dylan. He sat next to me, the lowly intern, listening intently to tracks he was producing. "Sounds good" was all he said to the room. More words than usual, I was later told.

"What about the acoustic guitar?" I blurted. In the off-hours, I had done an unauthorized acoustic guitar overdub that I was hoping would catch Dylan's ear. Dylan was probably stunned that an assistant would have such nerve. But all he said was "I liked it."

"Josh is our star intern," Hechtman perked up effusively. "His dad was Mad Bomber Melville."

I could have done without the moniker, but I compressed my shoulder blades, sat up a bit arrogantly, now toe-to-toe with the man who literally defined the '60s. "My dad was a big fan of yours," I said. His glazed and baggy eyes looked right into mine. "That's cool. Let's take a break," and he abruptly stepped out of the room.

A bit too abruptly.

I rose and began to empty the ashtrays, feeling stupid for my ham-handed comment. Hechtman tried to put a happy face on it: "Y'know, if he was my dad, I'd be writing a book about him." I reminded Hechtman that I was a diagnosed dyslexic, which he already surmised because every other word was misspelled on my session reports. I didn't mind if Hechtman knew I was practically a functional illiterate, but the idea that anything I wrote might be seen by others was horrifying.

On the last day of Dylan's booking, I found myself alone with him in the hall. I was keeping my head down, stocking mics when Dylan spoke to me: "He didn't make it . . . at Attica . . . your dad. He didn't get out."

"He was not murdered, if that's what you mean," I said, echoing what Robin had told me. "It was random. The rest is just willy-nilly '60s paranoia."

"You ever think about speaking? About him? Y'know, publicly?"

"He made some bad choices. I don't really see what there is to say."

On a random Friday, the woman who would change my priorities came into Rogue. She was part of a wannabe three-girl pop group. To the annoyance of the other two, JILL and I stared at each other through the isolation glass for what seemed like hours. I was twenty-four, she was twenty-one, a gutter-mouthed textile-design student at the Fashion Institute of Technology (FIT) whose Stevie Nicks hair and fashion-model figure excited me as much as her awkward wit. "I live in the Riverdale of New Jersey," Jill proclaimed into the mic, flirting with me between takes, "*Livingston!* But everyone calls it 'Living-*stein*,'" she delivered the punchline referring to the town's largely Jewish demographic and laughed at her own joke.

I hit the talk-back button. "I'm not into bridge-and-tunnel chicks." But starting that night, we spent the weekend in my bed surviving on Chinese delivery and saliva. On Monday, channeling the kind of free-wheelin' choices Sam would have made, I asked her to move in.

Mom hated her on sight. She pretty much hated all my girlfriends for reasons offered without solicitation: too much makeup, too earthy, too Jewish, not Jewish enough. Jill was too skinny.

"Mom, what type of woman *would* you approve of?"

"Educated—a BA at least. Professional. Classy."

"Can you picture such a woman dating me?"

"No."

When I met Jill, all I wanted was a partner in crime who sang, wrote songs, and marshaled the wandering eye I had inherited from my father. She loved my smile, my passion for music, and saw kinship in the home recording studio converted from my second bedroom. We formed a folk duet, instantly reducing ourselves to a music scene cliché and the kind of relationship that would not likely outlast our immediate infatuation.

However, the subconscious need attracting me was her warm family, something I had no experience with. And so, in her, I began to see a chance for a normal life. She could help me get my shit together. She could be the mother of my children, and we could live in a townhouse in the Village whose basement would be transformed into a recording studio. Each weekend, we could host salons. Rock legends would stay for a day or two and give our kids music lessons, in exchange for Jill's charm and my advice on their careers. I saw this dream every day in Jill's warm smile and big brown eyes. After a few months, we began to finish each other's sentences. On Halloween, she surprised me by dressing like a Vulcan princess from *Star Trek*, complete with pointed ears and the crewwoman's sexy uniform.

If that's not love, what is?

It was my first real live-in relationship, and one that I was determined to make last. Step one was keeping my family history a secret. I hid everything I owned about Sam, including the black folder of my dad's newspaper clippings. It would now live in the bottom of a closet.

Sometime in mid-1986, with Wall Street savings dwindling, I picked up shifts as a bartender via a six-week bartending school where I earned a "degree" in mixology—to keep my hip gig at Rogue, Hechtman in my life, and my apartment with Jill. One week, the dispatcher asked me to report for a special event at the Palladium. Once a theater on Fourteenth Street, the Palladium was now a garish nightclub famous for its expensive drinks and Neanderthal doormen defending the velvet rope. The event was organized by Yippie founder Jerry Rubin. Rubin had convinced his old partner in crime Abbie Hoffman to do standup comedy and staged debates at the most bougie venue in town. The buzz was that this was kind of pathetic. Hoffman had been in hiding since 1973 and had grown progressively more paranoid while underground. (He repeatedly told his brother as well as reporters that if he ended up in Attica "I'd be killed just like Sam Melville.")

Recently he surfaced and was desperate for cash. He agreed to participate in Rubin's satiric show, cheekily titled "Yippie Versus Yuppie."

In "Yippie Versus Yuppie," Hoffman ranted about Nixon and Watergate like an obsessed throwback, while Rubin played the recovering liberal-turned-capitalist. He was an early investor in Apple Computer and had defined the emerging class of 1980s ex-counterculture millionaires. At the show's climax, Hoffman would throw his hands up like he was being arrested and feign losing to Rubin as Rubin shouted, "Wealth creation is the real American revolution!"

Jill rejected the free passes. She hated the club scene as much as I did, but the reason she gave me was that her father had known Rubin from his hippie days and claimed he was an asshole and a hypocrite. That night's event would prove him right.

Early in the evening, I was setting up, half watching the many TVs mounted above the bars. President Reagan was reaffirming that he had no knowledge of Colonel Oliver North's secret plan to divert money Congress earmarked for rescuing hostages in Iran to rebels in Nicaragua. The new twenty-four-hour news station CNN was calling it the "Iran-Contra scandal," and newsmagazines called Reagan "the next Hitler."

Every generation has a Watergate. Iran-Contra was ours, so I was trying to pay attention when suddenly I heard, "Hang on a sec." It was Rubin, wearing a T-shirt that read, WANT TO START A MOVEMENT? EAT A PRUNE. He was walking purposefully toward me, and I thought perhaps he had caught a glimpse of my last name on the worksheet. I was bracing myself for the words that triggered me since I was twelve: "Your father was a hero." But I got something very different.

"You're gonna get a lot of vodka martini calls tonight. When the server asks for a call, on the first round, you use the brand. But when the server asks for a second round, you use the well. Y'dig?"

This was bartender lingo. Rubin was instructing me to make the second round with cheap vodka and charge as if it were the premium brand. I asked, "Can't a vodka connoisseur tell the difference?"

Rubin guffawed. "Vodka connoisseur? Let me show you something." He lined up three shot glasses, grabbed the soda gun, and sprayed seltzer into each. "Pretend these are filled with three top brands of vodka. I'll bet you a hundred bucks a *connoisseur* cannot pick out his favorite in a taste test. Every yuppie asshole takes the bet," he grinned, "but after the first shot, your palate is burned, y'dig?"

I could not decide if Dad would approve.

After the event, I was in the locker room, changing back into street clothes, when I heard, "You're his kid, aren't you?"

I turned to find Hoffman, sporting his trademarked ultrawide grin.

"Whose kid?"

"I'm not an asshole, man. The Bomber. From Attica. You're his son, right? He was a righteous dude."

"You knew him?"

"Hell yeah. Everyone in the movement knew him. I knew the asshole who turned him in too. George fuckin' Demmerle. A major phony fuckhead. Man, you should not be behind the fucking bar. You should be up on the stage with me and Jerry."

"You think so?"

"What else do you do?"

"I write music."

"Man, you should write a book."

"About what?"

"About what?!" He scooped his face under my chin, getting nose-to-nose. "Your dad changed the world with dynamite, and you're gonna tell me you got nothin' to say about it?"

I did not understand his persistence. Like many of my peers, I only knew about Hoffman's contributions in the abstract. And I was just so tired of this rap from what I saw as gray-haired Boomers, growing comfortably old in the greatest economy the country had ever known while telling my generation what *we* should be doing to make the word a better place when we could barely pay our rent.

Your father was a hero.

You should write about him.

You should speak about him.

Damn it. We were just trying to survive.

"You know what I'd really like to say?"

"What would you like to say?" Hoffman grinned and folded his arms like he was about to win the argument.

It took every ounce of discipline not to scream, "When will the '60s be over? When all the Beatles are dead?"

7 | JUDITH REGAN

THE MEETING THAT WOULD CHANGE everything for me was only a few months away and in a place I never knew existed. A gothic brass plaque with the engraved words THE YALE CLUB was bolted high and out of sight on an inconspicuous Times Square building.

Outside, the streets were abuzz with rumors that the three-decade-long Cold War with Soviet Communism would soon be over. Inside, pairs of leather club chairs were segregated for privacy, and a soothing library-like environment created the vibe that all was healthy in the world of the wealthy. This is where Yalies would take someone whom they were trying to impress. Today, I was the focus.

The person doing the impressing was thirty-six-year-old publishing rainmaker Judith Regan, a celebrity editor at Simon & Schuster. Her reputation as a sensational marketer offended those who still saw publishing as the last citadel of intellectuals. In coming years, she would disappoint them by publishing bestsellers by Howard Stern and Rush Limbaugh. But in '87, Regan was pinning her hope of a Pulitzer on a series of books about the American family. The angle that fascinated her was what it was like to be the child of a famous '60s radical. One of my oldest friends, who worked at Simon & Schuster, pitched *The Mad Bomber* at the Monday editorial meeting. A phone call later, I was sitting across from the power editor.

We were quite the pair, she in Donna Karan and I in an ill-fitting dress jacket the maître d' insisted I borrow. "I remember the day that the elevator shaft blew up," she said. She was referring to Dad's Standard Oil bombing in '69. "I worked in the RCA building. We had to walk through layers of bag checks and about a dozen flights of stairs for the rest of the month. What about other children in your father's group? Do you know any of them?"

"As far as I know, only the informant had a son. He was my age, I think."

"You should try to get in touch with him," she suggested, but it sounded like a requirement. She recommended, "Call the book *Growing Up Melville*." And this was decades before reality stars would own the "Growing Up" moniker. She also mentioned that she had already contacted America Hoffman, the son of Abbie; the mother of three-year-old Juliet Clifton Rubin, who was Jerry's daughter; and Karima Al-Amin, H. Rap's longtime spouse. So far, none had bitten. Given their history, I guess they did not appreciate the Yale Club.

I did.

Regan was not a recalcitrant hippie telling me to resurrect my father as a cathartic exercise. She represented corporate leverage, six-figure advances, and reviews in the *New York Times*—the kind of things that could impress Jill's parents and abort my mother's career criticisms.

She scanned the pricey side of the menu, ordered the most expensive dish for both of us, and then focused her intense almond eyes on me. "Do you think you can get me a book proposal in a few months?"

Her strength drew me deep inside her reality distortion field. Suddenly, I saw the historical significance of my father. I saw myself at book signings and doing TV talk shows, neither of which Dad would have approved. I began an inner dialogue about how I would pull this off without alerting Jill. I was scared to death about my ability to deliver. But instead, somehow, I blurted, with no control, "I can definitely do it."

Maybe this reflex was my way of getting back at my father for leaving, to have the last word. Maybe, like him, I wanted to have some social impact. Maybe I was tired of random people from his past showing up in my life or of being confronted by his targets on my way to work and school, and this was my way of taking control. Maybe I just wanted to know as least as much about my own father as everyone else seemed to.

Or it could have just been the money.

I did very much like Regan's family hook. The one thing omitted from the memoirs and manifestos of radicals was how their choices would affect their children. Most did not have any when they blew up buildings where fathers and mothers worked. Maybe it was time the world heard from us.

For the first time since I was twelve, I wanted to learn all I could about my one-man amusement park. Sadly, every memory I had was tethered to the fantasies of a child and my mother's rationalizations that he was a led astray by "crazed hippies."

I left the Yale Club thinking of the black folder at the bottom of my closet. After Jill was asleep that night, I moved a dozen pairs of her shoes to dig it out. Except for a few dog-ears, it had not changed since I was eleven. The front page of the *Daily News* was just as I had remembered it, like the poster of an action movie. Large photos of Dad and his coconspirators were spread beneath the lurid headline BOMBING SUSPECTS CAPTURED. Dad looked desperate and crazy, not the poem-writing folk singer I knew. Next to Dad's picture was Jane Alpert, the twenty-two-year-old Bonnie to his Clyde; she seemed vigilant, like a Manson girl, as if her arrest with him was her proudest moment.

The next photo was of a man about my age; the paper captioned him as twenty-six-year-old David Hughey III. He sported a dark, mysterious glare with intense eyes.

Finally, a fifth photo in the sidebar claimed a mysterious twentysomething woman, named Patricia Swinton, was "wanted for questioning." The article said she had a toddler daughter whom she had abandoned. Her daughter would be very close to my age today. Regan would like that.

But what about Robin Palmer? He was supposedly part of his group . . . and John Cohen, my father's "best friend" who compiled *Letters from Attica*. From his writings about my dad, he seemed close to the events. How did they escape? And could there be others involved who were still unknown? Others who could tell me why my father changed? Others who owed me an explanation as to why he left me? Others who could help me to see my father as the hero they saw? And suddenly I knew how I was going to seduce Ms. Regan. With the FBI still secretly looking over my shoulder, dead, alive, or still in hiding, I would find each of these fuckers.

PART II

THE STATE IS OUR ENEMY

8 | THE SONOROUS BARITONE OF WILLIAM KUNSTLER

WILLIAM KUNSTLER WAS THE FAMOUS LAWYER who had written the foreword to *Letters from Attica*. Being politically apathetic at the time, I did not know much about his résumé, only that if there was an important civil rights event between 1965 and 1975, William Kunstler was somehow connected. He defended the Chicago Seven and the Black Panthers and was asked by Attica inmate leaders to enter the prison yard to mediate during the four-day uprising. Getting him on the phone before 1972 would have involved layers of assistants. However, by 1987, the revolution was over. I looked him up in the Yellow Pages and within minutes heard his sonorous baritone: "To whom am I speaking?"

"Umm, my father was Sam Melville."

"Yes. I've been expecting your call."

Was he? Kunstler's assumptive style was his superpower. "The last time I saw your father alive, he was linked arm-in-arm with the Attica Brothers, guarding the hostages."

"I've put off wanting to understand my father for some time, Mr. Kunstler, but now I'm trying to get to the truth about a few things. Like, if his death was an accident."

"He was murdered, Josh. There is no doubt in my mind. When the shooting started on Bloody Monday, your father was one of the first victims."

"I've heard different from Robin Palmer. He told me Sam *wasn't* murdered. Do you know him?"

"Yeah." It did not sound positive.

"He told me he was with my father when he was shot."

"I had heard that, yes."

"And that my father stood up when the shooting started. I can't understand that. Do you think he wanted to die?"

"I saw Sam on the last night before the state troopers came over the wall. I didn't get the feeling that he thought he was going to die, other than the feeling that everybody had . . . that they were *all* going to die."

"And you believe Rockefeller murdered him?"

"I called him a murderer in the press, and then, a few years later, I was invited to a dinner at his house, and I was sitting next to his daughter Mary, and she said, 'Why did you call my dad a murderer?' And I said, 'Because he refused to go to Attica to meet with the inmates. He was a supreme capitalist who didn't want "niggers and spics" telling him what to do.'" Kunstler then changed subjects abruptly: "What kind of work do you do?"

"I'm a musician. I'm performing my own material in the Village in a few weeks."

"Your father would've been very proud." I could almost feel Kunstler smiling at the other end.

"I'm not so sure," I told him, referencing my tenure on Wall Street.

"Trust me," Kunstler assured, "a father is always proud of his son. You know, there is a lawsuit pending against Rockefeller for $30 million. And, Josh, your father's estate is part of it."

He explained about a class action against the State of New York on behalf of Attica inmates for "wanton disregard of human life."

"It's going to be argued in June. The woman to call is Elizabeth Fink—Liz. She is your lawyer. Call her right now." And he changed the subject a third time: "Have you gotten your father's FBI files?"

"I can get those?"

"Yes, you're entitled to them. They're your property, in fact, as a citizen." And he told me about the Freedom of Information Act (FOIA) that made it possible for any US citizen to get previously classified FBI documents. He said he would put in an application for files on Dad, Mom, and me as well.

"Me? You think I have a file?"

"I'm sure of it."

Perhaps I was being naive, but I decided my ace in the hole was the one source only I had easy access to. "Mom, did you ever get a visit from the FBI, back in the day?"

"They came by my office right after the arrest." She was working at Met Life, a very conservative insurance company that took up an entire forty-story landmark building on Twenty-Third Street. "And I was an assistant manager. Do you know what that meant in those days? A woman—a Jewish woman—managing Irish Catholic men in 1969? And the FBI comes in and talks to my boss. I was lucky to keep my job." Mom worked tirelessly in the computer department adapting the early computer programming languages Fortran and COBOL so Met Life could be on the cutting edge of risk assessment.

"Did you ever look into whether you and *I* have an FBI file?'"

"What for? I wanted nothing to do with them. Why are you asking about this?"

"Simon & Schuster wants me to write a book about Sam."

"Oh?" She held that hard stare parents get when their child asks for money. She never wanted to subject herself to my queries as a teenager. Now, when I was twenty-five, impressed by the glamour of a major publisher taking an interest in her son, she was willing to sit for two three-hour tape-recorded interrogations.

I thought learning about their marriage in the early '60s would give me the kind of grand insight Regan would salivate over. However, after six hours, all I had gained was her impression that *she* was the catalyst of Dad's dissent. When I asked why she wanted to split up, she said, "He was cheating on me and not letting me work." I got the feeling it was the latter that bothered her more than the former. "I asked him to leave, and that's when he became involved with radicals. He was not political before we split up. He was normal. Very normal."

That wasn't precisely what Diane had told me regarding Sam's salty relationship with his father and his red-diaper friends from the Bronx. "I think there might be more there, Ma. I have put together a list of the people he was underground with. I hoped you would help me find them."

"Josh, you shouldn't mess with those people! They are crazy. I mean it. Crazy! I tried dealing with them—with John Cohen, in particular, about your father's letters when he wanted to do the *Letters from Attica* book. He was a total bastard. He was not a real 'best friend' to him, believe me. That Robin Palmer is another crazy one. I never should have let him near you. They don't know Sam. They think they do, but they don't. They knew him for a short time, the last couple of years of his life, after he lost his mind. I was married to him for six years. I knew the real Sam Melville."

"Perhaps they knew a different Sam Melville."

"No! All of them are nuts!" She stewed. "Your father's body—" She finally said, "They wanted to burn it."

"Burn it?"

"That's why the Black Panthers guarded his remains at the memorial."

"I thought you told me the Panthers were there to pay their respects."

"No. The Weathermen were going to steal Sam's body as revenge for Attica. They wanted to burn it on Governor Rockefeller's lawn."

Elizabeth "Liz" Fink never answered her own phone. Minions at her Brooklyn law office did everything from proofreading briefs to picking up her dry cleaning. Mom may have been a decent launch point, but if there was an Oz at the end of my yellow brick road of Sam's legacy, my guess was that Fink would be its wizard. Kunstler described her as David taking on Goliath—the State of New York—for the "Brothers of Attica," inmates who were injured, tortured, or killed in what her newsletter called the "Attica Uprising." "*Riot* was the state's description of the event," Fink would correct me later when I used that term at our first meeting.

When I introduced myself to the intern who answered her phone, I heard, "Oh my God, hang on!" I sat with the phone to my ear for several minutes, reflecting on the irony of her hold music—"Father Figure" by George Michael, which had been released around that time. A moment later, I was speaking to Fink's assistant, Cathy Wilkerson, a former member of the Weather Underground. She was, for lack of a better term, radical royalty. In 1970 three of her comrades were killed when their pipe bombs exploded prematurely and destroyed her father's townhouse in the West Village.

Wilkerson disappeared for a decade. While underground, she had a daughter. In 1980, she surrendered, having spent half her life on the FBI Ten Most

Wanted Fugitives list. However, Wilkerson would escape terrorism and man-slaughter charges and serve only eleven months for possession of dynamite, I presumed thanks to her father's connections. Our conversation started with a few personal questions to verify that I was who I claimed to be. "Why would anyone pretend to be Sam Melville's son?" I asked her.

"You would be surprised." Wilkerson explained that as Sam's only heir, I was entitled to potential millions in damages for his wrongful death. Then, I asked her if she knew other members of my father's collective. I presumed the radical underground was so small that everyone knew everyone. I rattled off the names of Dad's coconspirators I received from newspapers and *Letters from Attica*: David Hughey III, Pat Swinton, and John Cohen. However, the only name she offered was one I had heard in passing from Diane as Robin Palmer's girlfriend. "You should talk to Sharon Krebs. She knew many people."

Wilkerson gave me Sharon's number and said she would add me to Fink's Attica Brothers mailing list. I asked, "Could you perhaps make me an intro-duction to Sharon? I mean, I don't have any real credentials to call her up out of the blue."

"You have the best credential you could have and the only one you will ever need: your name."

"What about Jane Alpert," I blurted. "I'd also like to speak with her."

Her tone became forceful. "She wrote a book about your father. I doubt she would tell you anything different from what she wrote in there."

A book about my father written by the woman who was closest to him? The same woman who dedicated her profile of my father to me, personally? Why hadn't my mother ever told me? Or why hadn't Robin or Diane? Or anyone? I got off the phone and dashed to Barnes & Noble.

The clerk found one copy in the back. Jane Alpert titled her memoir *Grow-ing Up Underground*. Lucky enough to get a seat on the subway, I cracked it open, anxious to discover my father's lost years told by the last woman who had loved him.

By the time I got to my stop, I realized why Wilkerson tried to deter me. Jane's view of my father was anything but heroic. For most of the chapter she titled "Sam Melville," she righteously redefined his polyamorous episodes of free love as "affairs and infidelities." His sexual preferences were also relevant to her story, apparently, since she embellished page after page with them: positions, kinks, and smells. What a thing for a son to read. She said my father used the words "slut" and "cunt" to describe women, absent all the respect for women that my mother and Diane claimed that Sam displayed to an almost mythic fault. I recalled one of his prison letters in which he denied the renowned radical magazine *Ramparts* its request for him to write an opinion piece because the male editor made a single demeaning remark about his female secretary. Chauvinism should be made of sterner stuff.

Next, Jane claimed that when Dad was not "cheating" and disrespecting women, he would bomb targets with little care for who was in the buildings. She related that he was so out of control the group "took away his blasting caps." She concluded that it was sheer luck that he didn't kill anyone—not the careful planning to "only destroy property," as Mom had spun. Finally, and for me worst of all, she alleged that despite the warnings about Demmerle by those in the group, Dad named names to a "known informant," leading to everyone's capture.

Somehow, these opinions being in a book from a legitimate publisher made it more real than all I had been told. All the conflicts I had for my father's actions were now in play. *Maybe Mom was right to keep his footprint in my life as small as possible.* Jane now made three women I knew of who loved my father once, only to criticize him later. Did he break Jane's heart like he had Diane's and Mom's? And if so, what was the price for breaking the heart of a woman who threw bombs?

9 | THE COLLEGIATE AND THE COLLECTIVE

SHE HAD THOUGHT HERSELF INVISIBLE TO HIM—too young, or maybe too square. In 1968, twenty-one-year-old Jane styled herself as the demure girl next door with the placid gaze of an icy academic. Underneath, however, a passion burned to join the revolution of her peers. On days when she was being honest with herself, she wished she understood it better.

She often eyed the older campus troubadour whom she had also seen at rallies. Most afternoons he played a nylon-string Martin on the majestic steps of Low Library. "Blowin' in the Wind" and Bach toccatas were his perennials when coeds found reasons to linger.

On a September morning, she waited there reading the *New York Times*. Eventually, Sam blocked her sun. She looked up, smiled into his silhouette, swiped her short brunette bangs from her squinting eyes and introduced herself with emphasis on her middle name: Jane *Lauren* Alpert.

"John assured me you would be at the next Morningside Heights Committee," Sam said, skipping the platitudes.

"I had class."

"Class? Have you considered that your tuition goes to displace people of color in an imperialist land grab?"

"I considered how I might help them with a Columbia PhD."

He glanced at her *Times* with disdain. "By getting your facts from the pig media?" he asked, and produced a copy of the *Guardian* from the stack under his armpit. He insisted it was the trusted source for those serious about the movement and that he was the paper's campus distributor. Jane bought a subscription. Although she knew her address was embossed in the corner of her checks, to ensure that Sam had everything he needed to reach her, she wrote her phone number on the back, making the zero into a peace symbol.

On their first date, Sam flared his plumage with his tales of his commitment to the coming American upheaval. He was presently collaborating with Black Panthers and their mutual friend John Cohen to create an East Village stop on the radical left underground railroad.

Jane studied his wage warrior's attire: farmer's overalls, T-shirt, and work boots. She asked, with more curiosity than concern, "How do you sustain yourself?"

He was happy to make only fifty dollars a week distributing the *Guardian*. He had quit his teaching job because teaching young kids how to become corporate slaves was "part of the problem." Before that, he had quit a high-paying "pig gig" as a plumbing designer for a prestigious architectural firm. "They wanted non-White bathrooms on the plans for a mall in South Africa," and moving closer to her face he whispered, "I told them I didn't have the drafting talent to design racist toilets."

She pulled back, not ready to end the conversation, and parried with her academic résumé: "I was finished with Swarthmore. Too many rules—*pig rules*." She added the tag to give herself some edge. "Columbia is overrated too," and without a breath segued that in addition to carrying a 3.8 GPA, she found time to be the youngest editor for the conservative Cambridge University Press. "I'll probably be running editorial by the time I'm twenty-four."

But all Sam heard was the subconscious fear of many women who had invested in higher education: *rescue me from the destiny my parents have planned, the one where I marry a suburban doctor and grow fat with his babies.*

They saw each other regularly over that week. Each visit was a lesson on Marxism and passionate lovemaking. Sam was not like the other men on campus. He took his time, cared about her needs. And soon she began to understand why Communist China, Russia, and Cuba were the inevitable paths for a declining America—so much so that she now saw her privileged life as an impediment. On Sunday Jane asked Sam to be her Sherpa into the radical left. But he shook his head and eyed her embroidered leather satchel with the *Times* peeking out like a joey. "Only those who are willing to yield every privilege will make the revolution."

The next morning, she skipped class to entertain the unthinkable for a middle-class girl from Forest Hills: dropping out of Columbia. At Prezy's Hamburger Joint across from the campus, she sat for the balance of the afternoon and over a burger and a Coke drafted a spurious resignation letter to the university board. When finished, she shoved it in her new bag, thinking that should really do it. But for two nights it beckoned her. By Wednesday, reading to herself, to a boy from her Greek class, and on the phone to a girlfriend, she finally liked the way it sounded enough to show it to its intended audience. "It's a manifesto of protest," she said to Sam, as he lounged naked on her bed. "My leaving Columbia itself is a protest. Y'see?"

Sam looked up, halfway down page three of five. "Thousands of people each week are dropping out. I've never heard of any one of them writing a press release." Sam crumpled her words into a ball, lobbed a swish into the waste can, and watched her smile fade. Then he rose, positioned his broad chest close to her face, and cradled her cheeks in his palms. "If you really want to join the revolution, Lady Jane, then you should just quit. Today."

She thawed at his words "Lady Jane"—mocking yet intimate, pinning her in a penumbra between wanting to either kiss him or punch him.

Was there any difference?

Sam broke the good news to Diane. "She is willing to sign the lease."

Sam and Diane had found a seven-room railroad flat for only seventy-four dollars a month. The cavern of chipping plaster and musical pipes was on a Latin-controlled block near the FDR freeway on Eleventh Street. The catch was that even though Sam offered the landlord several months as key money, the landlord still needed someone with both decent credit and no arrest record for the signature.

Diane recapped: "So, you, me, Gil, John, and this Jane as the square?" Cramming half a dozen activists into one downtown unit was not uncommon. Diane admired John Cohen, and "Gil" was the shaggy twenty-six-year-old activist GILBERT BERNSTEIN. He earned his street cred by being busted as part of the initial conspirators who became the Chicago Seven.

"Yes," Sam agreed, "plus David and Pat."

David Hughey III was a twenty-five-year-old heir apparent to a popular South Carolina Methodist clergy lineage. He had rejected his legacy by becoming an atheist, moved to the libidinous East Village, and got a job at the *Guardian*, where he met Sam.

Patricia Swinton, or "Pat," as she preferred, was David's sometimes lover of the same age and one of the most vigilant downtown activists Diane had ever seen. Her shoulder-length blonde mane framed a jugular that pulsed when she shouted vulgar poetry at cops who carted her away from demonstrations. "One, two, three, four, we don't want your *fucking* war! Don't be a sheeple! The state is the enemy, enemy of the people!" Sexual confidence preceded her, and she was easily noticed from half a block away by both men and women in the East Village due to her often-worn safety-orange sleeveless knit, revealing a dense underarm shag and a preview of her liberated breasts.

Jane was the random element. By Sam's description, she sounded like a preppie who, were it not for Sam's romantic portrait of the underground, probably never would have agreed to sign a lease for a cold-water flat, let alone share a man. Jane would not last.

"This will be amazing," Diane said. To celebrate, they rolled a joint and consulted the *Kama Sutra* for something new.

It took less than two weeks for Sam's master plan to unravel. When Gil and John saw their Latino neighbors setting fire to a rusted convertible in front of the tenement with boarded-up windows and layers of graffiti, they backed out. Pat had a toddler from her brief dysfunctional marriage to an alcoholic. She could see him using the place's condition to jack their shared custody. Instead, she and David opted to shack up in a tenement on Sixth Street, near the far safer Hells Angels headquarters. John moved into a tenement down the street from them. When Sam asked Sharon and Robin to replace Pat, David, and John, Sharon reasoned that the nearest restaurant was Veselka, and they had "lousy Joe." She preferred the French Roast Café in the West Village for her morning latte and half a pack of Kools. These changes of heart left just Diane, Sam, and Jane to dwell in the revolutionary commune. And for Diane, Jane was developing into something of a problem: she needed Sam to walk her to the subway in the morning and, due to nerves from the sirens at night, to comfort her in bed. Diane decided a bit of sabotage was in order.

Her plan revolved around introducing Jane to a women's action group run by a former sitcom actress, Robin Morgan. Morgan had been a rising star of the American feminist movement for nearly a decade and had perfected the aggressive valence of contemporaries like Bella Abzug. (Two years later, in 1970, Morgan would publish *Sisterhood Is Powerful*, a compilation of feminist writings. It was the first book to use the term *herstory*.)

Morgan was not a random choice. Diane knew that eager-to-belong Jane would quickly adopt Morgan's views about how *women are the nigger of the world* and that a slave revolt was long overdue. By the first week the topic became a garnish at dinner. By week two, Jane had elevated the plight of woman to the main course. Meanwhile, Sam saw the entire working class as being crushed by capitalism. He had little patience for diatribes about women as its sole victims; Jane came from Forest Hills and waltzed into an elite job at Cambridge Press, earning more than any male activist he knew. She began to sound like Ruth, nagging constantly about needing more. He pushed back at Jane one night by suggesting that she channel her newfound misandry into an article: "maybe something like, 'Holding That Door Open Is Closing Her Self-Respect: The Subtlety of the Male Conspiracy.'"

Diane's gamble paid off.

An uncomfortable silence loomed over the weeks of October. Jane would come home from work some nights to find Sam giving a guitar lesson to a female activist he discovered camping in Tompkins Square Park. Seeing that Jane was floundering, Diane developed empathy for the woman she had at first seen as a rival. In fact, she had begun to admire her intelligence, her dedication to understanding her new world, and her sharp wit. To keep her from leaving the apartment, Diane introduced Jane to someone with a more balanced view of feminism: the single mom who had backed out of the commune: Patricia Swinton.

Pat worked for the North American Congress on Latin America (NACLA), which provided research on Latin revolutions for SDS and the *Guardian*. In the afternoon she sold advertising for the underground East Village newspaper *Rat Subterranean News*. In the evenings, she would plan on getting arrested. And all the while, she took care of her three-year-old, Jenny. *How did she do it all?* Jane marveled, and latched on to Pat's sexy empowerment as if Pat were her with-it older sister.

Soon Pat would drop by the Eleventh Street apartment regularly in the middle of the day, bouncing Jenny on one hip, eager to share movement news with Diane and Jane. But knowing that both had day jobs, Pat was not disappointed to find Sam home alone.

Within two months, by mid-December 1968, a clique had formed.

Most nights, the group met at Veselka, where Jane found herself sandwiched between charismatic men about ten years her senior, and women closer in age but with weighty radical résumés.

"Man, I spat at this pig on St. Mark's Place," Pat grinned one night as she cut chicken into bite-sized bits for Jenny. "I was putting up posters for the MOBE, and the pig nailed me for *loitering*."

Robin had also been busted (again). He and George Demmerle stayed up till 4 AM one morning using yellow and blue paint to stencil Viet Cong flags on dozens of East Village mailboxes. "When the pigs caught up to us, Crazy George and me laid flat on the sidewalk. It took ten blue meanies to scoop us into the paddy wagon. We yelled, '*Sieg Heil!*'"

Gil and John had become something of a dynamic duo by editing New Left documentaries for the production company Newsreel, famous for its handheld guerrilla quality and acid rock soundtracks. (Newsreel's offspring would blossom into what today might be called "independent film" and spawned the LGBT film movement.)

As for David, his plans for sabotage of the army's draft sounded charming due to his smooth-as-molasses southern drawl. "The RC [Revolutionary Contingent] has had some creative ideas for that horrid little induction center on Whitehall—the one with young men lining up to become bacon?"

Jane's most subversive credit so far was that she had quit grad school. She cleared her throat one night and announced proudly to the table that because she left Columbia without notice she was probably a person-of-interest to "the fuzz."

"The fuzz," Pat laughed.

"Oh yes, the fuzz," Sharon repeated, suppressing a grin. *Fuzz* was TV slang on pandering shows like *The Mod Squad* and *Batman*.

Robin ruffled Jane's short hair. "Hey, Lady Janie, we need to get you some love beads."

Jane steeped in silence. *The women are fools*, she thought, parroting Morgan's sentiments, *tolerating condescending men who are dim slaves to their dicks*. Jane would wait for the right moment to make her contribution to the movement, and when she did, she was confident it would transcend coffee-shop bullshitting.

Toward the end of December, they dropped acid as a group at the *Guardian*'s twentieth-anniversary rally. The featured speaker was Bernardine Dohrn. She had just broken away from SDS to help form the new more militant splinter group called the Weathermen, whose name was inspired by the Bob Dylan lyric "You don't need a weatherman to know which way the wind blows." The other speaker was SNCC leader Rap Brown.

While Jane scribbled notes on Dohrn's demand for women to take a more proactive leadership role in the movement, Sam was glued to Brown's talk of armed revolution taking over the streets and how SNCC was siphoning off the more militant Black Panthers to form a militia. Brown slammed his fist on the table chastising their sponsor, the *Guardian*, for selling out, since it had raised its cover price and begun catering to "honky advertisers."

At the reception, Brown remembered Sam from the Columbia takeover earlier that year. His angry resting face growled, "Why is someone like you a house nigger for this bullshit rag?" Mentally, Sam quit the paper at that moment and, to impress Brown, offered up his spacious new apartment as a safe house for Brown's soldiers. Brown took the address.

Shortly after New Year's, Brown and his entourage of ex-Panthers were led into the Eleventh Street apartment by Pat and Sharon. The two sold the space like radical real estate brokers. "You'll be very safe here. Pigs are too chicken to come east of Avenue B," Sharon pitched, as Pat released three-year-old Jenny from her hip to the ground.

The first thing Brown noticed was a smell like cat's spunk poorly masked by sage incense, followed by a view of Sam, David, and John smoking cigars on the fire escape with no coats, as if resisting the January cold were a contest. With no door to the bathroom, it was also impossible not to notice a lathered Jane and Diane pairing up in the shower to save hot water. Brown's men, dressed in khakis and black berets, sidestepped Pat's toddler and took notes on the exit routes to the roof, service entrances, and garbage areas.

"What do you think?" Sam asked as he climbed inside, pulling a long draw on his stogie.

"Brothers and sisters, I love your enthusiasm," began Brown, scanning around. His eyes came to rest on the two naked women in the bathroom. "But a safe house suitable for my soldiers will not be a brown rice kibbutz with a stable of White sorority chicks." Brown had something else in mind. He wanted to use the empty bedrooms as a stash for a downtown arsenal.

From the fire escape, David shouted like a hippie hillbilly, "Right awn!" But as the conversation shifted from supplying asylum to storing assault weapons, Jane and Diane were drawn out of the shower and huddled by the doorjamb. Their jaws dropped as the words "M1 rifles and grenade launchers," were casually uttered while, on the floor, Pat's child crawled through a forest of camouflaged legs. Then Sharon grabbed Sam's cigar, blew a smoke ring, and said, "We're in."

Jane suppressed a gasp and looked back at Diane. The rebellious pool into which she had dipped her toe was about to swell into a vast ocean.

Jane and Sam, shortly after meeting in 1968. *Courtesy of the Rivchin Collection*

10 | BOMBERS AND BESTIES

THE SHARON KREBS AND PAT SWINTON I met in mid-1988 looked nothing like the pictures of them I had found in archives at the Donnell Library. The one of Sharon was originally published in an underground newspaper and showed her walking naked; her subtle curves and long hair were the backdrop to a slaughtered pig's head atop a serving tray. She, Robin, Demmerle, and a few other Crazies had infiltrated a Waldorf Astoria political dinner in 1969 disguised as waiters. They stripped to their skin and served the swine to a room full of appalled Democratic donors. A year later, in 1970, she and Robin were busted while trying to bomb a Chase Manhattan bank. She served about two years for conspiracy.

The day we met, Sharon was living a more sedate life in a Brooklyn Heights townhouse with a new husband and new last name. The remains of the fierce radical were reduced to an earthy sundress and a turquoise pendant. She kept her long hair. However, to train the frizz, she wore it like a nest atop her head. She worked in a civil litigation firm part time, as did other ex-radicals I had met. I guessed working with the law kept them connected to the cause. When asked what she did by strangers who did not know her past, she would reply, simply, "I'm a mom." She must have been good at it too. Her hug took the wind out of me.

"My God, it's like being in a time machine. You look so much like him." I was still not used to hearing that.

She apologized for not wanting to converse on the phone, saying she was concerned about security, and immediately segued by saying that she loved my father and named her daughter Samantha after Sam. "No, you don't have a secret half sister," she clarified.

She produced an old spiral notebook and folded it back on a page with a poem called "Contra-diction." "I wrote this right after Attica."

> I think Sam was relieved
> to have died
> without killing anyone.
> A gentle man, he once agreed that he would be
> pleased
> To spend his life disturbing
> not one
> blade of grass.
> And yet, once he said
> that some of us
> are only good for the
> destructive phase
> and will not be useful
> for the building.
> And he meant himself.
> I once asked him
> what he would do
> after the Revolution.
> "Blow things up," he said,
> And I imagined him
> blowing up
> lily pads
> in heaven.

I was speechless. I had read my father's poetic letters expressing his feelings to many friends in the movement, but this was the first thing I had seen where one of his close friends had written something poetic about him.

"The one thing that we all wondered through the years was, what happened to little Jocko? We all knew you existed but not what became of you."

She meant it as praise, but it did not hit me that way. They all knew about me, but none of them encouraged my father to reach out or reconsider his choices because he had a son? It was like I had been abandoned not only by one man but by an entire movement.

I caught her up on my old life as a Wall Street broker and my new life in the world of music.

"Well, that is quite a transition. I'm glad it wasn't the opposite way."

"Yes, me too. I know Sam loved music."

Settled in, I turned to my agenda by producing *Growing Up Underground* from my bag. "I wanted to meet you because I'm trying to understand how much of this is true."

Her face fell at the sight of Jane's book, as if her child had brought home a bad report card. "Well, I'll try to help you, but Jane is so angry."

"How could Sam have destroyed whole floors of large skyscrapers with not a single casualty, and yet, as Jane claims, be 'unmindful of safety?'" I asked. "You think parts of the book are exaggerated?"

"Yes, *of course*! Jane had a bone to pick with Sam." She laughed, causing some of her hair to fray lose. But my face remained serious, and Sharon could see I was annoyed that Jane had become my father's accidental historian.

Over the next hour she imparted her version of the events, eyeing my hand as it scribbled during the parts where she disagreed with Jane. I looked up at one point to address what I thought might be her concern. "I want to get everyone's perspective. I don't want to play favorites." I asked if she recognized any of Jane's altered characters, remarking that I wanted to talk to them too.

"Well," she said getting anxious, "that woman,'" she pointed at a name on one page, "that's mostly me. Well . . . it's me."

"I already figured out that this other guy is actually John Cohen."

She looked at the name under my finger. "Yes. She's quite pardoning to John. John loved her and would do most anything she asked."

"My mother said that John and some Weathermen wanted to burn Sam's remains on Rockefeller's lawn."

She straightened up in shock. "I've never heard that, and *I* was in Weather. John is a pacifist, and I cannot see him setting fire to anything."

Another Mom-sponsored inconsistency, I thought.

Sharon stopped verbalizing there, realizing that she was getting caught up in reminiscing with someone she didn't really know. After that slip about Cohen, she became unwilling to confirm with a "yes" or "no" about other characters. She half nodded at some, looked away at others, until I asked about three characters Jane described: a "Tai Chi instructor," a "Rutgers University professor," and the "Puerto Rican radical." Sharon put down her tea. "They weren't arrested, and I'm not going to *out* anybody. I need to be clear about that," she proclaimed, establishing a stern division between her moral universe and Jane's.

"I thought you wanted to help me?"

"I do." She paused, probably mulling over how *help* might manifest in a way she could live with. To let her off the hook I asked, "How about Jane herself. Could you put me in touch with her?"

"I haven't spoken to Jane in over a decade. As part of Jane's deal, she told the feds where they could find others. Nobody talks to her anymore." Then, Sharon got quiet and eventually offered, "I can put you in touch with Pat Swinton. I think she'd talk to you since she's already out, and her involvement is public record."

I arrogantly played lawyer: "I don't think the state can arrest anyone anymore for these crimes. It's been two decades."

Her face turned serious, her eyes big and scary. "They can think of all kinds of reasons to reopen cases. And they probably know about your visit here today."

I laughed in my head at her hippie paranoia. But I would soon learn she was right.

Jill's dad was starting to become suspicious. After moving on from Rogue, I was now supposedly managing a hip-hop studio in Queens for nine dollars an hour, and then, in the daytime when I should have been working for twenty-five dollars an hour in my home studio, I was having clandestine meetings with people connected to the Columbia takeover, Attica, the Weathermen, Dad's childhood friends, and anyone else I could find who had a good Sam Melville story, as well as doing marathon research at the library. There I came across radical newspapers from 1969. One was a copy of *Rat Subterranean News* that had Jane and Pat's name listed as staff. Wild.

Before Jill got home from class, I would mislabel the cassettes of the interviews I had done that day as rough mixes for clients and stash the research under heavy boxes of recording tape. However, my cleverness came to a crashing end when I returned one evening to find Jill sulking on the couch. Her pale face stared at an opened letter on the coffee table as if it were the results of a disappointing blood test. The Department of Justice had taped the letter to our apartment door. Even though it was addressed to me, her curiosity got the best of her. In three short paragraphs, it responded to the FOIA request Kunstler filed for my family's FBI files. They turned up six thousand pages and wanted $0.25 a page for copying and $50 for postage—a total of $3,050 (about $7,000 today). My income for several months. They did not accept credit cards.

Jill had called her ex-hippie dad and asked him, "Who was Sam Melville?" He remembered the Mad Bomber.

"I have wanted to tell you," I pleaded, "but your dad resents radicals, and I figured he would make you move out." I confessed that the "recording sessions" I was scheduled to engineer upstate, at BearTracks, were a ruse to take the Amtrak to New Hampshire and speak to Patricia Swinton.

"Who's Patricia Swinton?" Jill drilled.

I went to the closet and moved aside several coats to reveal a big plastic bin where I had kept my research and showed Jill the 1970s newspapers I had found. They had weekly updates on Pat with headlines HUNT FOR FOURTH BOMBER CONTINUES and COPS HUNT WOMAN BOMBER, paired with a grainy photo of Pat. Jill scanned them with her brown eyes grown big enough to light a path through a forest. Then I began blathering: "I reached out to her from the number Sharon gave me. I wanted to just interview her on the phone, but these radicals won't talk on the phone, and she said she could be more forthcoming in person." I added that I had a potential book deal with a major publisher and that this interview could provide the kind of inside scoop that would be irresistible to Judith Regan.

But Jill's cold stare owned the moment. "Who's Judith? And who's Sharon?"

I finally gave in to the fate of our relationship, "I see where this is going. OK, I'll help you pack. Call your dad."

She rose from the couch and moved in for a surprise kiss. When my tongue was gripped between her teeth, she slurred, "Do not ever fucking lie to me again."

Around 5 PM we pulled up in Jill's silver Nissan Sentra to a magical clearing in the forest. It glowed as if one might expect elves to appear. This cottage was what the bomb-throwing career radical Pat Swinton now called home. Pat opened the door, greeting me with wide blue eyes and a broad smile. "I would have known you were Sam's son even if I saw you on the street." She had retained her slender build but dressed modestly, like Sharon, in a sundress that only implied her curves.

Once we were inside, Pat fixed Jill and me sandwiches composed of alfalfa sprouts, peanut butter, and hot sauce on oat bread. To my surprise, it was delicious. "I call it my hippie sandwich," Pat said. "I taught it to Sam, and he used to make them all the time." I was not expecting Susie Homemaker. Like Sharon, she had found post-underground peace, hiding in plain sight.

Seeing I was relaxing, she announced a surprise. "I invited John Cohen over. Is that all right?"

After avoiding arrest with my father, in 1970 John had moved out of the city to be a courier for radicals on the run, transporting money, clothes, and messages. He made frequent visits to Sam at Attica. After the uprising, he showed up at the coroner and claimed to be Sam's brother looking to collect the body. Mom found out and, thinking that he was part of the rumored plot to burn Dad's remains on Rockefeller's lawn, initiated a legal tug-of-war over his remains. This cost John all his leverage when it came to *Letters from Attica*. He ended up handing over the copyright to the book in exchange for her permission to allow Sam's body to be put on display for a three-day memorial in a Greenwich Village church.

It was the kind of spiteful enfilade I knew Mom was capable of, so I was ready to disregard every dig she had told me about Sam's "best friend." As it would turn out, John would not need my mother's help in making a sour impression.

John entered timidly, took a seat across the room, and looked at the floor with an innocent, almost boyish face. His full salt-and-pepper 'fro and John Lennon glasses were the only remaining traces of the dynamic organizer Jane had described in her book.

"You had nothing to do with the bombings?" I asked him directly once we had settled into the conversation.

"No," he fired back, but it sounded like *Yes*.

"You didn't know about them?"

"Of course, I knew," he said, packing his pipe. "Sam asked me if I wanted to join the group, but I didn't."

"You didn't approve of what he was doing?"

"I approved of it. I was proud of him for what he was doing." Then he looked down again. I wondered what he wanted from our meeting and if he, like other ex-radicals I'd met, was working out some form of catharsis through me. He glanced at Pat out of the corner of his eye. "I had great respect for Sam. But . . . Sam wasn't careful. He wasn't . . ." He didn't finish the thought. His lips tugged on his pipe as if it might dispense absolution.

To break the tension, I asked what I thought might be an easier question. "Why bomb buildings at all?"

"We felt the state was our enemy," John said.

"And you still feel that way?"

"Yes. Definitely."

"But why not just protest?"

"Well, that wasn't working." Pat picked up the thread. "We wanted to be proactive." She segued into the time when some in their group created a stop on the underground railroad and helped freedom fighters on the run. In her memoir, Jane wrote about the collective helping Canadian radicals from a separatist faction called the FLQ hijack a plane in order to escape a life sentence for blowing up the Montreal Stock Exchange. I was about to ask a follow-up question about the Canadians when John stood for the first time. "Some people were born to build, some were born to lead. Sam was born to destroy." He said it as if it were a famous quote, but it was almost word-for-word what my father had written to John in one of his prison letters. "Our work came from the concept that to effect change you have to tear down the old regime and start again. But Sam never thought about rebuilding. He thought the people who were doing the tearing down were not supposed to be concerned with the rebuilding. That would have been someone else's job."

"I see," I said, thinking this was dangerously close to a rationalization for violence. John seemed very calm for most of the night, with only one or two bursts of aggression that would then quickly subside—as if he were getting control of an animal that had been constrained for some time. I tried to release it. "You said Sam wasn't careful. What did you mean?"

"He brought in the informant. And he told others what we were up to."

"I'm confused, John—I thought you weren't involved. How did you know what Sam told Demmerle, or others?"

"Jane told me."

Jane's book described a scene in which Sam disclosed names to the flamboyant FBI snitch. But even in her account, Jane was not in the room. I hoped that perhaps she had withheld something from her memoir that gave her authority, something that she had told John privately. However, John's answer was not helpful.

"She heard Demmerle's testimony at the hearing," John continued.

"I see. But didn't you tell me I shouldn't trust the FBI? That they would lie or say anything to get Sam?"

"They would."

"Then why do you think Demmerle is telling the truth about this? Even if Sam said nothing, an informant would have to testify otherwise. Otherwise, they're not much of an informant."

John looked at the floor again. A pattern began to emerge: many details on the collective's capture came solely from Jane, the one person who had cut a deal with the FBI.

This moment seemed to be a good time for me to introduce her book. Like with Sharon, their faces expanded as if I had just produced a feisty skunk. I turned to a page marked with a Post-it and asked if they agreed with Jane's analysis of my father's motives:

> [The radicals] had seen bombings as the means to a particular end. For Sam, politics was an excuse. He was as likely to turn his violence toward me or toward [David] or Pat or WBAI or the *Guardian* as toward the people we agreed were the enemy. He clung to the movement not because he believed in its ideas, but because he needed its rationale for his insanity.

Pat chucked the celery stick she was munching, saying, "What total nonsense." But John seemed to agree with Jane. "Sam's war was extremely nihilistic and *very* personal," he said to me. "It went beyond politics. It was *personal.*"

"Come on, John." Pat's jugular was pulsing as she added, "We *all* wanted to bring the war home. We *all* wanted to show the destruction wasn't just in some third-world country. It was here. That's why the state was our enemy." Pat then looked right at me. "And that's why the FBI would do or say whatever it took to catch us."

"Do you think Sam was deliberately shot?" I asked both.

John sprang up. "Yes! They passed around his picture to troopers. He was definitely murdered."

Recently, I had read a book on Attica by Arthur Liman. It was a summary of the McKay report, a published investigation about what went wrong at Attica. Mom had bought the book for me shortly after that memorable day when she told me about his death. Since meeting with Regan, I had highlighted the ten or so places where Dad's name appeared, including the part where a nameless state trooper claims he shot my father as he was attempting to throw a bomb. I spoke directly to John: "Even if that were true, the trooper was sixty feet away, shooting through tear gas and scampering prisoners. Do you think some weekend warrior could identify Sam from that distance through the mayhem?"

John went back to brooding.

I must have been a colossal disappointment: the son of the man to whom he devoted himself was questioning his twenty-year reality. Pat sucked her cheeks as if she were seeing an old friend losing a job he had held for life.

Although John and Pat initially regarded Jane's book with wary attention, that changed once Pat took possession of my copy. In her hands Jane's serious treatise about a Swarthmore girl's descent into radicalism was reduced to pulp fiction. Jill joined in, taking a role here and there, turning John and me into the audience of an actors' roundtable reading. Eventually, Pat put down the book and laughed. "Oh, that is funny. But that's not the way it happened." She surrendered the book to John, who scanned the pages frantically. "I don't know," John said, "I thought Jane's description of you was quite accurate."

"Maybe my bright orange sleeveless, but that's about all that's accurate." Pat continued laughing.

I asked Pat, "If you had to make a choice, which makes you angrier—the fact that Jane helped lead to your capture or that she wrote this book?"

"They both make me mad. Her talking about me to the feds and, well—"

John cut her off: "She knew the FBI didn't have enough evidence against you. And you were miserable being without Jenny."

John was becoming not just Jane's apologist but also the omniscient narrator of the Melville Collective: he knew what Jane saw at trial; he knew what Sam told Demmerle; he knew what the feds had on Pat; and apparently he also knew what Pat had felt in 1974 about her then five-year-old daughter, Jenny, whom she had seen but once in over two decades.

Pat pointed a stern finger toward John, her jugular now able to slice bread. "But that wasn't Jane's choice to make for me! That's *my* choice!" Then she looked at me. "When you're on the run, there's always a part of you that wants to get caught, just so the nightmare will end. But I stayed underground for five years, so deep down I must have not wanted to get captured!"

That sadly also meant her freedom was her priority—not her child.

Pat capped her screed: "And the book was a piggy thing to do! She talks about crimes that people committed but were never arrested for!"

I let the air settle and asked my core question. "Did anyone ever mention that eventually someone would get killed?" Pat's frustration finally peaked. She shouted at me, "Yeah, it occurred to us!" and stormed into her bedroom, slamming the door.

––––––––––––

The six-hour drive back from Pat's the next morning was a blur. Jill volunteered to take the wheel as I organized pages of notes that I had rapidly scribbled during bathroom breaks the night before. I was getting close to being able to reverse engineer all the redacted, altered, and composite characters in Jane's book, *Letters from Attica*, and the people mentioned in newspapers:

There was Sam, of course.

Pat—The hip radical with a small daughter.

David—Pat's sometime boyfriend and militant son of a southern preacher.

Robin—The organizer of the Crazies who denied to me that he knew Demmerle; also alleged witness to Dad's death at Attica.

Sharon—Robin's girlfriend who ran FUNY/Alternative U.

John—Sam's "best friend," rival for Jane's affections and compiler of *Letters from Attica*.

Diane—who brought Sam into the movement.

A still unknown Tai Chi instructor.

A still unknown Puerto Rican radical.

A still unknown Rutgers sociology professor.

And, finally . . . Jane herself—Sam's lover and protégé who blamed him for everyone's capture.

Eleven collaborators in total, far more than the four alleged by history or by Mom.

As I was learning different versions of reality about Sam, things were getting worse between Mom and me. My visit to Pat's was the backbreaker. When

Mom learned that Jill had accompanied me, she was livid. She had wanted to come with me, she said, not just to New Hampshire but now on my entire search for Sam. She had her own questions, she insisted.

I fired back, "You had two decades to ask questions." From there, our communication hit a brick wall.

After a few sessions, the family therapist we agreed to start seeing dismissed us. The doctor got way more than she bargained for, learning about the bombings of banks and '60s radicals still railing against society. But her stated reason was that Mom could not control her temper, drawing noise complaints from other doctors in the complex. In fairness, I was also unreceptive. At this time, I had pretty much felt it best that we boil our interactions down to the limited business of mother and son. But the unintended consequences of shutting Mom out was that I did not have the phone numbers for any of our family doctors. I did not care. Sam's letters had taught me the wisdom of fatalism. He never saw a doctor. Why should I?

Then I developed a cavity.

When I stopped by Mom's to get the number for our dentist, the conversation deteriorated into a probe about my visit to Pat and my direct contact with the radical she hated most: John Cohen.

"John was not as good a friend as John would like to think he was," she stated between tight draws on her cigarette. I could not help but notice that, like John, Mom also had a monopoly on knowledge of how people felt, which she deployed whenever she was losing an argument. "Sam said people were not sending him things—things that he needed in prison."

"Ma, when you are in prison, deprived of contact with people and of necessities, you probably feel that nobody can do enough."

"Bullshit! Your father was the most selfless man alive," she shouted, and I could see in the subtlety of her lowered eyes that she still loved the man.

Hitting a conversational cul-de-sac, her comments then turned to an area where she could control all the facts. "Did John tell you about *Letters from Attica*? He wanted all the money for himself."

I had heard this from her before. "I brought that up to him, and he said that he gave his half to Jane so that she could stay underground."

"I have all the letters Sam wrote *and* the contracts. I know what I'm talking about. John changed stuff in the letters. John knows why he feels guilty about Sam."

"You still have the original letters? Unredacted? Can I see them? And the contract?"

"No. You have your new facts. These are my old ones." She hesitated. "People don't just walk around for twenty years feeling guilty for nothing. I don't trust John. I would have trusted your father with my life."

I began thinking of the hijacking of a jet by two Canadian radicals Jane talked about extensively in her memoir, which Pat confirmed as the only part of her book she agreed with. With Mom insisting that Sam was selfless and trusting him with her life, hijackings seemed contradictory. By now I had adjusted to the idea that Dad doing political bombings was "reasonable." A hijacking took me to a new level, and for some reason seemed far, far worse.

"Did you ask Pat if she ever considered what might happen if someone got killed?" Mom barked.

"Yes. She just stormed into her room and slammed the door." But the part I withheld from Mom was what happened the next morning, when things were quite different. Jill and I appeared from our bedroom around sunup. John was long gone, and Pat was sitting alone, staring out the window like Thoreau. "I'm sorry about last night," she said, holding her gaze. "Of course we thought about people getting hurt. But none of us wanted to talk about it."

I joined her at the table. "Do you know what I wish? I wish you would tell me something I'll never learn from Jane's book."

So, over egg whites and kale, Pat Swinton unpacked the story of what turned eight fed-up pacifists into bombers.

11 | CANADIAN TERRORISTS?

JANUARY 1968 SAW ONE of the most tumultuous election seasons anyone could remember. The breaking of the cease fire by the North Vietnamese, known as the Tet Offensive, was followed by President Johnson's withdrawal as a Democratic candidate after an unexpectedly close race in the March New Hampshire primary. Three months later, in June, Democratic candidate Robert F. Kennedy was shot and killed, just moments after his victory in the California primary. His death left a weakened and divided Democratic field to challenge the powerful Republican front-runner, Richard Nixon.

Even though Nixon's campaign promised to end US involvement in Vietnam, nobody south of Fourteenth Street believed him. The draft was ramping up to over thirty thousand a month, and to avoid coming home in a body bag from Vietnam, young men were fleeing to Canada. The liberation of South Vietnam from the Soviet-controlled North was only one of several separatist movements around the world. Nation states everywhere were pulling away from the powers that dominated them: Ireland from the UK, Palestine from Israel, Hong Kong from China, and several of the Soviet Union's acquisitions: Ukraine, Bosnia, and East Germany. Even in the United States, the polarization inspired discussions about the secession of New York and California; once absurd notions now seemed acceptable as the unacceptable now seemed probable: Nixon, a perceived right-wing dictator, would likely grab hold of the Oval Office. The shit had finally gotten real.

One of the most violent separatist movements was the Front de libération du Québec, or FLQ: Marxist-Leninist radicals demanding Quebec's independence

101

from Canada. Inspired by Fidel Castro's 1953 raid on the Moncada Barracks, the FLQ robbed armories in 1963, looting over thirteen thousand rounds of ammunition, automatic rifles, bazookas, rocket launchers, and grenades. In the following years, they used them in over fifty-two attacks, including an attack on the US consulate in Montreal and the Montreal Stock Exchange, and the group allegedly engaged in occasional kidnappings and an assassination. Often their actions involved crossing the border into Buffalo, New York, to meet US contacts. But despite repeated pleas for assistance from the Royal Canadian Mounties, the FBI only chose to help when it was learned that the FLQ was plotting to blow up the Statue of Liberty.

Finally, in May 1968, the FBI assisted the Mounties in capturing the FLQ's leaders, and they were sentenced to over one hundred consecutive life sentences. But the two chief lieutenants escaped and fled across the border to New York. Their plan was to hijack a flight from JFK and force it to land in Cuba, which routinely granted asylum to enemies of the United States. Their Manhattan contact was Sharon Krebs.

FBI files allege that Sharon provided a safe house in Harlem. When I asked her about this in 1988, she said the group had eventually thought better of it, because Red Squad agents were becoming more noticeable. The Red Squad was a street term for NYPD's undercover cops, the Bureau of Special Services and Investigations. By late '68, BOSSI had several deeply embedded undercover agents in the Black Panther Party and the Yippies. (Today, BOSSI is called the Intelligence Division, and infiltrates mosques to report on Islamic extremists.)

A consensus among Sharon, Robin, Pat, Gil, and Sam was that the FLQ fugitives, with their long hair and pale skin, would better blend downtown. They were seriously entertaining Sam's offer of the empty bedrooms in his Eleventh Street apartment. However, it had only been a few days since Rap Brown's arsenal idea was vetoed by "Sam's old lady," and the concern among them was what some had begun to call "the Jane problem."

In order to devote full time to helping the fugitives, Sam took Brown's advice and quit the *Guardian*, going entirely off the grid. He would live off the $14,000 insurance settlement he had received from the 1966 auto accident he got into with Diane's Bug. He convinced David and Robin to also drop out. David quit his post as a layout artist for the *Guardian*, and Robin quit his job as a deep-sea diver.

Henceforth, the three men rendezvoused at the Yippie headquarters next to Veselka and smoked a joint with Abbie Hoffman. Sam tried to convince

Hoffman to arrange asylum for the FLQ brothers, while Hoffman tried to convince Sam to be an organizer for the Yippies. When this exchange reached an impasse, the three men left the Yippie storefront and met Gil in Washington Square Park to strategize how to get their Canadian guests out of the country. They used Gil's karate coaching as a cover. Red Squad agents who posed as panhandling hippies would observe the four men pretending to tone their bodies. Sam, David, Gil, and Robin whispered messages as they exchanged full-contact countermoves.

Jane's first indication of Sam's new direction was two weeks later, when she opened the refrigerator to discover Sam had thrown out sugared cereals and fat-heavy products and filled the shelves instead with goat's milk, nuts, and something called lecithin.

"What the fuck?" she screamed.

The next week, Jane overcame her fear of the neighborhood dealers and bought a joint. She needed to take the edge off to deliver bad news to Sam about a crossroads she had reached. Sam had insisted repeatedly that she get in the movement full time and shake off Cambridge University *Pig* Press, calling it a "bougie dependence." Jane had decided to do the opposite. As the prelude to a promotion, she had accepted an assignment that would have her spending the better part of a month in England. She was expecting a long lecture from Sam as he prepared a smoothie of spinach and barley malt after a day in unemployment heaven. But ignorant to Sam's agenda regarding the FLQ fugitives, Jane was in for a shock.

"I think that's great, Lady Jane. A break will do us both some good." On February 18, 1969, Sam drove Jane to the airport in Robin's dented Chevy wagon. He kissed her farewell and that same day moved the fugitives to Eleventh Street.

With the Jane problem resolved, at least for a while, friends would come over almost nightly to hear stories from the "guests," as they called them. One caught Sam's attention: how the FLQ had gotten away with almost fifty bombings. They used a timer. Timers not only afforded the ability to establish alibis, but they were also the standard MO for bombs used by movements abroad, like the Irish Republican Army in its war with the English.

Sam wanted to know more.

The guests sketched out a bomb design that consisted simply of a common mechanical windup alarm clock called a Baby Ben made by Westclox, one foot of solder, an arm's length of single-gauge wire, three packs of sulfur matches, and two flashlight batteries: everything one needed to make what the FBI would call a "high-order device"—except of course for the dynamite. All for about two bucks.

The next lesson was the use of disguises. "When you talk to people, make sure they like you, but not to the point that they remember you," one told them, in a thick French Canadian accent. They had learned this from a stolen CIA training manual.

After a few classes, attendance dropped off. Gil and John were nervous about getting too extreme, but they blamed their absences on a busy schedule at Newsreel; Robin was organizing guerrilla theater with the Crazies, and Sharon had a school to run. On the night when the guests taught the final and most dangerous step—how to wire the timer to the blasting caps—Sam, David, and Pat were their only students.

Halfway through the lesson, Sharon interrupted with an urgent communique. The Montreal chapter of the Black Panther Party, which had financed the fugitives' escape, had procured passports and money. Sharon said someone needed to make direct contact with the Panthers at the Canadian border. Sam had grown up near Niagara Falls.

"Canada already has our share of hippies," a border Mountie in Quebec said as he sized up Sam's long hair and army jacket. According to New York police records, after a few more insults, my father threw a punch and was arrested. The post commander called the FBI.

The agent who took the call ordered a clerk to see if the FBI had a 167 file on Sam Melville. He found one, very thin, revealing only an arrest at the Columbia takeover, his name change in 1964 from a Jewish name, his father's ties to the Communist Labor Party, and, finally, his recent application for a Cuban visa. The last item was the trigger. A pro-Castro hippie trying to enter Canada through New York probably had had ties to the FLQ. The agent asked the Mounties to release Sam near the border in hopes he would lead the Mounties to the FLQ fugitives.

With two Mounties following stealthily, Sam was uncuffed and started down the interstate on foot. When the sun set, he strolled off the macadam into dense woods, where he felt at home from a lifetime's experience of camping. Then he disappeared.

Quite perturbed by the Mountie's incompetence, the FBI launched a small investigation the following week, which swelled Sam's file from three to ten reports. Still, the FBI would learn very little: he was arrested in 1961 for refusing to take shelter during an air-raid test; he had cashed a large check from an insurance settlement related to a car accident but never deposited the money; he had worked for several engineering firms, but nothing for over a year; even his last known address with Ruth was over two years old.

No bank account, no address, no employer. My father was a ghost.

The investigation was closed.

When Jane left for England in February, the flat on Eleventh Street seemed cavernous. The one she returned to in March resembled an Amsterdam youth hostel. Two strangers with thick French Canadian accents were lounging on the couch with Sam and all their friends who had been coming over for nightly soirees.

John could tell by her tight lips Jane did not approve and saw an opportunity to comfort her, but before John could rise from the couch, Sam and Pat ushered the jet-lagged Jane onto the fire escape, pushed a joint into her mouth, and explained that the Quebec radicals were in a fight for liberation from the fascist Canadian government and these two revolutionaries needed a place to hide.

Jane rubbernecked between them. Her focus was less on the FLQ history lesson and more on the way Pat occasionally placed a too-familiar hand on Sam's back.

In the morning, Sam carefully slid his arm from under Jane's sleeping head, rose from their mattress on the floor, and began to shove clothes into his knapsack.

"Where are you going?" she asked, still groggy.

"I have to go upstate again, remember? To get the cash for the boys." Unlike two weeks ago, when he was deported, this time he was going to travel undercover as part of a couple on honeymoon. He was taking Pat.

She sat up quickly. "I could go."

"You just got back. And it won't be the Ritz Carlton."

"I know that."

"Don't you have a deadline for Cambridge Pig Farm?"

She did—one that her promotion depended on.

She stared at the lover she was losing, and just like quitting Columbia, she called her office and resigned.

Three days later, Sam and Jane returned from upstate with Cuban passports and $1,000 Canadian. Upon entering the apartment, they saw Diane, Sharon, and Pat huddled in a panic reading the *Rat Subterranean News*. While Jane ran for the shower, the three women showed Sam an article about the 124 life sentences given their Canadian guests, who were tried in absentia. Next to it was a psychedelic comic strip that depicted the fugitives dining—at Veselka!

That evening, their guests, along with Sam, Robin, and Sharon, piled into Robin's Chevy station wagon, along with Sharon and Robin's two Labrador retrievers. They were bound for the original safe house Sharon had kept in Harlem. Approaching One Hundredth Street, they encountered a police blockade and watched the line of paddy wagons corralling over a dozen Black Panthers arrested that night for allegedly trying to bomb the Twenty-Fourth Precinct. Going farther north to Harlem was out of the question.

Over the next few days, almost two dozen members of the Black Panther Party were charged for a widespread conspiracy to blow up three police precincts, kill several police officers, and destroy several buildings, including five department stores and the Bronx Botanical Gardens. The defendants became known famously as the Panther Twenty-One.

More cops appeared on the street as the week progressed. It was clear to those in the collective that they had little time to get the boys out of the country, and they still needed one key element to pull off the hijacking.

Guns.

Forty-one-year-old Rutgers sociology professor LESTER BARNS sat at his kitchen table reading a letter from the assistant dean. A recent convert to Rastafarianism, he scratched his budding dreadlocks as he reread the letter's harsh words. The dean had cautioned Lester several times for overly left leanings in his lectures, as well as his leadership of students in antiwar rallies. The final straw was that he was having an affair with a twenty-one-year-old economics major. The letter stated that Lester had been fired.

The ringing phone interrupted his brooding. At the other end was Sharon, his ex-lover. After a few requisite exchanges about him teaching at Alternate U, she wanted to know if Lester still had the revolvers he kept after his army service in the Korean War, the ones he had often shown off to her. "What for?" he asked.

She handed the phone to Robin, who had also served in Korea. Lester had been to several of Robin's guerrilla street-theater productions and repeated, "What do you need them for?" thinking that perhaps Robin wanted them as props.

"Uh . . . ask me no questions, and I'll tell you no lies," he responded, with a jocular air.

Lester knew that he'd probably never see his mementos again. Since his religious conversion, he decided that he didn't care much either.

The next day, with one of Lester's guns taped to each of the would-be hijackers' ankles, Sam, Jane, David, and Pat drove the fugitives in Robin's Chevy wagon to LaGuardia Airport. The collective watched from the visitor's lounge as the Canadians moved past security, unchecked.

That night, around 10 PM, a report announced the hijacking of Pan Am flight 301 to Miami. The plane landed safely in Havana. No passengers were harmed. The broadcast finished, and everyone stepped out on to Eleventh Street to celebrate.

Among Hispanic neighbors tagging shuttered windows, someone had started to paint the letters *GM* on the boarded-up plywood window of their building. Pat joked, "Think they meant to write 'Fuck General Motors?'"

Sam picked up the discarded spray can from the gutter and aimed it between the letters, filling them instead with "George Metesky was here."

The collective raised knowing eyebrows and bowed whimsically to Sam as if he were the shah. Jane had no idea what was happening. The next day she went to the Tompkins Square Library on Tenth Street and looked up George Metesky.

Metesky terrorized New York for sixteen years, between 1940 and 1956, by bombing iconic structures, including Grand Central Terminal, Pennsylvania Station, Radio City Music Hall, the New York Public Library, the Port Authority Bus Terminal, the RCA Building, and the New York City Subway. He was apprehended based on letters he wrote to a local newspaper, found legally insane, and committed to a state mental hospital where he resided to that day.

He was known in New York City history as "the Mad Bomber."

12 | A PENITENT YIPPIE APPEARS AT FOLK CITY

IT WAS ONLY THREE BLOCKS LONG, but the MacDougal Street strip in Greenwich Village was referred to as "folk city" by the acoustic musicians that still frequented its clubs as both performers and supportive voyeurs. One club was actually named Gerdes Folk City. Lining its crown moldings were photos of the folk legends of open mics past: Bob Dylan's intensity judged you while Judy Collins's deep eyes softened your soul. In an era when beatbox hits filled the airwaves, Gerdes was a rare oasis for music made from wood. (The club closed in 1986, and became a sports bar called Kettle of Fish.) After months of Monday open mics Jill and I had landed a coveted Friday-night spot at folk city's lesser-known survivor around the corner, the Speakeasy.

My thirty or so friends were already halfway into their two-drink minimum by 7:30 when I noticed, standing in shadows, a mane of dirty blond hair and thick sideburns I'd come to recognize as Robin Palmer's. Like the proverbial bad penny, he somehow had learned about my gig.

When our set finished, I made my rounds among friends, while Robin waited patiently at the bar. I tried to send Jill home, but she threw me her *no effing way* look. So the three of us walked a block south to Le Figaro Café for a confrontation that was long overdue, one where I cornered him with new facts about Dad's death, who was involved with the bombings, and how the hell he always knew where I would be.

He began with banalities. "You know Sam played guitar, right?"

Of course I knew.

"Yeah man, you sound like him. Amazing."

This was not even half true. Recordings I had of Sam revealed he had a fantastic tenor and was an accomplished classical guitar player. I strummed a few chords and sang some notes correctly, praying Jill's voice would cover.

Robin talked about his local public access cable TV show, *Free Wheelin'*. It made him something of a celebrity in Ithaca. He wanted me to appear on the show with Jane Alpert and do "A Tribute to Sam Melville."

But I wasn't buying his ass-kissing. "How did you know about my gig tonight?"

"Sharon said you two had a great talk, and my buddy is one of the owners of Rogue."

Was there no getting rid of this guy?

"Sharon? Yeah, I saw her last month. She said you told her Sam was shot in the *back* from a sniper on the roof."

"She's confused."

"You told me that he was *not* shot deliberately. She said you told her the opposite."

"I don't recall ever telling her that. Yeah, no, there was tear gas everywhere, Josh. You couldn't see a hand in front of your face," and he demonstrated by holding his open palm an inch from his nose.

"But you said you heard the shot."

"Yeah?"

"You heard a shot from sixty feet away? Among hundreds of screams and bullhorns and helicopters? You could differentiate a shot that was meant for Sam? That means the shot was close. Distinct. Not sixty feet!"

His face sagged, as if he might be trying to recall exactly what he told everyone.

"Ithaca might be fun," Jill interjected.

Robin looked toward her for a rescue with his mouth of big smiling teeth. "Yes, of course. I have plenty of room. You were beautiful up there tonight. How long you two been together?"

I dragged him back to my line of questioning: "Mom told me that you and John Cohen wanted to burn his body on Rockefeller's lawn. Will we be talking about that on TV?"

"I wanted to put him in a cemetery upstate so people in the radical movement could pay their respects. Where is he buried?"

I suddenly realized that I did not know exactly where my own father was resting. I knew only what Mom had told me. "Somewhere on the Appalachian Trail. Why do you want me to do this show?"

"Because he wasn't the Mad Bomber. I want the world to know that."

Or at least the people who watched Ithaca local cable. "Did Jane say yes?"

"Well . . . She's pretty mad, y'know. She just wants to move on."

"It's nice that she has that luxury." Then, sensing some leverage, I said, "I'll tell you what. I'll do the show if you give me information on other members of the collective." I had found all but three. Referencing Jane's book, I mentioned the Puerto Rican radical. "I didn't know him," Robin said, looking happy to be off the hook. "There really wasn't just *one* group. He was part of another one Sam was building devices for." Then, I mentioned the Tai Chi teacher and the Rutgers sociology professor. "According to Jane's book, you knew them quite well." He stared at me, his ethics twisting like dirty linen on a clothesline. "I'm not in touch with them."

I held my glare. I had almost everything I needed to reconstruct what had happened in the summer of '69. Everything that Judith Regan would want. The missing piece was speaking to the remaining members and, of course, Jane herself.

Then, he softened. "The Tai Chi instructor is Gil Bernstein. And the Rutgers professor is Lester Barns."

"You don't mind outing them to me?"

"I don't care anymore. And you deserve to know the truth."

"And Jane? You said you asked her to do the show. That means you have her number."

He looked defeated. "Yeaaah."

"Give it to me and I'll convince her."

He must have been looking for a trace of the innocent twelve-year-old he met over a decade ago, now replaced by the Wall Street closer. Robin sighed, "I bet you could too." Then he became pensive as he dug out his little black phone book.

"Why are you shaking your head?" I asked.

"I'm just glad that right now, I'm not Jane Alpert." Showing me Jane's number, his brow wrinkled even more, like I had pushed him to some philosophical brink. I was hoping it was the one Sharon had not been willing to cross. "A'right! I'm gonna tell you what I know about the dynamite," he said grumbling, "the dynamite, the bombs, and what we did. Yeah. You deserve to know, damn it."

13 | RAT AND THE MASTURBATORS

AT 1 AM ON A HOT MID-JUNE NIGHT IN 1969, Robin, Sam, and Gil burst into Jane's new Fourth Street studio apartment two floors below Pat's. Sweat oozing, muscles taut, Sam, out of breath, plopped two heavy crates on the floor next to Sharon and scampered onto the fire escape to light up a cigar. Gil and Robin heaved their crates onto the kitchen counter, panting and giving each other handshakes and hugs.

Jane folded her arms in a huff. "That's it?" After all the planning, they had stolen only four crates.

Robin ruffled her short brown hair. "Hey, Princess Janie, there's enough boom-boom in there to blow up five Grand Centrals. In fact, like I said in the car, we should put it in the refrigerator. Y'know, keep it cool, daddy-o."

"I asked you not to call me 'Princess Jane' or 'Lady Jane,'" she sniped. It fell on deaf ears, as the men opened the refrigerator and removed all the goat's milk, organic celery, and farmer's cheese. In their place went the four boxes of TNT.

According to Robin, the origin of what the FBI would call the "Melville Collective" began three weeks earlier, when conversations about stealing dynamite would redefine friendships.

In late May the group gathered on what they would come to call their "war room": the roof of Pat's Fourth Street tenement. On a particularly hot afternoon, my father delivered a prophecy: "There is no individual change without social change, and there is no social change without fierce political upheaval."

John stepped forward with doubts. "So, we're breaking with SDS and civil disobedience?"

"Honestly, as I see it, the Yippies and SDS haven't answered the immediate needs of the people with civil disobedience. Civil disobedience has not gained hegemony over apathy. Only when action escalates from desperation will Whites become as committed to the revolution as Blacks and Hispanics have had to be, merely to survive."

David, usually the quiet one, leaned away from the ledge and in his southern drawl added, "There are enough people in SDS schooled in Marxism-Leninism who should have by now come up with answers that could deal with Latin America and Vietnam. We have a fascist in the White House. Soon this will feel like Stalin's Russia. Sam's right. We do not have the luxury of being concerned about SDS, or anyone who still thinks that marches and sit-ins will do a fig of good."

The rest of the group began to nod. Small bottle bombs had already been set in police stations and ROTC centers by the Panthers and a rising Puerto Rican radical group while SDS, the Weathermen, and the Yippies were still building floats.

My father pointed to the building behind him. "Right there is the heart of the pig." The sixty-story phallus in Foley Square known as the Federal Building housed the Department of the Army. He then swung his arm around and pointed north toward Midtown, "And there," stating his desire to attack the seat of Rockefeller's money: Standard Oil, located in the RCA Building.

"And Whitehall," David added, meaning the army induction center near Wall Street. Destroying it would cripple the New York draft.

John tugged anxiously on his pipe. "We might want to caucus with the other groups." He was ignored as Gil, Robin, and Sharon added other locations, and within ten minutes the group had named over a dozen potential targets. Pat reminded everyone what the FLQ taught them: each target required about twenty-five sticks of dynamite, and each building should be cased by a three-person team for a minimum of a week.

At this point it was Robin, the activist in the group with the thickest arrest file, who oddly enough shared John's dovish reservations. There were only six people on the roof that day—seven, if you counted Jane. He recommended they bring in more committed activists from the Crazies—Demmerle, in particular, who was deeply militant. "George is blowing up the Brooklyn Bridge, he said."

But Gil shut Robin down. "Jeez, Robin, don't you know bullshit when you hear it? George is a fed! The Crazies are filled with feds!"

"Hey, I'm in the Crazies, y'jackass. So is Sharon," Robin retorted as one of his Labradors barked at Gil. "And I can tell you George and I go back to the Workers World Party in '66 and the V&R. And George was the lookout for us at the Waldorf," referring to when he and Sharon stripped naked at a Democratic fundraiser and served pig's heads to delegates. "And you were with us in Chicago, Gil. You saw what George did. No fed is gonna destroy a cop car. Never, man, never!"

"Right on," Sharon punctuated.

Gil had remembered that it was Robin who threw the brick at the cop car, while Demmerle instigated. But rather than getting roped into a labyrinth of Robin's rhetoric, he turned to the ledge and studied the traffic six floors down.

David had reservations regarding Demmerle as well. "I've been in RC meetings with him. He *could* be a fed—but he certainly acts like a kook."

Sam waved his hand, putting an end to the pointless debate. "We need to keep this tight. Just us. And if we need more, I'll talk to Rap [Brown]."

"Whatever," Robin grumbled, and pointed a long finger at Gil. "You think everyone over thirty is a fed."

And then they advanced the agenda to the next subject: acquiring explosives.

John was now having trouble hiding his concern. He knew that Sam had kept one of the four weapons Robin procured for the FLQ escape and had it hidden in an ankle holster. John didn't like guns, particularly at this meeting. *We may be musing for fun about a bombing, but we're still pacifists,* he thought, and he wondered how Sam would react if he did not see the humor in this "meeting." But then there was Jane. He gazed wistfully at the woman who had chosen Sam over him. She was constructing a paper quilt from copies of *Rat Subterranean News* so she could sit on the hot tar. She looked up when David suggested that they could probably steal dynamite from a construction site. Jane had grown fond of David. He had Sam's passion and dark energy, but he was closer to her age. However, still mired in the conventionalism of monogamy, she avoided David's occasional long glances out of respect for Pat.

"That's a myth," Sam corrected David. From his career in engineering, Sam knew there was never much TNT kept at construction sites. "The city gave a monopoly to one company, Explo Inc. They have a warehouse in the Bronx."

Sam chose Gil and Robin as his extraction team. Robin was ex-military, and Gil was their resident martial arts expert. The three men began casing Explo the next day while Pat and Sharon went to various hardware stores to procure Baby Ben alarm clocks, reels of solder, and boxes of batteries. Jane was assigned the provisions. She went to the health food shop, where she bought wheat germ, lecithin, and fish oil, resenting Sam's chauvinist role for her as much as she did the store's pungent smell of its open barrels of yeast. Without her prestigious editing job or the grandeur of the Columbia campus, being treated like the group's intern began to chafe at her sense of purpose. Pat came to her rescue. She sold back-page ads throughout the neighborhood for the number-two underground Village paper and suggested, "You should write for *Rat*."

Jane pouted. She had been so close to a window office at Cambridge. *Rat's* covers looked like head-shop posters, and its vestibule at 241 East Fourteenth Street smelled of urine. Pat cocked her head. "Oh, come on. I thought you didn't want to be Princess Jane. I'll introduce you to Jeff."

Jeff Shero was a twenty-six-year-old former SDS organizer from Austin, Texas, who spoke with precision, as if mentally auditioning each word before he spoke it. He arrived in New York in 1967 with twelve dollars and a mission: to raise enough to start *Rat Subterranean News*. Since then, his daily challenge was figuring ways to integrate *Rat* into the movement like the more established number one underground paper, the *East Village Other*. He targeted major record labels as advertisers with competitive rates for full-page spreads. In June 1969, Shero was concerned about offending his favorite, Apple Records, by leading with a story his competitors would not touch: that Paul McCartney had secretly died two years earlier and the person performing with the Beatles was an imposter named Billy Sheers. Shero complained to Jane, who was sitting pert and overeager before him, that he could not afford the kind of intel mainstream papers paid for since he spent what crumbs of capital *Rat* earned on overhead. "There is no budget for reporters either," he told her. "Seasoned writers consider their articles in *Rat* a contribution to the movement."

Jane was forcing a commiserative nod. She knew the McCartney story was ridiculous. As for working for free, to assure Shero that attending Columbia didn't mean that she was unwilling to start at the bottom, she attempted some humor. "Contributing isn't deleterious. It's needed. Your food section last month was quite the farrago with its recipes for hash brownies." And she laughed at her own joke.

Could she be a cop? Shero thought. He assumed at least one of his twenty-four volunteers was Red Squad, and he knew that Columbia was a recruiting hotbed for the CIA. A smart woman agent would have been a big step up from the usual crazy losers, photographers, and "helpers" without newspaper skills who tried to worm their way into *Rat. Potential agents are the people an editor embraces, not pushes away. You want your adversaries close, where you can watch them,* he thought.

But then, without even meaning to, Jane disabled this suspicion. "You remember the FLQ hijacking story you ran last month? Well, how about "How to Hijack a Commercial Jet" by Jane *Lauren* Alpert?"

Shero sat up in full attention.

———————

Later that afternoon, a loud knock on Pat's door was her introduction to Jane's upsetting news: Sam had been tripping on LSD and become violent, breaking things and waving his fists.

Pat tried to calm her. "Sam never raises his voice or makes sudden moves."

"Well, now he's doing both. He was so mad that I pitched Jeff a hijacking article. *'Why don't you just give an interview to the Boush York Times!'* he was shouting. I mean, does he really believe that the pigs read an abstruse monthly with cartoons, printed on recycled paper?"

Pat sighed, conflicted between wanting to quiet her without disagreeing. Now was not the time to bring Jane up to speed on how thorough the feds were—Jane was caught up in her rant. "He can channel Che Guevara and convert the apartment into an armory. I don't care anymore."

This was an overdue breakup that Pat was glad to facilitate. She knew of a vacancy in her building two floors down.

Jane's withdrawal was Sam's opportunity to reoffer Rap Brown the Eleventh Street apartment to store munitions. But Diane was now the obstacle. She brought Sam into the movement three years ago and fell in love with his gentle pacifist nature. But she had gotten closer with Jane in the past month and could not see herself going down Sam's militant path. Diane had hardly spoken to him since he helped FLQ fugitives escape, and she had given up on lassoing Sam's affections. She had moved two Black Panther lovers into the empty bedrooms. Diane refused to join the rooftop war council, and the next day, when Sam asked her to join their efforts to discuss some bombings, she asked him to move out.

David and Pat were also taking another break since she could not agree to David's provincial terms for monogamy. Earlier that week, he moved into a sublease on Third Street but kept leads on multiple crash pads for potential safe houses. Learning of Diane's change of heart, he told Sam about a place on 67 East Second Street. It was a quiet Russian/Ukrainian immigrant quarter with a gaggle of Slavic yentas cursing the homeless who used their stoops for a lounge. A Russian Orthodox church dominated the block, and David assured Sam that the cemetery across the street would make it impossible for "the pig spotters" to get a vantage point into the windows.

Court testimony by FBI agents claimed that my father used the name on his fake passport, David McCurdy, for the lease and paid the landlord six months in advance, $180 in cash, for the top floor apartment, number 48. He never bought a stick of furniture, nor did he risk having Mom's attorneys finding him by turning on the utilities. Instead, he contacted people connected to Brown and told them that he now had space to store arms. Sam would refer to the apartment in code as "the McCurdy place." Unknown to all, around the corner, an apartment was recently rented by FBI informant and Abbie Hoffman bodyguard Prince Crazy, George Demmerle.

The next day it began. The FBI speculated that Black and Puerto Rican radicals linked to Brown dropped off rifles and grenades at McCurdy. Sam must've wanted to sleep elsewhere, because for a few nights he hopped beds, then eventually, needing a reliable base free of possessive boyfriends, he called Jane. He told her she was right to leave. He now understood how vital journalism was to her and that they should probably not be together—all the things she needed to hear. He sounded sincere. Despondent. Alone. She invited him over to talk. Sam brought a Labrador puppy, gifted by Robin and Sharon from a recent litter of their dogs. Sam named him John Keats, after the poet. He also brought bits of desks and scrap wood he found in the alley and used them to build her a queen-sized loft bed. Jane would tell Pat that it was the most romantic thing any man had done for her. Sam would spend that night with her in the bed he built and nearly every night thereafter.

Just two nights before the dynamite heist, Sam's mood swayed. Feeling melancholy, he asked Jane if he could be alone. Jane obliged him by meeting the volunteers of *Rat* for drinks. As she was leaving, she caught Sam slumped in a chair, pining while looking over a strip of paper. It was the only pictures he still had of him and me together, a four-shot montage from a Woolworth's photo booth he kept in his guitar case.

"Why don't you call him?" she said from the doorway. Sam didn't answer. Soon he would point a gun at night watchmen to steal explosives. There would be no turning back after that. When he heard the locks tumble, he stood up, flexed a yoga pose to center himself, and, with a deep breath, picked up the phone and dialed. Mom's voice pierced his mellow. "Hullo?"

"I was calling to speak with Jocko. Is he home?"

Her tone changed when she recognized him—"Of course he's home. It's seven o'clock. Where else would he be?"

"Please, let's not fight."

But they did. "When will you see your son again? Where are you living?" It went on.

I was playing with the latest child-development toy, LEGO, and could hear fragments of their conversation from my room, when Mom called me to the phone and extended the receiver. "It's for you" is all she said.

"Hullo?'

"Jocko? It's Daddy." The voice sounded like many others.

"Are you sure?" I said.

"Yes, I'm sure. It's Daddy."

I could hardly remember the last time I'd seen him. I thought it was our camping trip on the Appalachian Trail when he taught me how to safely build a campfire and said he was going away. That was last year, an eternity to a six-year-old. "I don't think you can be my daddy. Because my daddy said he was leaving to help Indians."

"Yes. I know. I know I said that. But I'd like to tell you something . . . Jocko? Hullo . . . ?"

But I'd gone back to my LEGOs.

Next for Sam came the harsh drone of a dead line. My voice became a memory, fading against the distant sirens on Avenue C. We never spoke again.

Two days later four boxes of TNT were stolen from Explo Inc., and the Melville Collective was born.

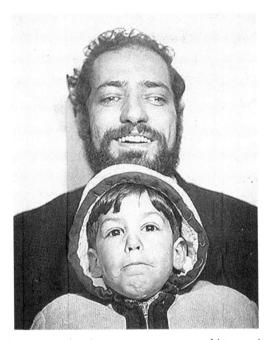

The only photos Sam carried in his guitar case were of him and me, taken at a photo booth in 1966 or '67. *Author's collection*

Two weeks later, Jane scowled. Instead of being kept at McCurdy, four boxes of TNT were tucked against the coil of her Frigidaire to "keep it cool, daddy-o," as Robin had insisted. She saw the condensation forming on the boxes and thought Robin an imbecile.

Earlier that night, everyone was high on achievement. The men praised their coordination, as Sharon dropped to her knees grinning like an evil child while sensuously stroking the stenciled words HIGH EXPLOSIVES. However, the celebration quickly faded into an argument about the wisdom of bringing dynamite to Jane's new place instead of to McCurdy.

The group agreed on only two things that night: to meet back at Jane's the next day at 2 PM to discuss their first attack, and a pledge to tell no one else about "the stuff."

The pledge would be short lived.

An hour later, when Sharon and Robin returned to their West Village apartment, it was to answer the ring of an insistent phone. Lester Barns, her middle-aged ex, wanted to know what had become of the four pistols he'd lent Robin two months ago. "I thought Rasta meant renouncing all implements of violence?" she postured.

He didn't want to discuss it on the phone.

While Robin took the dogs for a walk, Sharon met Lester at the Waverly Coffee Shop and confided that she had given the weapons to the FLQ hijackers that he had probably read about.

"There were only two hijackers. What about the other pistols?"

Unprepared with an elaborate excuse, Sharon trusted her ex with her biggest secret: his remaining two mementos had been used that very night by her and couple of friends to steal explosives. Their intent was to do what she called "responsible terrorism."

Lester itched his matting hair. "Have you thought about universities?" On his mind was bombing Rutgers, the school that had fired him only six months before his tenure. Schools were not part of the group's vision, but she was relieved, thankful really, that her ex, with his awkward dreadlocks paired to his Queens accent, was not leveraging this sensitive information into sex. In fact, Rasta Lester had another form of leverage in mind.

Sam had also not kept the pact. In an attempt to persuade his best friend, John, to join the group, the next morning he spent two hours over a late breakfast at Veselka telling his comrade about "the stuff" and pressuring him to attend the first collective meeting later that day.

John reluctantly agreed, and by 2 PM they sat on Jane's couch along with Gil in wait for the activist power couple—Robin and Sharon. As foreplay, Sam talked excitedly about the pipe bomb at the Loew's movie theater on Eighty-Sixth and Broadway (five blocks from where Mom and I lived) set by an anti-Castro radical faction, Acción Cubana. John grew ever more uncomfortable as Sam mused about what it would feel like after their first device exploded on the thirtieth floor of the RCA building—the offices of Standard Oil. He was counting on that happening next week. Maybe even tomorrow.

At 3 PM, Robin and Sharon finally arrived, somewhat bashfully, and to everyone's surprise, with Lester Barns in tow. According to Jane's memoir, Sharon's introduction sounded more like an apology. "Lester supplied the guns, and he has many connections in the movement. I think he should be involved."

Sizing up Lester, Sam was not impressed. A middle-aged White college professor sporting an army jacket with Bob Marley silk-screened on the back and a "People Get Ready" T-shirt seemed like a perverse cultural appropriation rather than a religious awakening. Jane mirrored Sam's skepticism, and with her hands on her hips, said, "I never heard of him."

Sharon spun around. Her frizzy hair tussled. "*You* have never heard of him? Remind me again, Jane, how the Sam-Jesus-long you've been in this movement?"

As quarrels detonated, Sam shook his head and turned to the kitchenette. He wished David and Pat were here. In honor of Pat's absence, he started to prepare several sandwiches of alfalfa sprouts, peanut butter, and hot sauce on oat bread. Behind him, he half heard their war over minutiae. Lester had strong opinions on everything: he had supplied the guns, so technically, he was already involved; Pat and David were the real security risk because she worked for NACLA, which was under FBI surveillance; finally, Lester disagreed with Robin—keeping explosives in the refrigerator was not smart since it was a confined space. And Rutgers should be their first target. The shit was already getting out of hand and the collective was less than two weeks in the making.

Lester's intellectualized activism reminded Sam of his father. *Action was all that counts today*, Sam thought. Action was what he wanted the group to move toward. Thinking of the conversation he and Pat had the other night about the Cuban Revolution, he turned with a tray of sandwiches to announce that July 26 was the anniversary of Castro's attack on the Moncada Barracks. "Is that enough time for everybody to get their shit together? Who wants a sandwich?"

John waved his hand, no thanks, but like teacher's pet, Jane's shot toward the ceiling. Sam handed her a corner and looked at the room full of career activists who had grown darkly silent. "Who else?"

Sharon eyed Jane competitively and took a sandwich from the plate. "Well, of course, I'm in. But I think before we do anything, we need to consider our brothers at the Black Panthers."

She elbowed Robin, who perked up. "Yeah, yeah, she's right. We can't go willy-nilly without making them hip. It would be racist."

Gil shook his head in violent rebuttal. "No, no, no! *Dude!* The Panthers are crawling with UC pigs!" Gil always seemed to be informed about where to find informants. Robin and Sharon defended their plan by presenting an asset they assured would remove all risk of exposure to undercover cops: the Young Patriot's defense captain, appointed by Panther national president

Bobby Seale himself, George Demmerle. The three of them, Robin, Sharon, and Demmerle, were going to the Black Panthers' national caucus in Oakland, California, next week to represent the Crazies. Sharon felt that getting Seale to approve their bombings would be tantamount to an endorsement from the entire New Left.

To Sam, this stall read not as White guilt but as bourgeois approval, as well as an added security risk. "What if Seale says no?"

"He won't," Robin guaranteed as he took the last sandwich corner and looked hard at Gil. "Not if we go through Crazy George."

Gil buried his face.

By 4:30 AM the following morning, Sam did his usual one hundred push-ups, two hundred sit-ups, and a half hour of yoga on Jane's rug while she slept in the loft. At 5:30 AM, he met Gil on the stoop for a clandestine mission. Pat had just returned from an overnight in lockup. Sipping her morning coffee by the window, she watched from five floors up as the two men quietly carried four heavy boxes out of the building.

About a half hour later, Sam came back to walk John Keats. With the dog in tow, he stopped by Pat's apartment; through her door, he could hear an argument. David was accusing Pat of lying about last night's arrest. He suspected that she had really been making love with another activist. Sam knocked hard and called sarcastically, "I'm looking for Fidel Castro. I have his shipment of cigars."

Pat jerked open the door, wearing little more than a grin. "I'll take a cigar." She beamed seductively and invited Sam into their spat.

Sam pivoted with big news: last night he had liberated four cases of dynamite from Explo.

Pat asked, "That's what you were carrying this morning?"

Sam nodded and said he wanted the two of them to come with him right now to meet Gil at McCurdy and start making bombs. David's eyes narrowed. "What about the others?"

"You mean, the Masturbators."

David drawled, "*Masturbators?*"

The Masturbators was Sam's new spoof name for Robin, Sharon, Jane, and John. The hybrid formed from splicing the well-known downtown activist group the Motherfuckers with the word *procrastinators*. He retold the scene from last night of Sharon involving a White Jewish Rastafari convert named Lester, who did not want to include her or David because *they* were too conspicuous. "Sharon also talked the room into thinking that they needed to get Bobby Seale's approval to set off a bomb."

Pat lit her first cigarette of the day as John Keats began licking her toes. She had heard about Lester's toxic machismo from others. She didn't like him. "That is ridiculous. *Sharon* said that?"

"Masturbators," repeated Sam, and extended a ten-dollar bill. "We'll need more flashlight batteries and several Baby Ben alarm clocks."

She took the money.

A half hour later, the Ukrainian yentas of Second Street shook their heads in shame as a braless hippie jostled down their street in a funky orange sleeveless knit, clutching a bag from the hardware store. Pat flipped them the bird as she climbed the cracked stoop of the McCurdy tenement, and in a moment, the young militant found herself in a four-hundred-square-foot studio, with three lovers and four cases of explosives.

While Gil and David nervously spied out the window for suspicious cars, Sam and Pat dumped the bag and began dissecting the alarm clocks to make three sets of timers.

As the hour progressed, Sam realized that since he was staying at Jane's practically every night and would be making trips to Milwaukee to connect with Brown, someone else would have to look in on the stuff once a day. He turned first to Gil, but Gil was trying not to look anxious, inching away from the stockpile of munitions. "Newsreel is like, fourteen-hour days, man." His justification was that both he and John were cutting a documentary about the CIA's penetration into Cambodia. Sam shook his head. *Prioritizing a movie about imperialism less than a few hundred people will see over actually ending imperialism?* Gil was sounding like a Masturbator. He turned to David with the same offer. His illegal sublease was a two-minute walk to McCurdy. David took the key.

Although two days prior Jane was adamant about getting the dynamite out of her refrigerator, now she was feeling left out of the loop again. Sam refused to give her a spare key to McCurdy. When she learned that he had given one to David and invited Pat to make detonators, Jane and Sam fought. "If you want to be sexual with her, you don't have to use the movement as an excuse."

"First . . . Jane, you need to be less possessive sexually. Second, you're way out of line!" Sam defended David and Pat as serious revolutionaries and pointed out that she had barely done anything constructive in the seven months since they had moved from the decadent Upper West Side, other than work on her bougie and potentially dangerous hijacking article for *Rat*. Finally, she was still siding with Robin and Sharon as they whined about getting the Panther's permission, like schoolkids in need of a hall pass.

She brooded for the rest of the evening and while in bed that night defended her hesitance. "What harm is there in getting the Panthers on board, other than waiting a week until Robin and Sharon get back from Oakland?" Sam answered by rolling her on her side, spooning into her curves, and repeating a phrase that he often used.

"The revolution ain't tomorrow, Lady Jane. Y'dig? It's *today*."

14 | THE FBI'S BOMB EXPERT

AROUND JANUARY 1989, Kunstler had passed on my FOIA case, citing "a full plate." LARRY, my new attorney, had taken Kunstler's referral pro bono since I was a struggling musician and he admired my dad. At a health food restaurant in the Village, Larry had both good news and bad. The good news: "I was able to get some of Jane Alpert's file, yours, and your mother's." He handed me a slight manila envelope. I flipped it open and saw that what few pages they released on Jane had many thick, black redaction marks. "This is it? Larry, tell me the truth, if I were the *New York Times*, would I have been given everything?"

Not really. Larry explained that before the DOJ can release a file, it is scrutinized by people in several departments who redact anything still classified. Since my father's file was enormous, it would take years. The DOJ had released the files for my mother and me because they were very thin. The only way Larry was able to get a small part of Jane's very thick file was because a grad student from the School of Foreign Service at Georgetown was doing a paper on the Weathermen and requested these exact pages.

"What about Sam's file? Didn't the grad student want that?"

Apparently not.

The waitress deposited our order. His was black coffee. Mine was something new I had to explain slowly: alfalfa sprouts, peanut butter, and hot sauce on oat bread.

"They've changed the rules at the DOJ," Larry explained. "All requests over a hundred pages take a while." If I knew exactly which hundred pages to ask for, I could get them in a few weeks. But if I wanted Sam's complete, unredacted file, it would be a court battle, one that would probably take years. But how could I know which hundred pages to ask for without knowing the contents of the entire file? A nasty catch-22, which I was learning was typical of asking the government for anything a citizen is entitled to.

Larry cleared his throat. "I have a number for you. You can never say that it came from me." He handed me a Post-it.

When I got home, I tore through my thin FBI file. It had almost every part-time job I held since I was fifteen, including Rogue Studios; report cards; college professors' notes; and small clubs I belonged to as a child that I'd long forgotten about, like the Official Star Trek Fan Club. (Really?) It had a redaction of a name and address of a "known Key Activist" I'd gone to visit in Brooklyn just a few months back. It was obviously Sharon Krebs.

I put it aside and called the number on the Post-it. Per its instructions, I punched in a five-digit code on the touch-tone keypad, then hung up. The Post-it said to wait. About five minutes went by until the phone rang. "Hullo?"

"Mister, um . . . Melville?" said an older, froggy voice, clearing his throat.

"Yes."

"You can call me Oliver. Write down this address and be there tomorrow at 10 PM."

It was in Queens, underneath the Fifty-Ninth Street Bridge near the film production company Silvercup Studios—a very sketchy part of town in those days.

The next night, I stood in near panic on deserted Vernon Boulevard. High above my head, adding to my terror, were the billboards for the competing top-rated family TV shows that year: *The Cosby Show* and *Roseanne*. The actors' ten-foot-wide grins were a creepy comfort as I drove across the Fifty-Ninth Street Bridge into Queens. But as I stood directly underneath and looked up into the lascivious smiles and nostrils of Bill and Roseanne, their faces seemed distorted and grotesque. The massive warehouse they were anchored to had no directory, buzzer, or any visible way to enter. When the phone in a lone booth on the corner rang, I grabbed the receiver.

"Oliver?"

"Yes. I only have a few minutes."

Oliver said he was the bomb expert at FBI in 1969 who profiled my father. What he told me would change the entire scope of my investigation.

"The DOJ is not going to give you your father's file, because the charges against your father should have been dismissed; we had no search warrant, and his due process rights were trampled on when we extracted a confession while denying him a lawyer."

"But he had a lawyer," I said.

"At trial. He was denied one at his interrogation. The Judge . . . Pollack, I think it was, covered for many mistakes made by the Bureau and the munies"—the municipal cops. "Your father's trial lawyer only exposed a few of them when he cross-examined the case worker, Joe Anderson, and his informant, Demmerle. You should get those transcripts."

No kidding. As if I had not been trying. Then I got skeptical. Who the fuck was this guy, really? "I thought they caught my father red-handed with bombs in his duffel bag. So, why all the cloak and dagger BS?"

"Your father's case came during a time of a management turmoil at the New York Office, which was mostly to cover for bad actors there. The head of the NYO in '69 was John Malone. We called him Cement Head. He was retiring in a few years and wanted an agent named HENRY BYERS to succeed him. Anderson wanted out of the Intelligence Division and had his sights set on special agent in charge. So, in return for promotions, Anderson and Byers would clean up the dirt done under Malone—mostly to do with Yippies, Black Panthers, and a handful of Weathermen that were set up with planted evidence."

Oliver claimed Hoover was desperate to quash the New Left and asked Congress to classify Panthers and the Yippies as "enemy combatants." (Today, this would be like declaring them a "domestic terrorist organization.") If Congress agreed, it would grant the FBI constitutional privileges for warrantless surveillance and detainments. "Sam's case meant that this wasn't just about the Black militants. Educated White men engaging in domestic terror in 1969 were considered a national security threat."

"And conspiracies make a better argument than lone assailants?"

"Yes. If you can make a case for one, conspiracies are career-makers and budget-expanders."

But to make a case for conspiracy, the FBI needed Sam to give them names—hopefully names like Rap Brown and other well-known organizers. "That's why you're not getting the files," Oliver continued. "If you did, you'd learn that your father never gave them *any* names. I was there for his interview."

Without names, only an informant could link Sam to other cells. I interrupted: "But Jane's book claims my father *confessed* the names to Demmerle."

"Jane's book is almost a complete fiction, at least when it comes to the bombings. She gets many facts wrong, like the placement of the bomb in the Federal Building. I have a lot of FOIA files that I can send you. You can see my initials on virtually every internal document."

"I need to know who you are. I'm trying to write a book on Sam, and I can't just write about all this without quoting a source. And I know your name isn't really Oliver."

"It's Wesley Swearingen. I owed Larry a favor, but I would tell you this anyway, since I think the Bureau has a lot to answer for about that era." (Six years later, Swearingen would write *FBI Secrets: An Agent's Expose*, published in 1995 by South End Press.) "What really led us to Sam and the others was not an informant. It was Jane's articles in *Rat*."

15 | *BOOM!*

"HOW TO HIJACK A COMMERCIAL JET" was published in *Rat's* June 1969 issue. Shero subbed out Jane's sensational headline for the FAA posting at airports:

AIRCRAFT HIJACKING IS A FEDERAL CRIME
PUNISHABLE BY DEATH

Shero changed the title because he was concerned. "There's a big difference in reporting what hijackers have done and advocating hijacking. This article would get us arrested."

While Jane was correct that few above Fourteenth Street read *Rat* or knew of its existence, so was Shero. The FBI on East Fifty-Sixth Street was keenly aware. They had had the paper under surveillance from the day it opened. *Rat* was not exceptional in this regard. Teams of clerks scoured underground newspapers for leads. Articles were clipped, labeled, catalogued, and distributed to various divisions.

Jane's piece was flagged and placed in a folder for Special Agent Joe Anderson, who had been assigned the investigation into the FLQ Pan Am hijacking. Anderson felt the FLQ was the clear inspiration for the *Rat* article. He assigned an agent to do a background check of the author. However, Jane's name in the byline had been misspelled as "Jane Albert." Thus, Anderson missed her thin, recently created 167 file. At that time, it included only an interview with a Columbia provost about her sudden departure and an interview with her editor at Cambridge University Press about her equally sudden resignation.

While Jane's file would remain buried, Hoover had authorized a special task force of two thousand agents to scour the 167 files for downtown subversives who might be connected. Within the over 1,250 selected 167s were the eight, as-yet-unrelated files of Sam Melville, David Hughey III, Pat Swinton, John Cohen, Lester Barns, Gilbert Bernstein, and perennial FBI favorites Robin Palmer and Sharon Krebs. Robin had been upgraded the previous year to "Key Activist," due to Demmerle's reports, and now had regular "welfare checks" (when an agent pretends to be a salesman or Con-Ed worker to get a peek inside the home of a subject). Finally, Sharon Krebs was peripherally involved in so many investigations that her 167 was often stored in the mimeograph room for convenience, right near the files for Abbie Hoffman, Jerry Rubin, and Rap Brown.

But, for the moment, the files of the collective remained unconnected due to the veil of a single typo in *Rat*.

Sam and Pat were waiting at the curb when Robin's dented Chevy station wagon returned from the Black Panther conference in Oakland. Something was missing. Sharon was riding shotgun. Jane, who had nagged Sharon to take her with them, was in the back trying to distance herself from crushed cartons of Kools. But there was no George Demmerle. Robin whispered privately to Sam that George had grown suspicious of Jane after talking with her for several hours at the conference. "She claimed she was on assignment as the 'star reporter for *Rat*.' And Crazy George says, '*Rat's* infiltrated,'" Robin told Sam. "George thought *Jane* was a fed." Robin also claimed that the reason for Demmerle's absence was that he had decided to stay in Oakland to help the Panthers drop grenades into manholes. But the good news was that before departing, Demmerle also told Robin that Seale had no objections to their doing a bombing.

"Outstanding," Sam whispered back, unconcerned. He removed Jane's bag.

Once Robin and Sharon's car turned the corner, Sam and Pat huddled with Jane in an attempt to seduce her away from the Masturbators. They briefed her about the plan they had hatched in her absence, to blow up the United Fruit Company loading dock on the West Side Highway.

United Fruit exemplified the banana republics of Central America. It bottlenecked distribution with bribes, creating a virtual monopoly. In 1954 it played a notorious role in encouraging a CIA-backed coup that deposed Guatemala's democratically elected president Jacobo Arbenz. Also, its ships had been instrumental in the blockade of Russian ships during the incident known to Americans as the Cuban Missile Crisis, thwarting Russia's "perfectly reasonable right" to store nuclear weapons on Cuba's shores. Bombing United Fruit was an appropriate way to celebrate the anniversary of the Cuban Revolution. Sam and Pat had biked to its docks on the Hudson the night before and had seen that they were deserted by 10 PM without even a night watchman. Sam wanted to do the job that night.

Jane's bloodshot eyes shifted back and forth. Sam and Pat had that same giddy enthusiasm as when she returned from her monthlong trip to England. They were very high and had probably just screwed minutes before she arrived. "I smell like an ashtray," Jane moaned.

Sam kissed her forehead. "You don't need to smell pretty to blow up a dock on the Hudson. C'mon, Lady Jane, it's time to ride the horse in the direction it's going." Pat nodded, hoping Jane would stop straddling the divergent camps.

But Jane held her ground. "A couple of days' wait would be efficacious. The country is distracted." She was referring to Neil Armstrong's one small step on the moon a few days before, as well as Senator Ted Kennedy's accident, in which his car had gone off a bridge on Martha's Vineyard, drowning his female passenger. Both stories dominated the national conversation.

Pat nodded in agreement with Jane. "The anniversary of [Castro's raid on] the Moncada Barracks is not actually until July 26." But Sam tensed at a forming pattern of delays. "United Fruit would get a headline," he said, trying to appeal to Jane's thirst for one.

Jane shook her head. "The munitions dump. Remember?" She was referring to Pyronics, a New Jersey hand grenade factory. While she was in Oakland, Sam and Pat practiced by placing a small device in their dumpster the previous week. "It was all but ignored by the press."

Sam agreed to wait two days.

Two days later, Sam opened the door of the McCurdy place to greet the face of a significant asset to the Melville Collective: IVAN LOPEZ. Ivan was where Sam wanted to be, planting myriad bombs with several well-organized Puerto Rican nationals who were interested in Rap Brown's growing militia in the Midwest. He had dark, thick eyebrows that contrasted with his face's soft features, like a real-life version of movie actor Montgomery Clift.

Ivan gave Sam a duffel bag of grenade parts that Brown needed to be kept secure. Sam added this to the arsenal, and they shared war stories for an hour, becoming fast friends, after which Sam asked Ivan if he wanted in on their United Fruit caper later that night. He rested his hand on one box of TNT from Explo for emphasis. Ivan was very impressed. He would be happy to learn of the destruction of United Fruit, an enemy of the revolutions in Latin America, but he was leaving for a bombing in Miami at midnight. Instead, Ivan countered with an invite to the christening of the New York Chapter of the Latino activist group the Young Lords. The Young Lords began as a Puerto Rican turf gang in the Chicago neighborhood of Lincoln Park in the fall of 1960, but by '68 had become a civil and human rights movement coalition with chapters across the United States. Within the hour, in a loft near the Hells Angels headquarters, a room filled with Latin revolutionaries; there, they first learned through Ivan of Sam Melville—a person worthy of their respect. (The Young Lords also had a strong presence at Attica.)

With his adrenaline peaked, at 9 PM Sam banged on Pat's door. "Get some clothes on, and let's join this revolution."

At 10 PM, Sam, Pat, and Jane set out to the pier by bike. Sam had the bomb in his backpack, and Pat carried the detonators. Once at the pier, Sam set the hour hand of the alarm clock to a little past 12 AM, so that the blast would synchronize to the actual date of Castro's raid. Pat wired the blasting cap. Jane got the job of lookout, half a block down.

When they got back to Fourth Street, Jane beelined to her typewriter, finally able to deliver her contribution to the collective: the press release. But . . .

"No notes," Sam said, reminding her that Metesky was caught due to writing samples.

"But I'll type it," Jane argued.

"Baby, the FBI can match typewriter ribbons easier than handwriting. I'm surprised you don't know that."

They walked to the corner pay phone. Sam produced a bandanna and placed it over the mouthpiece to disguise his voice and called WBAI. The only person answering the phone during the graveyard shift was the DJ, who thought the call might be a request and patched it into the live feed. To the DJ's shock, an assertive, muffled man's voice said, "The United Fruit Company pier was blown up tonight in honor of Cuban Independence Day." Sam hung up and smiled at Jane. She looked annoyed. "Cuban Independence Day is January 1," she corrected him. "Today is National Revolution Day. I'm surprised *you* don't know that."

The action that was supposed to unite the Masturbators with Sam, Pat, and David did the opposite.

At 8 AM the next day, David was cleaning the seeds from his stock of weed when the CBS morning radio carried a report about the destruction of Pier 3. A phoned-in warning claimed the bombers were honoring Fidel Castro. The jocks added some witty banter. "But, uh, bad news for these bozos, according to AP, United Fruit owns the dock, but it's been rented out to some tugboat company. Sorry, boys. Do your homework next time."

David jammed his legs into his shorts, remembering, *Pat has United Fruit stickers all over her refrigerator.* He ran the half mile to Fourth Street. After several knocks, he went downstairs to Jane's place, where he found her, Pat, and Sam, naked and interlocked near the radio, the pungent smell of sex and pot thick as steam. He smiled, produced a joint, and joined them.

Around 10 AM, Pat and David dressed and left Jane's to avoid the Masturbators, all of whom had heard the news and called to say they were rushing over.

By 11 AM, Lester, John, and Gil were pacing an angry hole into Jane's carpet as Robin and Sharon chilled with a joint on the fire escape. Lester's negativity was, as usual, most authoritarian: he thought they were going to decide on targets together and Pat would *not* be involved. Gil agreed, stunned at how real everything had suddenly become. John gaped at Jane. He was unable to pair the violent act to the demure girl-next-door brooding on the couch. She was still heavy-headed, coming down off her high, when she suddenly perked up, clutching the morning edition and crushing it into a ball with uncharacteristic expletives. "The *Times* is a shit paper. They are still obsessing over the fucking moon bullshit!"

Robin took a moment to sidebar that he heard that the Apollo 11 moon landing was staged in a TV studio in Nevada. Jane ignored him, started pacing quickly, and stated that she could write a quick press release and then "accidentally find it" when she opened *Rat*'s mail that day. "It would guarantee that our message is clear."

Sam shook his head. "Forget the pier. We need to go bigger. Standard Oil, Chase Manhattan."

"Well, I dunno," said Robin. "I think we should wait until after August 15."

Jane stopped pacing. "Yes, he is right! The fifteenth!"

Sam couldn't wait to hear their next creative delay. "OK . . . What is August 15?"

"You mean Woodstock?" asked John.

Lester perked up. "Everyone will be upstate. That settles it. We wait."

Jane and Shero had created a map to be published in *Rat* called "Movement City," an area within the massive music festival set aside for almost two dozen New Left groups, like a job fair. "Everyone important will be distracted," Jane related. "It would be horrible timing for an action."

"Not to mention disrespectful," added Lester.

Sam had no interest in partying with thousands of hippies at a pop festival. But grasping the depth of procrastination from the Masturbators, he was developing interest in meeting the man who Sharon and Robin had claimed was dropping grenades into manhole covers, who was connected to the upper echelon of the Black Panthers, and who would be staffing the Crazies booth in Movement City—George Demmerle.

While the NYPD sorted through what was left of United Fruit on the Hudson that morning, Jane, intent on messaging the attack, pushed Jeff Shero for her monthly column to be harsh words aimed at the Latin imperialists.

"They deserved the attack," Jane repeated several times as Shero sipped coffee.

Shero warned her of being too much of an advocate. "I was concerned that the FBI might think *she* was the bomber," he told me when I interviewed him in 2017. "But I'll never forget what she said with that practiced New England tone, that *Rat* is not worth the recycled paper it is printed on if it 'hides in the shadow of indifference.' That's how she spoke to people."

Shero gave in that day, but he cut her piece down to a single column, sandwiched her article between ads, and printed it with no byline. Still, it caught the eye of an FBI research clerk who routed the article to the head of Bombing Investigations, Wesley Swearingen.

Swearingen was a tall, stone-faced outlier Malone handpicked not only because he was a dogged investigator but also because bomb investigation was the dirty job no agent wanted and Malone did not like the man. Swearingen didn't smoke, drink, or frequent nudie bars. His froggy voice reminded Malone of the stuffy high school homeroom teacher who predicted how you will fail. Worst of all, Malone felt he was a persistent conspiracy theorist who was right just enough times to keep him overconfident.

In 1961, Swearingen filed a report outlining a theory that the Chicago mob was planning to kill President Kennedy. To punish him for rumormongering, Hoover transferred him to the remote field office in Eastern Kentucky, where he covered six counties—alone. After Kennedy's assassination and hints that linked organized crime to his murder, in 1967 Swearingen wrote Hoover a stern I-told-you-so memo claiming that he might go public if his instincts were not acknowledged. Hoover granted him a transfer to the New York Office—a reprieve from isolation but the toughest place in America to be the smartest agent in the room.

After Kennedy, Swearingen was hard pressed to back down off a hunch. And that day, *Rat* caught his attention. Since its inception, *Rat* mostly lampooned the movement more so than it took serious positions—until now. To Swearingen, that meant the paper might have connections to the United Fruit bombers.

He called the NYPD and wanted to know if the pier bomb used plastic explosives, which he could have linked chemically to other bombings he was investigating. He was told the device used dynamite, which, once detonated, could not be traced. The NYPD had already concluded that the blasting caps were stolen from Explo Inc., but did not think the tip was worth sharing with the FBI. Instead, it misdirected Swearingen by telling him that the pier job "looked like the work of an amateur," evidenced by the use of a common windup alarm clock as the timer. The NYPD insisted that this was a local matter and not a concern for the Bureau.

Not swayed, Swearingen rang his counterpart in the Intelligence Division, Joe Anderson, who was working other cases involving pro-Castro/anti-imperialist radicals, like the FLQ. After Swearingen showed him the *Rat* piece, Anderson dug out the previous month's *Rat* article about hijacking a plane, written by "Jane Albert." To Swearingen, the writing styles and pointed intolerance of US involvement in Latin America were similar and confirmed his hunch that *Rat* was somehow connected. He suggested a standard *black bag job* on the author: tails, illegal wiretaps, and hidden cameras.

Black bag jobs were severe steps, used in important cases, that sometimes included spreading rumors to a person's boss or wife that the subject was a Communist, child molester, adulterer, or person of interest. Anything to pressure subjects to cooperate. Anderson told his counterpart he had already thought of doing a black bag job on Jane Albert last month but could find no information or current address and presumed it was an alias. Without a hard link, Anderson agreed with the NYPD that this was a local matter and not one in which Swearingen should involve federal resources.

Sam awoke to the sounds of mic checks over the distorted PA system. A lifeguard chair sat atop a knoll overlooking the festival. Sam climbed its ladder to watch the massive field filling up with flamboyant scarves, long locks of hair, and bare breasts painted over with flowery pinwheels. About fifty thousand tickets were sold, but nearly four hundred thousand people converged on a farm in Bethel, New York, during the three-day celebration of love and peace known as Woodstock.

The terrain resembled that of the Appalachian Trail, where he camped with his Bronx buddies in the early days of his marriage to Ruth. Most had families now, making hay from their PhDs and sitting in their safe spaces, hearing Vietnam casualty reports between toothpaste commercials. Even many in the herds before him were numb to the real pain of US imperialism. How many had hitchhiked for days to just hear music, get high, and get laid more so than listen to speeches that might end US dominance? Today, as concert-goers migrated like buffalo toward the stage, they were speckled in mud from last night's heavy rains, and breakfast tents sagged with rainwater. T-shirts and tree branches were refashioned as loin covers, emulating Adam and Eve.

To Sam, the damp morning nip felt good; he decided that history's biggest hippie festival was the appropriate moment to have his final toke of Mother Nature. Tomorrow, he would hold the Masturbators to their word to begin attacks in earnest. And if they defaulted, he would move without them.

In the tents of Movement City, representatives from the Yippies, the Black Panther Party, the Motherfuckers, the Crazies, and many more had erected their booths before dawn and now had food, Kool-Aid, and posters to contribute to the flamboyant energy. Missing only were the crowds they had expected. Most opted to stake out rain-soaked patches nearer to the stage or were getting high by the stream where skinny-dipping was on the political agenda. At the Yippies' booth, a megaphone began the morning address with a recap of incidents ignored by the "pig media":

> August 4, Chicago—A police car was shot up by Black militants;
> August 6, Denver—Five Points police station was fire-bombed;
> August 8—the "People's Park Massacre": a peaceful demonstration turned into a riot where one person was killed;
> August 10, San Diego—Black Panther operative Sylvester Bell was shot.

The announcer offered one piece of mainstream interest: the day before, on August 9, police discovered the bodies of actress Sharon Tate, coffee heiress Abigail Folger, and several friends at the home of Tate's husband, Oscar-winning film director Roman Polanski. The words pig and die whitey were written in blood on the walls. Hippies around him cheered, "Right on!" praising the Hollywood homicide of the rich and privileged by fed-up Blacks. It would turn out that a White songwriter, Charles Manson, engineered these killings because of a record producer who rejected him months earlier when renting the same house. Manson instructed his followers to stage the scene like a race crime.

Sam found Jane sleeping in the main tent. She had formed rain ponchos into a makeshift bed in hopes of keeping mud from the paisley blouse she bought for the occasion. They located Robin and Sharon at the Crazies' booth in Movement City. Front and center was what looked like a drunk in a purple cape and pink Roman centurion helmet: Demmerle pointing a javelin into the air, yelling, "The revolution is today, motherfuckers. Why are you wasting time at a bougie, fucked-up music festival?"

Upon Robin's introduction, Demmerle got right to work. "So, you're the Sam that Abbie raps about." Sam shrugged humbly, and the three over-thirty men instantly began to impress each other with war stories of the Chicago DNC, Washington MOBE, and Columbia University. Jane became bored with tales that she had heard many times by the old farts of the movement. She wanted to get closer to the music, where people her age were dancing. She would check back with Sam in a few hours. "I'll be right here," Sam said to her, implying that this was the place to be if she was serious.

"A bit of frivolity won't wane my passion for change." She kissed him and turned toward the stage as the three men watched her incredulously.

Demmerle faced Sam. "Articulate. Writes for *Rat*?" He recalled Jane telling him this in Oakland.

"Yeah."

"George thinks *Rat*'s infiltrated," said Robin.

Demmerle seconded. "You should get her out of there."

Sam nodded and pivoted to his agenda: "Who have you been working with?"

Demmerle dropped his list: Hoffman, Seale, and Ivan Lopez. When Robin left them to hand out some fliers, Sam asked Demmerle for referals: Who did he know who might want to help take down the Financial District? Demmerle's reply surprised him: "Palmer."

"Really? Robin? Any chance he's a fed?" asked Sam, testing him.

"Zero chance." Demmerle squinted. "You should have seen him throw a brick through a cop car in Chicago. Feds ain't allowed to break the law." Demmerle was riffing on the counterpropaganda that undercover cops were legaly prohibited from doing drugs or performing criminal acts. "Right on, man," Demmerle shouted above Jefferson Airplane singing "Volunteers." "It's all about action. Talk is BS I got no time for."

By the next morning, exhausted from the long drive back to the city, Jane crashed in the loft. Meanwhile, Sam smoked a cigar on the fire escape, jazzed by his talk with Demmerle. Freedom fighters around the world were doing daily damage, but almost a month had passed since the Explo heist and the Masturbators had been like a lead weight around his ankle. Robin and Sharon had decided to stay upstate to hear more music, and John and Gil were always too busy at Newsreel. Jane was too concerned with PR. Sam wanted to call the only two people he felt would want to plan an attack with him that day: Pat and David. However, Pat was out of town seeing her daughter, Jenny, and David had gone to Sarah Lawrence College to court a coed.

By noon, impatience felt like ants crawling over the back of his neck. Sam gazed at the soldering station under the loft. Quietly he wired up a blasting cap, hoping that would release tension. Next, he wandered into the bathroom and cut short his shoulder-length hair, preparing to blend in with corporate culture as he had during his marriage. Still restless, he finally went for a bike ride, hoping that it would settle his soul. Soon, he found himself at McCurdy.

Four lonely boxes of TNT stared at him from the corner.

Jane was reading on the fire escape when Sam returned around 7 PM. She had spent the afternoon on a date with John. As she highlighted a page, she reminded him, "You said that I needed to become less sexually possessive."

"Yes . . . John and Jane . . . Did you have a good time?"

"John is very sweet."

"Good. Well, I set a bomb on Wall Street today."

"Really? What time will it go off? I need to plan dinner," she said dismissively, her face still in the book.

"Three hours."

Something in his voice made her look up. Sam was wearing a suit. His hair was short and face clean. "Woodstock is over. And we cannot afford to look like hippies anymore."

He told her he had chained his Schwinn to a parking sign outside a target he had picked at random: Marine Midland Bank at 140 Broadway, a conspicuous smoked-glass monolith of capitalism. Jane went pale. "But what does a Wall Street bank have to do with the war?"

"Don't be naive."

Robotically, she meandered to the desk to start a press release, still not sure if the danger was real. "How did you know the building would be empty?"

"Ever walk through Wall Street after eight? You could play stickball in the gutter."

"But it's an international bank, Sam. Ten PM is around lunchtime in Tokyo."

Sam turned on the shower and began to undress. "Well, it's done."

Jane looked at her typewriter, contemplating the time lag to write a release. *Screw that.* She dialed information and got the number for Marine Midland's main desk and ran out to the corner phone booth. Sam called after her: "They're not going to listen."

The bank had received over a dozen fake bomb threats that month.

At 11 PM, an explosion blew a four-thousand-pound computer five feet from the wall of the eighth floor of 140 Broadway. Windows shattered, leaving a ten-foot hole, and a thousand shards of smoked glass fell to the street. Approximately one hundred people were still working on various floors. Many were covered in debris and plaster and received minor cuts.

Lester, John, and Gil were at Jane's within the hour, once again pacing on her carpet like disappointed parents. "This was irresponsible!" Lester shouted in his Queens accent while scratching his dreadlocks.

"People were hurt," Gil stuttered. "Next time, next time it could be worse."

John held his tongue, incredulously staring at Sam, who was lounging on the fire escape and enjoying a cigar like he had just had a massage.

Next entered Robin and Sharon. They knocked hard on Jane's door and, once inside, were shocked at the harsh vibes over what should have been their first celebration. "Sam put us on the scoreboard," Robin said, flailing his arms. "He has got a right to be fed up with us. We've become decadent, jibber-jabbering about a stupid pop festival."

Sharon raised a fist. "Right fucking on! Robin's right! Enough bullshit. We should bomb *two* fucking banks tomorrow."

"Or Standard Oil," Sam added from the fire escape.

"But banks have nothing to do with Vietnam," pushed Jane. "We should do something quick, while we have the attention, but it should be something relevant to the war."

Lester gave in. "OK, man, fine. Sam had the right idea." Then he added a condition. "But we need to take away his blasting caps," he said, as if Sam were not in earshot. "And the seven of us decide where and when they get placed—as a group." Lester glanced through the window at Sam, as if to get consensus. Sam was ignoring him.

After this meeting Jane's walk of shame at 2 AM was two flights upstairs to tell Pat that Sam had gone rogue and bombed a Wall Street Bank. Her timing could not have been worse. As she knocked on Pat's door, she could hear a WBAI broadcast of the story on the other side. Jane described Pat's response as resentful for being left out. However, when I was in New Hampshire, Pat had a different take: "I'd be a pretty bougie Betty if I thought Sam needed *my permission* to plant a bomb."

The only recollections the two women could agree on was what they produced next: a press release on how to message Sam's solo attack as a conscious group effort. Pat dug out some research she had been doing for NACLA. It turned out that the Marine Midland building was owned by the W. R. Grace Company. Grace was a major exploiter of Latin American labor. This would be their angle.

Jane crafted an anti-imperialist, pro-Latin epistle, and the two of them typed five copies and mailed one to each of the four key underground papers: the *East Village Other*, the *Militant*, the *Guardian*, and *Rolling Stone*. For expediency, they held on to the fifth, thinking that at first light Pat would insert the communiqué in *Rat*'s mail drop with her ad-sales receipts, and Jane, whose volunteer duties included sorting the mail, would "find" it when she got in around noon.

Less than a week later, Sam sat at his usual table at Veselka across from Robin. Both clutched the latest issue of *Rat*, with its full-page spread capped by the oversized headline:

WALL STREET BOMBING

Circulation had exploded due to the bomber's anonymous message.

FOR THE UNDERGROUND PRESS ONLY
NO COMMUNICATION WILL TAKE PLACE WITH THE PIG MEDIA

The explosive device set off at the Marine Midland Grace Trust Company was an act of political sabotage. Considerable damage was done to the security files and building structure of the W.R. Grace Company, which extensively controls agricultural and chemical holdings throughout Latin America. There was no intent to hurt anyone. The attack was directed only at property. This was the third of such acts, beginning with the explosion of a grenade arsenal in New Jersey on July 15th and the blowing up of the United Fruit Company on July 26th commemorating the Cuban Revolution.

Crimes against other peoples of the world are every bit as hideous as crimes against Americans. Jailing and killing will not deter acts of sabotage in the U.S. nor will the age-old placebo known as "liberal reform." Nor the longed for ending of the war in the U.S. Nor, in short, is there anything the government can do to placate the impulse to revolution that is in the blood of young America from coast to coast.

Robin loved it. "This is far out, man! Far freaking out!" All around them, people were reading the same page. But Sam was not smiling. Obsessed with selling Marine Midland as a small part of a larger plan, Jane's press release deliberately linked all three attacks to the same people. Sam also noticed that Jeff Shero stupidly placed Jane's monthly editorial on the *same page* as the press release. It was a piece she had pitched to Shero as "Why Marine Midland? What's the Connection Between the Bank and the War in Vietnam?"

Sam shook his head. *She just couldn't let it go.*

Shero was savvy enough to omit Jane's byline. Unfortunately, she was credited on the masthead as "Princess Jane Alpert."

This time, her name was spelled correctly.

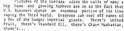

Jane's press release for the Marine Midland bombing and her editorial were printed side by side in the August 1969 issue of *Rat*. In the latter, she named the collective's future targets: Chase Manhattan and Standard Oil. This solidified the FBI's theory that all the major New York bombings that summer originated from one group connected to the paper. *Courtesy of Jeff Shero*

Shero listed both "Princess" Jane Alpert and Pat Swinton as staff on the August issue's masthead. (I've circled them here.) In the months following the arrest of the Melville Collective, *Rat*'s masthead became one of the FBI's best sources for leads on the East Village radical underground. *Courtesy of Jeff Shero*

Within a day of the August issue of *Rat* hitting the streets, Swearingen stood in Malone's office holding three of its clippings. His theory was that of all the Village weeklies, only *Rat* published the bomber's message, which meant at least one of the bombers was connected to the paper. Swearingen emphasized that the style and tone of the uncredited Marine Midland editorial matched:

- The bomber's press release on the same page;
- The article on the United Fruit bombing last month;
- Jane Albert's hijacking piece from the month before that;

And, finally,

- "Princess Jane Alpert" was credited on the masthead.

"These are clearly all the same Jane," Swearingen said to his boss. Five dots, connected. Swearingen wanted a one-hundred-man team to scour the 167s to see if he could connect more.

Cement Head sat back and put his feet up. "Since when do women throw bombs?"

"Well, they don't," Swearingen agreed, "but I think she's connected to the person who is, and I think I know their next two targets: Chase Manhattan Bank and Standard Oil."

"How the hell can you possibly know that?"

"It's in the first line of Alpert's column: 'Everyone can reel off names of a few of the hungry imperial giants. There's United Fruit, Standard Oil, and Chase Manhattan.'"

Malone leaned over Swearingen's long finger highlighting the degraded print on *Rat's* recycled paper. There was a goofy cartoon at the top of the page showing a line of hippies standing profile and evolving like Darwinian apes. "You want me to go to Hoover with a case about a female bomber built on information sourced from this piece-of-shit paper? They could be lying about the bombs being related. Terrorists do that, y'know. And *none* of those alleged targets are federal."

"Yes, but NYPD found almost no physical evidence, so we have to start looking at patterns of motivation. Clearly these bombers are pro-Castro."

Malone shook this nonsense from his skull and ordered Swearingen to drop this theory and join the squad investigating the recent hijacking of a Brinks truck.

Ignoring Cement Head, Swearingen phoned the NYPD and inquired about who was working on the Marine Midland bombing. He was routed to lead detective Pete Perrota.

Perrota had his hands full that morning. His boss, Chief Albert Seedman (who would a decade later cowrite the bestselling memoir *Chief!*, which featured this investigation), had assigned him only twelve detectives to call hundreds of disgruntled Marine Midland employees. Swearingen suggested instead that Perrota look at that month's *Rat Subterranean News*.

In the coming days, all three major New York dailies carried headlines on or near the front pages about the "Mad Bomber" destroying Marine Midland. This story ran right next to others about the escalation of troops in Vietnam and its "Butcher's Bill"—that is, the rising count of soldier casualties. The editorial sections carried the view that the Mad Bomber, while extreme, was ultimately on the side of the angels.

As the mood south of Fourteenth Street embraced the Marine Midland attack, the Masturbators softened and began to look to Sam for guidance. Jane and Robin both asked Sam to choose one of them as the next courier. Sam said that before any Masturbator could be a courier, that person had to do as he, Pat, and David had already done: scour thrift stores for establishment attire as "bomb clothes" to blend in.

By the end of August, the collective completed a list of targets:

- The Department of the Army (in the Federal Building)
- Standard Oil (in the RCA Building)
- Chase Manhattan Bank
- General Motors
- AT&T
- Dow Chemical
- Met Life
- The Chrysler Building
- ROTC at the Rutgers New Jersey Campus (Lester's contribution)

And David's all-time favorite since his days at the Revolutionary Contingent:

- The Whitehall Street Army Induction Center

Each agreed to make an appointment in one, don their bomb clothes, and mime their way through contrived business, only to then wander the premises in search of Sam's checklist:

1. Bathrooms near stairwells, preferably ones with no locks
2. Damaged or open air ducts
3. Janitorial closets near elevators or utility stations
4. Although rare in 1969—security cameras

Sam told them to note the average number of people moving in and out of the lobby at 3 PM, when they were likely to plant the packages.

After a few weeks, they had narrowed their targets down to one: the Federal Building, which, despite having whole floors of judges' chambers, had the worst security.

On September 12, Sam called a rooftop meeting to choose the next courier. Pat abstained from the meeting, preferring to take her three-year-old Jenny to the zoo with David. Both were still unwilling to work with Lester.

With the Masturbators assembled, Sam motioned first toward Gil, who had waffled between Masturbator and committed radical. "How about you?" With the intense attention suddenly focused upon the man whose mane of curly black hair made him resemble the peace-loving folk singer Cat Stevens, Gil scanned the faces of those who had become his closest friends that summer. He sighed, "I'm sorry, man, but I'm out," and quickly moved through the steel fire door. It sprang shut with a loud thud and left the group grim. He would never speak to most of them again.

John stepped forward and removed his glasses, surprising everyone that the biggest pacifist was volunteering. The surprise died like a spark landing in water. "I'm gonna go too." He had not bought any bomb clothes, nor had he cased any of the targets he was assigned. Sam nodded sadly as the man he thought of as his brother-in-arms shuffled across the tar and through the fire door and back to his film-editing cave with Gil.

Now there were five.

Sam drew back the focus. "Right . . . Robin?"

"You betcha, daddy-o. Fuck yeah!"

"No," objected Lester. "No offense, but the guard desk at the Federal Building probably has pictures of both you and Sharon pinned to the ledge, and in my opinion—"

"So who is left!" Sam interrupted, looking hard at the Rasta. He knew, with himself disqualified and the religious convert not volunteering, there was only one Masturbator remaining without an arrest record.

Jane Alpert was all smiles.

16 | CHILDREN OF THE REVOLUTION

BY OCTOBER 1989, IT HAD BEEN OVER a year since my first meeting with Judith Regan at the Yale Club. I had promised her a book proposal in a few months. However, the rabbit hole ran too deep, and I had moved past the bougie commercial aspects of this project. It had become personal, as it should have been from the beginning. Plus, I was mad now. At this point, Jane became for me what journalists sometimes call a rowback: a follow-up interview done with a source after contradicting facts have come to light. I had left two messages for her at the number I leveraged from Robin. There was no response. I assumed that John Cohen had warned her that I was investigating a narrative she had controlled for the better part of twenty years, one that shielded his possible contributions to their crimes.

While Jane was avoiding me, Pat's daughter Jenny had retuned my first call within a day. Pat had given me her number, perhaps in furtherance of my desire to talk to other children of the collective, or perhaps to help mend a fence.

Now in her midtwenties, Jenny told me she had stopped struggling with her feelings about her mother. *How did she do that?* When she said she was visiting New York, I jumped at the chance to find out how she managed to adjust. I took her to Serendipity 3, the home of the frozen hot chocolate and the uber-bougie venue of choice for every sweet-sixteen-year-old in Sutton Place.

Jenny was not at all like Pat. She spoke in a shy voice and said she was jealous of people who could confront the city's harsh life. It was hard for me to make the connection to the streetwise radical who was her mother at the same age.

"Until I heard you were visiting Pat, I had no real interest in understanding my mother. My dad said what she was involved with was something glamorous."

I had the feeling that glamour was exactly what Jenny sought—a relief from a small-town scene, where a conservative father discourages his daughter from discovering her own political truths. Eventually, Jenny did her own research and found Pat's address in New Hampshire. "I thought I would feel a lot of anger about seeing my mother because of the abandonment and kidnapping"—a claim by Jenny's father. "But I didn't feel any anger at all. I thought it would be like some big catharsis for me. But it really wasn't."

"Did you talk about the role she played in the bombings?'

She had childhood memories of playing with toys in the apartment where bombings were planned but no memory of the sex and drugs that were prevalent in Jane's book. It was interesting to learn that another child had identified holes in Jane's story. Did she care that Jane used her mother for commercial gain or that, by this same stage of her life, her mother had a lengthy FBI file and was planning the destruction of skyscrapers to stop an illegal war? "Not really. I just thought my mother was in the wrong place at the wrong time. I don't think she had these big political aspirations. I think your father had a lot more initiative than any of the others."

It was clear that she had no coping secret to offer me. The calm detachment of her responses revealed that Jenny was exactly where I was when I started this journey, parroting the lies we were sold as children: that our parents were somehow swept up in the times rather than defining them. But how could I get her to see that? "Your mom told me that she felt 'the state is our enemy.' She said she still feels that way."

Jenny processed this for several seconds, taking a long pull on the straw of her frozen hot chocolate. "I think your dad and my mom and Jane pretty much just wasted their life." And after an awkward silence, she asked, "What was the most difficult part about this process for you?"

I wanted my answer to start her onto her path. I wanted to set her free from the fantasy that our parents were not self-determined. But what came through my uncertain lips was, "The hardest thing for most kids, I think, is to forgive our parents for being human."

I realized then, the kid I was talking about was myself.

Around this same time, the Department of Justice had responded to my lawyer Larry's FOIA demands for more information. I had put in requests for all the names in the collective that I had at this time: Jane, John, Sharon, Robin, Pat, Gilbert, Ivan, Lester, and, of course, Demmerle.

The DOJ responded that before it would release anything I had to prove I was Sam Melville's son. Why they did not ask the FBI, who had been keeping tabs on me since I was eight, I never learned. They refused to send any files on the rest of the collective or the informant at all, citing national security. Larry told me this is the reason given when a request is on someone who assisted the government as an informant. Aside from Demmerle, who could that have been? Robin, who had managed to avoid arrest? Jane, who made a deal with the FBI after her arrest? Or John, who seemed to know more than someone "not in the group" should know?

I did not see an underlying reason for all these stalls, nor did I think Jane had any influence over the department. All I thought was that it would mean another round of lawyer letters to get the files and another delay of my ability to vet everyone's facts. Still, it did spark a thought: How many of the collective, deliberately or inadvertently, had assisted the FBI in my father's arrest?

Then, two months after I left my first message, Jane Alpert, her fame in retrograde and perhaps like other ex-radicals still haunted by my father's ghost, spoke to me. "Hello," I heard after the beep from my answering machine, "This is Jane *Lauren* Alpert." It was a poised voice, soothing, like that of a greeter at a hotel or luxury spa—someone who never loses his or her cool.

I grabbed the handset, hoping to catch her before she hung up. "Ms. Alpert?"

"Yes. I'm really happy to speak with you," she said with an eerie calm. After a few rounds of formalities, she got to her point: "Have you thought about writing a book about Sam? I'd like to help."

PART III

MOTHER RIGHT

17 | . . . AND JANE

THE BLEAK PHOTO OF A YOUNG, FORLORN WOMAN on the flap of *Growing Up Underground* bore little resemblance to the middle-aged woman who came toward me. This woman projected confidence and charm that grew brighter with each step. She still had what I had always known as a boy's prep-school cut, but the paisley blouse was replaced by a form-fitting spandex cycling jersey. In tow was her Renault man's racing bike. The sizzle of its precision gears echoed off the cement walls of my Section 8 hallway. "I'm so happy to meet you," she said, beaming. "You are certainly Sam's son."

I gave in to an awkward hug.

In our first phone conversation, when Jane asked if I had considered writing about my father, I was not going to tell her about Simon & Schuster. The radicals had made me paranoid enough to think that with her publishing and FBI connections she might know already. What if her agenda was to block me? So I spent the next week gathering intel on the Greta Garbo of ex-radicals. For the first time I co-opted Jill into my process, asking her to bring a women's perspective to learn what might have turned Jane from Dad's devotee into his demon lover. What we uncovered was only the first half of my answer. But it was enough to elevate my concerns.

In 1973 Jane was a fugitive. It had been almost three years since she jumped bail. She was living under fake names and couch-surfing through a chain of Weather's safe houses. Lying low must have been profoundly frustrating for someone with her ambitions. *Letters from Attica*, my father's posthumously published work, had begun to inhabit the same conversations as *Soledad Brother*

153

by George Jackson and *Soul on Ice* by Eldridge Cleaver—both revered radical bibles. Excerpts had been reprinted in the glossy hard-left political magazine *Ramparts*, turning her ex into a folk hero and a martyr. Meanwhile, Jane's then current contribution to the movement was the occasional "where could she be hiding?" speculation editorial in the underground press, as she was unable to publish or to leverage her recent fame.

At this point she asked John Cohen to arrange a clandestine meeting with her mentor, women's rights activist Robin Morgan. By '73, Morgan had become an editor for the popular feminist periodical *Ms.* magazine. At their meeting in a remote roadside diner, Jane expressed outrage that *Ramparts* painted an overly romantic picture of the radical left. Jane felt that it was time for the world to hear another side to the story: one where young women were manipulated like polygamist brides by the underground's surplus of macho satyrs. She felt *Ms.* was the perfect platform. Morgan agreed wholeheartedly.

Sometime in mid-1974, Jane delivered (via her attorney) a sharp-toned manifesto. She titled it *Mother Right: A New Feminist Theory*. The introduction characterized her association with the radical left as something akin to Stockholm Syndrome—particularly so with the Melville Collective:

> I was very much pressured, against my own sense of tactics and timing, into playing the role I did in the group of radical bombers Melville half-led, half-dragged along with him. The pressure was of the kind peculiar and common to male-female relationships: he constantly threatened to leave me if I backed out.

This was a stark contrast to what I had learned from Robin, Sharon, and Pat. They claimed Jane was a dilettante, anxious to leapfrog into the role of organizer. My father "leaving her" was an abstraction. In those days, the concept of monogamy was considered ultra-bougie. But the gut punch to Jill and me was how her manifesto included a biting eulogy for the victims of Attica:

> And so, my sisters and Weathermen, you fast and organize and demonstrate for Attica. Don't send me news clippings about it, don't tell me how much those deaths moved you. I will mourn the loss of 42 male supremacists no longer.

Whatever sympathy Jill might have held in reserve for Jane vanished. Now she saw Mother Right as a dangerous chameleon. But I needed a deeper understating of her betrayal. So, when I sheepishly confessed that I invited the chameleon to our apartment, Jill's jaw dropped.

Upon entering our small two-bedroom Jane abandoned her racing bike near the door and smiled at our Ikea furniture like they were museum pieces. "I love your taste."

I introduced her to Jill, who offered to take a photo like we were old friends. Then Jill retreated to our bedroom, offering only the minimum courtesy demanded by good manners. When our tour of the apartment continued to my second bedroom/recording studio, Jane's face brightened at my equipment's LEDs, sparkling like stars on a country night. "Sam would have loved this. He would be very proud that you are in music," she said, and rested a friendly hand on my arm, like she was comforting a child at a funeral.

From everyone's description, I thought Jane would be a conceited smart-ass. However, her soft tone and almost perpetual smile were disarming. I probed: "The Sam you knew didn't want to die?"

"Yes, that's right."

"Do you think it was possible that he stood up deliberately when the shooting started?"

"The Sam I knew would not have risked his life to make a vain point."

"But you do think he was self-destructive?"

"Yes, in doing things that could get you caught or doing something to get in trouble in prison. Suicide—that is something else."

I told her about my meeting with Sharen Krebs and how Sharon thought that my father may have been overwhelmed by being outdoors and under the stars for the first time in years. Sharon's poetic theory took Jane to another place psychically. "I have always been very, very fond of Sharon. It is unfortunate that we cannot be in contact."

I offered Sharon's number, to which she responded, "I doubt that she would ever want to talk to me."

"Sharon also told me to write a book. Do you think that's a good idea?"

"Yes, not because of Sam but because of you. I think you have a fascinating story."

"I have never written anything."

"I would like to help you. However, I would like us to be friends first."
What would that even be like?

Jane had started our dysfunctional relationship when I was ten, when she dedicated her profile of my dad in *Letters from Attica* "For Jocko Melville." At the time she wrote it, she had come to hate my father. Still, she was reaching out to his son. Then there were the memories I had as a young child being in an apartment where Dad lived after he and Mom split, but I did not know if it was Jane's or Diane's. The place smelled clean. The rooms were tiny. To think I might have used Jane's bathroom, wrestled with Dad in the bed where they slept together, and eaten at her kitchen table where they planned the destruction of a skyscraper. Today she was in my living room offering to help me complete a version of the man I had been seeking and the one she spent years denigrating.

"I'm sure it doesn't come as a surprise that some people are upset at what you've written," I said.

"No, it doesn't. " Her eyes widened. "Are you?"

"I'm not upset with anybody. And at the same time, I'm upset with everybody."

"Why is that?"

"For abandoning their principles, for joining the establishment."

"You're upset because they got on with their lives?"

"I'm not really *upset* with them. I just can't seem to forgive them."

"Yes, I understand." She served another comforting, deep-contact smile. I could see why men fell for her.

"John Cohen told me, 'Sam was definitely murdered.' He said the FBI was passing out pictures of him to the troopers before they stormed in."

"John tends to romanticize Sam a lot, but you can trust him. He's not like Robin. Robin has told me twenty different versions of how Sam died over the years."

"Do you think he was deliberately assassinated?"

"No. I don't think the trooper could have identified him from the distance that the bullet was fired. Sixty feet is pretty far—especially through gas."

Finally, here was someone besides me who put aside emotion and applied some science to the question. Jane didn't need Dad to be murdered, or a victim of a conspiracy, the way Kunstler and the ex-radicals did. Now I could see why she pissed off her peers. I hated to admit it, but I envied Jane for her ability to put Dad in the past and make a new life for herself. I wished I could do that. I had hoped Jenny might be able to give me a clue. Maybe Jane could. One thing was clear: I could see that with Jane I did not have to concur that the state was my enemy to get answers.

She would be an interesting addition to my collection of father figures.

Jane and I meet for the first time in 1989. *Author's collection*

"Jesus Christ, Josh, don't you know when you're being used?" Mom said, munching on a hamburger in her kitchen.

"What could Jane possibly want from me? If anything, I'm using her."

"You're joking, right? You think you're smarter than her? You didn't even finish art school. She wants to be your friend, probably so she can write another book, *How I Befriended Sam Melville's Son*."

"You know Jane agrees with you that Sam was a chauvinist," I said, desperate to show her that she and Jane had common ground.

"I never said that."

"You told me that he had very traditional expectations, that he wanted you to cook and clean and then entertain him at night. I have it on tape."

Mom went into normalizing mode. "By today's standards, a chauvinist, maybe. Today, if you scolded your wife for working late when you want her home making dinner, you're a chauvinist. Back then it was OK to forbid your wife to work at all, and even that was not called chauvinism."

I didn't know what to believe from her anymore. Then she added, "I don't want you to see her again."

"Excuse me! I'm twenty-seven."

"Well, I'm not going to stand for it. She's a manipulator, and she's going to hurt you, somehow. She's just like all the radicals. They are all liars, and they see things the way that benefits them, not you and certainly not the truth."

"You just can't stand the fact that I'm developing my own realities about Sam, and my own sources, can you?"

"What did Jill think?" she asked, still chewing.

I could not recall a single time Mom was interested in what Jill thought about anything. I lied. "She liked her."

"Well, if you see her again, don't say I didn't warn you, and don't come to me when she fucks you over."

"You know, Ma, for someone who thinks you have very little in common with the radicals, you sure sound just like some of them."

The next week, Jane and I made our first attempt as friends. We met at the Waverly Theater on Sixth Avenue. We sat in the dark, side by side, for two creepy hours watching *Roger & Me*. Afterward, in the more formal setting of a restaurant, we squared off: the ex-radical and the son of the lover she betrayed. Jane sat with perfect prep school posture, as if she had a yardstick taped to her back. I was a bit rougher around the edges, hunched over my coffee and no match for her pedigree. Channeling Dad's chess mastery, I opened with an aggressive knight leaping over the pawn: "Did anybody ever discuss what would happen if someone got killed?"

Her answer was more analytical than Pat's. "Yes, we did. And there was always talk about hostage-taking. I mean, you must understand that this was before the Symbionese Liberation Army took Patty Hearst. You read about it in the news almost as an accepted part of life in Lebanon or Iran. But in the States, it was on the fringe of radical bearing. We might say in a meeting, 'Let's kidnap some heir.' And what would happen if our bluff was called and we had to kill the hostage? Most of us felt that we couldn't do that. Now, your father, long before this point in the discussion, would have walked out of the room and started playing his guitar or fixing a meal."

That hit close to home. She continued, "Sam hated sitting around while people verbalized and had debates about things that were not about to take place. If it wasn't for your father, we probably would've sat around and debated until the Vietnam War was over."

"And how did my father deal with these discussions?"

She became flip. "Oh, he would go to the apartment where we kept the dynamite, and make a bomb and place it somewhere, and then we'd have to deal with the consequences."

Where we kept the dynamite? I thought. It was stored at an apartment my father paid for and leased under his McCurdy alias and would not give her a key to. She had somehow co-opted it as *theirs*. I was starting to get a feel for how she filtered things. Her memoir was my witness. In it, only one of the bombings—Marine Midland—was performed by Dad without consent of the collective. Right after this inconsistency came another: "I haven't thought about this in a long time, but I could probably go back and think about every act the FBI called 'overt acts within our conspiracy' and explain how at the core of them was the need for Sam to go out and 'do something,' and then it got modulated into some kind of new process—something to do with our relationship."

Did Jane believe that my polyamorous father bombed buildings because he was jealous of her sleeping with other men, like John Cohen, who could barely look me in the eye, or Robin Palmer, whom she thought a jackass, or David, with whom she and Sam had a foursome with Pat?

"You know," she paused as if she had been holding her next thought in reserve, "Have you thought about talking to the FBI? I could put you in touch with Joe Anderson. He oversaw our case."

"You are still in touch with the agents who put you in prison?"

"Yes," she blurted as if it should have been obvious. "I surrendered, and I spent every day with the agents prepping for testimony and for years after when I check in."

None of the others who were arrested stayed in touch with the FBI. Moreover, I was thinking about what Swearingen had told me in our second conversation, which focused on the Federal Building bombing. Swearingen claimed that Jane's recant was a "complete fiction."

"You took pretty much most of the credit for the Federal Building attack," I said.

"Yes."

"And you wrote that it was successful action by the collective?"

"I believe that, yes."

In *Growing Up Underground*, Jane described it like a scene out of Hollywood. Her bomb clothing was a second-hand Jackie O–style designer dress. Sam wired ten sticks of TNT into the bottom of a knockoff Gucci handbag, reached inside the purse, set the hour hand at 2, and twisted together the remaining wires that would turn a fashion accessory into a high-order explosive. He sealed the deal with a strong kiss and watched his lover enter 26 Federal Plaza at 4:45 PM. Jane claimed she took the elevator to the spot scouted by another collective member: the thirty-ninth-floor ladies' room, which was directly below the Department of the Army. She scanned the ceiling above the stalls for an air vent cover that was loosened for her the day before. She emerged to the street twenty minutes later with the outflow of clerks and lawyers, empty-handed.

The flash went off at 2 AM and could be seen from every south-facing window in the Village. It must have seemed glorious to the collective watching from a rooftop. But according to Swearingen, the bombing left the clues that would be the collective's undoing.

18 | AN EXPLOSION IN FOLEY SQUARE

IN THE HAZY 3 AM TWILIGHT OF SEPTEMBER 19, 1969, a hive of law enforcement acronyms engulfed the Court House District.

When Swearingen arrived, he met NYPD Detective Perrota face-to-face for the first time and asked him if he had a chance to look at the *Rat* articles. Perrota had forgotten the conversation. He shrugged and shifted their focus toward the water that was presently gushing down from the forty-first floor of the Federal Building to the street, taking out the electrical and telephone systems. "The Department of the Army was the clear target," Perrota told Swearingen as he escorted him up to the blast area and pointed out the remains of the timer—a common windup alarm clock.

By 5 AM an anxious Swearingen was told to wait outside Malone's door. His boss was livid. The Mad Bomber had gone federal and had blown up the offices of personal friends of his and J. Edgar Hoover's. Swearingen, dressed in his standard charcoal suit, like he had been up all night waiting for the call, watched in frustration through the glass as his counterpart from the Intelligence Division, Joe Anderson, in wrinkled T-shirt and sweats, got first shot at briefing their director. He could hear pieces of Anderson's hard sell through the glass: Anderson wanted this case badly and pushed for Malone to take it away from the annoying know-it-all bomb expert. His theory was thin: that the Federal Building was probably done by the FLQ. "The bomb tonight was the same MO: a thick bundle of dynamite, similar to the one used at the Montreal Stock Exchange."

Standing next to Anderson were three gruff people Swearingen knew well, also clothed like they had just rolled out of bed: SAC Joe Sullivan and his two lieutenants, SA Joseph MacFarlane and SA Joseph Corless—"the three Joes," as they were known. Swearingen had a bad feeling. Not one of them had bomb experience, but they were all FBI veterans with landmark cases.

Eyeing Swearingen waiting outside, Malone suggested that if they wanted the case reassigned, Anderson needed to make a stronger connection to the FLQ. He recommended a call to the Royal Canadian Mounted Police to verify the design of the Montreal device.

Anderson and the three Joes exited purposefully, rubbing sleep from their faces and avoiding Swearingen's as he switched with them. Standing alone, looking gallingly crisp and clear-eyed, Swearingen pitched a completely different theory, one based on motivations rather than physical evidence: United Fruit, Marine Midland, and now the Federal Building all had phoned-in warnings and, according to the two "anonymous" press releases in *Rat*, all made mention of pro-Castro or Latin anti-imperialist sentiments. A smoky silence took over when he was done. Cement Head put down his first cigar of the day and stood eye-to-eye with the towering investigator. "Wes, I'm assigning a special task force for this. Sullivan will run it. Anderson thinks this is the FLQ, not some local amateurs. So I want both of you to coordinate through Sullivan."

"I see. Can I ask why you don't like my theory?"

Malone was happy to edify. Since the Marine Midland bombing on August 20, there had been multiple militant attacks across the country: a National Guard armory in Modesto was blown up, a police station in Denver was blown up the day after that, and reports of Panthers' assaults on police cars in several cities came the following week from San Diego; Lawrence, Kansas; and St. Louis. "But somehow," Malone concluded, "you think only these three bombings are connected to a single cell of pro-Castro unsubs? Why?"

Swearingen's lips formed his thin trademark gotcha smile, and he offered something he knew Malone could not deny: physical evidence. "The timers. All three bombs were triggered with Westclox Baby Ben alarm clocks. All the bombs you just mentioned didn't use *any* timers."

Malone tossed his cigar into a half-finished coffee cup and, to get Swearingen out of his face, granted what he had requested after the Marine Midland attack: a team to work the 167 files. Swearingen had wanted a hundred men back then. Today, Cement Head gave him five, and only one day to produce results. He was sure that by later that afternoon Anderson would have this case and Swearingen would be back on the Robbery Division.

For the rest of the morning, Anderson left messages at the offices of the Royal Canadian Mounties. None were returned. Over the past six months, the FBI had refused to respond to the Mounties' request to share intel on its investigation of the FLQ. With this tit-for-tat, Anderson came up empty-handed by day's end. Meanwhile, at 9:05 AM, only seven hours since the destruction of the Federal Building, Swearingen's small team would yield one suspect: Samuel Joseph Melville, age thirty-four.

Melville had the technical background required to ensure precise structural damage because he had designed the plumbing systems for government buildings. He had applied for a Cuban passport, and his late father was an executive in the Communist Party of America. However, what tipped the profile was that he was receiving his mail at an apartment on Eleventh Street whose lease was in the name of Jane Alpert—the *Rat* volunteer. Swearingen begged Malone to raid *Rat* in search of the original bombing notes it had published. From those, they could lift fingerprints or do a typewriter analysis.

And there it was again—the *R* word.

"Dammit, Wes," his Director snapped. "We need an informant—someone who can name names. We cannot build a case around articles in a shit paper like *Rat*. Y'hear? What else you got?"

"Melville's file claims he was spotted in Champlain, New York, meeting a Black Panther operative with someone who matched Alpert's description."

It was still not enough.

Malone ordered him to report to Sullivan from now on and waved him out of his office but wrote a general memo to the Intelligence Division about Melville receiving mail at Alpert's on Eleventh Street. Then, just to cover his ass, he called Police Chief Albert Seedman and suggested that the NYPD raid *Rat*.

About an hour later, two FBI agents dispatched by Anderson knocked politely at Sam and Jane's former Eleventh Street apartment. When Diane answered, they identified themselves and asked for Sam Melville. Diane claimed that she and Sam broke up months ago. She had no idea where he was. She waited until the agents were out of sight, dressed, and ran a half-mile south to where she knew Sam would most likely be. Sam answered the door, and between deep breaths she told him the bad news.

When Jane emerged from her shower, she found Sam pacing like a caffeinated tiger. Instead of panicking, she wanted to challenge the feds head-on by hiring a lawyer. My father used a trait rare for him: adamance. "Don't you get it, baby? They got the wrong place. We got lucky. We should leave town. Right now."

"What about the communiqué?" She meant the one she and Pat wrote about the Federal Building attack, which Sharon had placed in *Rat*'s mailbox the night before. "If I don't show up this morning and find it in the mail, there's no way to ensure the press release will make it into the next edition."

"Baby, that's nuts. It's time to get out of town," and he tucked John Keats's leash and bowl into his backpack.

But Jane sat on the couch in protest, continuing to dry herself, "We have to let everyone know what the Federal Building was about, or we just look like terrorists," she insisted. Then, seeing his bewildered look, she added, "I am not a fucking terrorist!"

That night, while Jane slept, Sam sat at the soldering station. Rather than wake her to wish her well, at about 5 AM he spent a somber fifteen minutes with John Keats. "You take care of Lady Jane now, y'hear?"

He biked to McCurdy, packed a .38 caliber pistol, several grenades, blasting caps, and two dozen sticks of TNT into a large duffel bag. He called David from a corner pay phone at 6 AM and explained he was heading to Milwaukee to connect with Brown. He would be gone for an undetermined amount of time and wanted to make sure David still had the spare key to McCurdy. David dressed and hustled three blocks. The young radical needed a detonator/timer assembled before Sam left so he could blow up his dream target: the Whitehall Army Induction Center. He trusted Sam's bomb-building skills more than his own.

Sam ushered Dave into the vestibule. "Who's helping you on this?"

"No one."

"*No one*? So, no press release?"

"I just wrote my own." He showed it to Sam.

> Tonight we bombed the Whitehall Induction Center. This action was in support of the NLF, legalized marijuana, love, Cuba, legalized abortion, and all the American revolutionaries and GIs who are winning the war against the Pentagon. Nixon surrender now!

It lacked Jane's collegiate verbosity. Sam loved it. "What about Pat?" he asked.

"We're not really speaking this week, and I'm not involving any Masturbators."

Sam looked up and down the street, then dug into the duffel bag and handed David a prewired detonator.

At the dusk of their goodbyes a tan van pulled around the corner and came to a quiet stop in front of McCurdy. The door slid open to reveal the Puerto Rican radical Ivan Lopez. Sam climbed inside with a raised fist to David, and the van sped off into the twilight.

Jane awoke later that morning to John Keats whimpering for a walk—a clear sign that Sam had left. She pushed past her mixed emotions, deciding that Sam did not have the maturity to deal with law enforcement head-on and called Sharon to get the number of the attorney who had gotten them off for their naked Waldorf Astoria protest. Jane hoped it was William Kunstler, but Sharon said that Kunstler was preoccupied with the Chicago Seven trial and had referred them to another attorney who was building his reputation as a movement lawyer.

In Jane's first conversation, the lawyer convinced her that he could pressure the FBI to back off. However, the reverse proved to be the case. On the call, one of Anderson's agents told the attorney that Jane was *not* a suspect and that they only wanted to confirm some facts about the FLQ, who they claimed were the actual target of the investigation. They recited Jane's address to make sure they were inquiring about "the right Alpert, who lived on East Eleventh Street."

Her attorney was relieved. Thinking that they had the wrong person, he proffered his client's right address.

The next day, in a farmhouse outside Milwaukee, over a dozen former Panthers and SNCC members, several Puerto Rican Young Lords, and Ivan Lopez surrounded Sam as he showed them how to wire a Westclox Baby Ben alarm clock to a bundle of TNT. There was no discussion about how deploying them might undermine a music festival.

Over the next three days, multiple devices were placed around the Midwest. Among them was a bomb in the Chicago Civic Center placed by Sam and Ivan. On September 26, the Madison National Guard Armory exploded, and in Milwaukee, the Selective Service Building's windows were blown out, causing hundreds of thousands in damages—but not a single injury.

All this destruction was good news for Anderson. He heard from the Chicago Field Office. An informant reported that Rap Brown was in the Midwest with a large supply of weapons and that the bomb the office found and disarmed in the Chicago Civic Center had a timing device identical to the one used in the Federal Building—the Westclox Baby Ben coupled with caps from Explo. Anderson had come to his first solid (although ultimately misguided) conclusion: the Mad Bomber was Rap Brown and had moved from New York to the Midwest.

Anderson informed Malone and was about to requisition a massive manhunt that would coordinate the New York and Chicago field offices. He would ask Malone to put him in charge of it. However, on the same day that he presented the "Rap Brown is the Mad Bomber" theory to Malone, a bomb in the Whitehall Induction Center leveled the entire third floor. Parts of a Westclox timer were discovered. The Whitehall attack punched a hole both in the building and in Anderson's theory.

Two days later, on October 9, the Weathermen organized a three-day protest in Chicago, dubbed the Days of Rage. The New York and Chicago field offices coordinated with Anderson to compile a group of his select East Village undercover informants to mingle with demonstrators and identify subversives. Demmerle was among them. As Demmerle was getting off a train at Chicago's Union Station, Sam was being dropped off by Ivan in front of McCurdy. There, Sam emptied his duffel bag, inventorying Brown's recent acquisition of arms. He packed a grocery bag with blasting caps, walked to a hardware store, bought more solder and flashlight batteries, and continued to Jane's to use the soldering station and perhaps charm her into some makeup sex. But today, the FBI, now with Jane's correct address, had two agents parked outside in a white sedan. Propped up on their dashboard were photos of known subversives they were hoping to connect to the *Rat* volunteer. Upon seeing a familiar face, they checked the picture they had of Sam from his Cuban visa application. It was a grainy copy of a copy, but from a distance it seemed close enough to merit further investigation.

The agents climbed three flights of the tenement and confronted the man outside Jane's door. "Excuse me," they said, flashing credentials, "We are looking for Samuel Joseph Melville."

Sam drew upon his best hippie voice: "That Sam cat? He split weeks ago, man." He could hear John Keats starting to scratch and whimper for him from inside the apartment. "I am just helping out one of his chicks. Y'know, feeding the dog," he winked.

They asked for ID.

My father put down the bag containing several alarm clocks and solder right next to the foot of one agent and produced his David McCurdy passport from the pocket of his overalls. In the photo "David" appeared clean-cut, as Sam did now. Up close neither one seemed like a match for the degraded Cuban visa photo, which displayed a hippie with a beard. "If you see Sam, you give us a call right away. There's a reward in it." The agents handed Sam their card.

Jane's ear had been pressed against the door and heart had pounded through her chest. She erupted after Sam used his key: "That was dumb, Sam! You know they're going to investigate the name McCurdy and find the apartment."

Sam smiled and fed John Keats the biscuit he had kept in his pocket since Milwaukee, speaking into the dog's chopping jowls. "There are a thousand McCurdys in the phone book. Mine is not listed and I'll be gone by tomorrow. You should come with me."

But Jane was scared for another reason that she had kept secret from Sam, as well as the rest of the collective: two weeks after Sam left, on September 30, the NYPD finally took the FBI's suggestion and raided *Rat*. Lieutenant Perrota corralled *Rat*'s dozen or so volunteers into a corner of the storefront and demanded the original typed message explaining the Marine Midland attack. One staffer claimed it was thrown out. Perrota had him handcuffed and fired off question after question in front of the others. Sandwiched in the middle was the only one he really cared about: "Who opens the mail in the morning?"

The staffer responded nervously with the name of the only volunteer who had not shown up that day: "Jane Alpert."

19 | TWO MOTHERS, TWO TRUTHS

"WHY DIDN'T YOU JUST RUN?" I asked her.

In *Growing Up Underground*, Jane wrote of her deep fear at this juncture but did not explain why she stayed in the epicenter of the investigation. In my interviews, one member of Weather speculated that, in hindsight, Jane might have already been cooperating as an informant. But I didn't buy that. So I pressed her. "You had been compromised—twice: once when agents came to the Eleventh Street apartment and then when you heard that the police raided *Rat*. But you never told the others about either? And you didn't run."

"You have to understand that when you write a story, you get granular. However, living it in real time is very surreal. Everything was happening very, very quickly."

This sounded like the same type of nonanswer Robin Palmer would give me about his version of Dad's death and not being associated with Demmerle.

By this point, Jill had had enough of Jane in our lives, especially when the biggest break of my music career came along. It was in the form of being asked to help rip off a major-label recording artist for about $100,000. At the time, I was rubbing elbows with the still-undiscovered Joan Osborne and hoping to discover the next Suzanne Vega. Faced with this reprehensible offer, I should have called Jill for advice, or maybe my mother, if I could stand a double dose of "you should have stayed in school." But for some reason, instead, I called Jane.

I waited outside her office, which was in the Hotel Chelsea. Many of the suites had been converted into small offices. In gold letterset, her door read, JANE ALPERT AND ASSOCIATES. In a moment, she came out and quickly closed the door behind her. "Let's get some coffee," she said. When we were seated, I described my conundrum.

KASHIF MOBUTU's real name was LAWRENCE JEFFERSON before he converted to the Nation of Islam. He was part of a family of record producers and songwriters responsible for a string of Top 40 funk/soul megahits. Kashif's productions were generally of hard-core rap artists with song titles like "Drop a Cop." I had no personal stake in the artists' freedom-of-speech choices, but I remembered when a rival rap group busted into Kashif's session at the studio I had been managing in Queens and took the master tapes at gunpoint. I told Jane, "His clients didn't know what my father had meant to the Black Panthers and the civil rights movement." Instead, they typically prodded Kashif as to why he would hire someone like me who was "a White devil."

I should have avoided Kashif. But cash talks in the Apple. I always took his calls, which were always in the middle of the night. On this night, Kashif said he had a project he had just signed to a major label: an R&B band from the Midwest called ONE LIFE. "You still charge forty dollars an hour for engineering, right?" he asked, already knowing the answer. "OK then, here's how it's going to work," Kashif cleared his throat. "You're going to bill sixty dollars an hour to the label. They will pay you, and then you're going to give me twenty dollars an hour on the side. Y'dig? You'll call it a commission on your taxes."

Jill had been a rising professional backup singer and knew this as normal. I kinda knew it too.

Jane also saw no problem, so I explained that since the recording budget is recoupable against the artist's royalties, the more that is spent on the album, the longer it takes the artist to see any real money. "It's not really a commission," I summarized. "It's a kickback. What would Sam have done?" I couldn't believe that I was asking Jane, of all people, to be my proxy for both mother and father.

"Sam saw everything as capitalist exploitation," she said, "even delivering newspapers. He probably would have walked."

It seemed if I wanted any type of career, maintaining my father's ethics was becoming hopeless. Wall Street took my moral virginity, so I left finance to pursue music—to do something noble. Now Kashif was ushering in my next betrayal. Everybody cheats, it seemed. Nothing is as advertised. I recalled what Closer Dan told me about the difference between rape and seduction. Now I was the one being seduced.

The studio recording schedule for One Life meant vampire hours. In the first week, I came home around dawn dejected from wondering if my father would still be proud of his son's pursuit of music. I tried to talk about it with Jill and told her that Kashif found many creative ways to pad the budget: unnecessarily long studio hours, union-wage musicians who sat around, probably all with the same kickback arrangement I had agreed to. No one else seemed to mind—even Jill, who knew Kashif by a degree of separation. "This kickback shit is standard," she said out the door one morning.

Then why did it bother me so much? Soon, my father's ghost was planning another sabotage. When the conflict kept me from sleeping, I once again asked Jane to defuse his bombs.

At one of our morning encounters, Jane pushed past my angst and revisited the idea of cowriting a book about Sam with the FBI as a source. She said Dad's files that she got through FOIA were helpful with her book. I had made zero headway in my FOIA quest and asked if I could see her files. "I think I tossed most of that stuff," she said, "It was years ago. I'll have to look around." As a consolation prize, she handed me the number for her attorney, who was to be my liaison to the FBI special agent in charge, Joe Anderson. I took it with hesitation. I had mixed feelings about calling the guy who branded my father a snitch just to make a case. But I could not live comfortably with the idea that my father outed his comrades, even by accident. Not without some proof beyond Jane's claims.

Instead of Jane's lawyer, I called an FBI source that Swearingen gave me: Henry Byers, the agent who presided over my father's interrogation. Byers said he was happy to try to answer my questions and offered no corroboration to Jane's versions. I rationalized to him, "If my father was trying to gain the trust of Demmerle—a man he had only met once—it strains credibility that he would mention people Demmerle barely knew: Swinton, Albert, and Hughey. Right?"

"True," said Byers.

"And if he was trying to recruit him, why would he omit mentioning people Demmerle was very comfortable with: Robin Palmer and Sharon Krebs?"

"Maybe he didn't."

"Well, neither of them was arrested with my father. How is that?"

He had no answer.

I brought all this to my next meeting with Jane. "I was wondering how you could've known what Sam said to George if you weren't at that meeting."

Remembering what Swearingen had told me about the absence of Dad's confession, I added a trap: "Was Sam's confession in his FOIA file?"

Jane glared at me for the better part of a minute and curtly changed the subject. "You haven't even asked me about my trip to Moscow. Aren't you interested in what I saw?" Somehow Jane, an ex-radical bomber, was one of the first Americans to visit the post-Communist Eastern Bloc just weeks after it had been announced that the end of the Cold War was near. I'd guessed her connections at the FBI helped.

"Of course I'm interested. But I'd also really like an answer to my question. Did you ever find those FOIA files?" I mirrored her deep stare technique. She shifted in her seat, probably surmising these meetings would never be ordinary coffee dates. "I have to think about this situation," she finally responded. "I want to help you. I do. But I need to think about opening all this up again."

I thought I had won that round. But by the next week I would learn exactly what she meant by "help."

At 2:15 PM Jane wandered into the studio where the One Life sessions were being recorded. She had a gift in hand. "Where is everyone?" Jane asked, since I was sitting alone. "Well, the session was called for two, but Kashif never shows up till about seven." She nodded, connecting to what I had told her about budget padding and kickbacks. "I am sorry I haven't been available," she said, apologizing for not returning several calls. "I needed to do some thinking." She handed me the gift, wrapped in secular holiday paper.

"Should I open it now?"

She nodded with a big grin, and I tore at the wrapping to reveal a fresh copy of *Growing Up Underground*. It had come out in paperback. "It's a second edition," she grinned. "I signed it for you."

I had marked up the first edition in so many ways that transferring notes would have been daunting. But I thanked her.

"I brought something else for you. But I want you to wait until I leave to open it." It was a sturdy envelope with JANE ALPERT AND ASSOCIATES embossed in the return address area. "After reading that, if you still want to talk about Sam, I can."

She left in a few minutes, and I opened the envelope to see that it was a two-page typed letter that stated, in a nutshell, that if we continue to talk about

Sam, she would need to have final say over what went into my manuscript. That would make her in effect my editor.

The letter required my signature.

―――――――――

I had not expected to hear Mom's voice. We had barely spoken in the past few months since she bolted from that last disastrous therapy session. She chose to break our silence for an urgent reason: her birthday.

She planned a double dinner at the Plaza with my grandmother, who was turning ninety in a few months. This was code that I was to put aside family acrimony and do something special for her. I thought I'd give her a gift of a big fat "I told you so" about Jane Alpert. Instead, I penned some verses on a homemade birthday card. They weren't going to win any poetry contests, but I thought they would soften Mom's heart. Jill added a touching doodle, and we both signed it, optimistic that this could be the start of mending a fence.

When Jill and I arrived at the Plaza, Mom was already into her second ten-dollar glass of Chardonnay, looking displeased at the sight of us. She read our card and put it aside, saying nothing. To break the silence, I told her about Jane. She said what I expected her to say, and I thought that would be the end of it. No such luck. She went on a rant while ninety-year-old Nana sat in silence, hearing every other word.

By the time the between-course sherbet replaced the appetizers, Jill had heard enough. "Ruth, I agree that Josh is a bit obsessed, but you can't blame him for wanting to know more about his dad. He's trying to get on with his life."

"You stay out of this," Mom shot back. "This is none of your fucking business."

"How is this none of my business?"

"You are not family. And this is a family dinner. And I didn't invite you."

The string quartet stopped playing. Things degenerated from there.

Soon half the staff of the Plaza knew my father was a bomb-throwing radical and a leader of the Attica prison riot. I thought the maître d' was going to ask us to leave, but Jill beat him to the punch. She pushed back her chair and stood. I followed her for a hasty exit.

When we got home, she jetted for the bathroom and closed the door, and I heard the shower. I focused on getting ready for bed and could see the red light on my answering machine blinking. I had a feeling it would be more bad news.

"Hello Josh. This is your mother. Your birthday card was inappropriate. And I'm very sorry that you felt it necessary to walk out. Nana complained of heart pains after you left. The thought of bringing Jill when you and I are not getting along is wrong. And I'm not the only one who feels this way. Your friends have been telling me that you and Jill have become stuck like glue and people are having a problem with it. They're not going to tell you about it but I am your mother, so I will be honest. You should join us and be a human being—like you used to be—by yourself, without bringing her. That's all. Goodbye."

I pulled the cassette out of the answering machine so Jill would never have to hear what a shit family she was buying into. How could Mom ask me to choose? I ran several blocks to her apartment, armed with far more information than when I first interviewed her almost two years ago. I used my key instead of knocking. She was in her robe. I came out swinging. "How much of what you told me about Sam is pure crap? How much?" I said, slamming the door shut.

"What are you talking about?"

Instead of more bullshit half-answers, I wanted documents—specifically, the original letters, the death certificate, official papers from the prison, photos, basically everything she had. "Why didn't you ask the state the hard questions about his death?"

She lit a cigarette. "You have to understand, Josh, they said his death was an accident. You didn't question the government back then." She was talking about 1971. "And what do you mean by 'crap'?" She sat up. "I've always been honest with you."

"Where shall I start? The crap about how Sam became political only after you two split up." I told her about my conversations with their former Bronx friends and the Communist Labor Party meetings they attended with their fathers. "Or him having little to do with planning the bombings when the reverse is the reality—he led the collective. Or being 'dragged from his cell,' when he was a key organizer at Attica. And letting me believe he was randomly shot when everyone thinks that he was murdered!"

She was breathing heavily. "I didn't want to encourage you. I've had my share of these lunatics."

"So you lied? You're deliberately blocking me with half-truths?"

"I guess you'll have to decide who's telling you the truth, because I'm not going to talk to you about Sam ever again." Regret spread across her face, and I sensed an emotion that I had never seen from her: fear. Her voice cracked. "You can't see how much of him there is in you," and she retreated to the bathroom.

There are those moments in every family when betrayal surfaces and with it, a choice.

The armoire in the hall contained everything I was looking for: an entire Sam section under some tax papers. I took it all, quietly closed her apartment door, and slid my key underneath.

Back at my apartment, I set my acquisitions aside and focused on the stack of mounting bills. Within them was a letter from Jane. It had been a week since she had given me her ultimatum. I had not responded. This could be her concession:

> *Josh, as much as I want to I cannot continue to have the kind of conversations we've been having without a stronger guarantee of privacy than you are willing to give. I realize that this will disappoint you. But you already have a great deal of material from me, from others and your first-rate brain. With or without help from me or anyone, you can write a first-rate book. I shall miss talking to you but I trust this is just a hiatus in our friendship and not an end. And I hope you're not too angry to believe that, from my heart,*
>
> > *I wish you the best.*
> > *Jane*

20 | IT WAS A GREAT NIGHT FOR THE REVOLUTION

IN THE SECOND WEEK OF OCTOBER 1969, Jane gazed at remains of the detonators Sam had built while she slept. Just yesterday she had listened to his tales of multiple attacks with Ivan and Brown in the Midwest. Now he was on another bombing spree—without her. Then, David had told her that he pulled off the Whitehall bombing days before, alone. Robin and Sharon were growing distant as they got more involved with Weather. The revolution was moving forward, while Jane made coffee and sat by the window.

On her first cup, she reflected on the ease of planting the bomb in the lady's room in the Federal Building. She sourced and planted that device. By her second cup she felt that except for wiring the devices, she did not need Sam at all, unlike the Masturbators, who needed pep talks even to buy bomb clothes. By the third cup, she had a vision: although the youngest, she would rally the Masturbators in an unprecedented antiwar bombing on the most significant of war-related dates, Veterans Day.

She took John Keats for his walk, barely noticing the white sedan still parked catty-corner on Sixth Street since the day before. Upon return, she went straight for her dresser. In it was a large tourist map of Manhattan she bought last month when they were casing targets. Rockefeller Center was its focus. The most traversed tourist center in New York, 30 Rock played host to Radio City Music Hall and Sam's favorite capitalistic entity, Standard Oil. She could see the headlines already.

When she revealed her plan to Lester, he laughed. "What did Sam say about this?"

"Sam's in Milwaukee."

"OK, I see," he said, dividing his matting hair with rubber bands. "Jane, do you have any idea how many pigs will be at Rockefeller Center on Veterans Day?" The annual parade traveled down Fifth Avenue in front of 30 Rock's skating rink. Lester added that to counter the Veterans Day Parade there would also be the MOBE demonstration. "It's the most significant antiwar event of the year and being promoted as a peaceful protest. A bomb would completely destroy their credibility and send a message that the movement is at best disorganized and at worst disingenuous." He picked up his dread comb. "They are finally long enough to braid, do you agree?"

Jane folded her map neatly. "My hair hasn't been long enough to braid since I was thirteen." She thanked him, left, and walked to Robin and Sharon's apartment just a few blocks south. Sharon was at Alternate U, and Robin was alone. He made Jane tea.

Steeping the bags, he admitted to still being a bit peeved that Sam picked Jane to be the courier for the Federal Building instead of him. Jane saw some leverage and produced a joint.

As they shared it, she complimented Robin on his guerrilla theater work with the Crazies and offered to massage the arm that he injured during an arrest. Within an hour they had sex, after which Jane showed him the map and offered him a meaningful place in her plan. But Robin also declined. "It is too crazy, Crazy Janie," he said, as he dressed. "Too many piggies in the pen. Plus, Sharon and I are tight with Weather now, and Sam split to Milwaukee. Without him the group is done, daddy-o."

"I see."

Now out of sympathetic ears within the collapsed collective, Jane decided to breach the very protocol for which she would criticize my father in her memoir—she confided in an outsider. That week, her mentor, Robin Morgan, would learn much that had transpired over the past six months, including how Sam was "controlling her," even in his absence. Jane wanted to perform a serious attack, something big on the same day as the MOBE, but her biggest fear was that she would get caught and then criticized by the movement for going rogue.

Morgan must have felt Jane puerile with her need for approval and to feel accepted. More so, she clearly was missing the big picture: the movement needed to show that it was not just macho fools who were taking serious steps to end the war. In fact, by this point, Morgan thought women should take over every aspect of the movement *entirely*. She brought up the underground and the liberties it had afforded several serious and effective radicals: the Catonsville Nine, the Chicago Seven, the Buffalo Nine, and the Panther Twenty-One. Forty-six activists arrested who had since risen as movement examples. But *barely a woman among them.*

Jane had had her brush with the underground when she helped harbor the FLQ fugitives in the Eleventh Street apartment. But the idea that she herself might have a life in it give her goosebumps; that she might even be more effective as a feminist icon if she went underground after carrying out an effective attack was a possibility she had not considered.

After this Jane felt like she had the potential to be a modern-day Margaret Sanger. *Whining about capture is bourgeois,* she thought, *Goddammit, stop thinking like fucking "Princess Jane."*

Two weeks later, on October 29, Jane was deep into her plans for the Veterans Day attack. She had realized Sam was right about the Masturbators and regrettably abandoned them, recruiting instead Sam's picks, Pat and David. Jane was impressed with herself. At twenty-two years old and barely in the movement for a year, she was leading experienced activists several years her senior. Things were going well. They were organized and focused on targets relevant to the war—unlike Sam, who to her seemed all over the map. Everything was under control. She credited this to her intellect, fine-tuned by an Ivy League education absent in the others. Then, she answered her phone one day and froze at the sound of Sam's voice.

"Janie . . . the heat is heavy out here."

Calling from a Milwaukee phone booth, Sam claimed that since the Days of Rage, security had increased and targets in the Midwest were not accessible in even the most innocuous of buildings. He was running out of money and would be coming back to New York tomorrow. And just like that, her confidence was shattered. *His dominance will destroy everything,* she thought. And in a moment of panic, she deployed a round of deflections, starting with a claim that Chicago police had disarmed a bomb planted in the Civic Center and that the FBI had figured out that the bomber was the same one who targeted Marine Midland. She warned that he should stay far away from major cities and offered to wire Sam $100 to a Western Union office—anything so he would stay out of New York.

All over an open line.

Perhaps it did not occur to her that a money wire would reveal his location or how all this might sound if the phone was bugged. Or perhaps she felt immune to arrest.

The backbreaker was when she mentioned that a white sedan had been parked outside for a few days. Sam hung up.

Flipping through pages in his address book, Sam made calls to half a dozen militants he had connected with over the summer. Did they want to stop talking about revolution and do something serious with him in the Midwest? Robin was the only taker and suggested that they bomb the courthouse at 100 Centre Street in New York City, where the Panther Twenty-One trial was starting that week. But as for joining him in Milwaukee, Robin served one of his more creative Masturbator procrastinations: he was anchored to New York until the end of his lease in November. As a consolation prize, Robin again suggested Crazy George. "He's always down, man. Militant as Christ. And he goes everywhere."

Following Anderson's instructions, Demmerle had been laying low in his Lower East Side tenement. He was watching a new TV series that premiered that week, *The Brady Bunch*, to distract himself from the stress of coming out as an informant when he would testify against Abbie Hoffman in the Chicago Seven trial in a few weeks. Other hippie CIs had already been outed when they were called to testify, and they had to go into hiding after. The next call was not the one he was expecting.

"It's Sam. We talked at Woodstock. At the Crazies booth."

Demmerle snapped into character and donned his disaffected persona. "I talked with a hundred losers at that bougie bullshit. Half of them were probably pigs."

"You heard about the bank on Wall Street the day after Woodstock. And the Fed Building downtown?"

"Yeah, so?"

"Robin introduced us . . ."

"Oh, Sam from Woodstock? Yeah! Those were *you*?"

"Where can we meet tomorrow?"

Demmerle gave Sam his address, hung up, and called Anderson, relaying that, although he didn't get a last name, "Sam," who he knew had ties to Abbie Hoffman, Rap Brown, and a group of Puerto Rican nationals organized by Ivan Lopez, was a strong suspect for at least some of the major bombings in New York that summer and was coming to his house tomorrow.

Sensing the biggest arrest of the year—and his path to SAC—Anderson opted not to share Demmerle's report with either Swearingen or Joe Sullivan's newly formed Section 22a (now called the Bomb Squad). Instead, he called the US attorney's office in Illinois to determine how essential Demmerle would be for the Chicago Seven trial. He was told that the evidence against Hoffman, Rubin, and Seale was not as strong as they boasted in the papers. Kunstler was winning points with the jury, the judge was incompetent, the trial was sure to go on for several months, and they needed Demmerle to lie low.

Regardless, Anderson felt bombings took precedent over a politically motived "conspiracy" trial. He called Demmerle first thing the next morning and told his snitch, "You are not going to Chicago."

———————

On the Sunday afternoon of November 9, just two days before Veterans Day, Jane was nursing a funk. She was still bothered that she could not move the Masturbators into giving her their full support. "I should have the acumen to formulate a consensus, right?" she said to John Keats, who was curled into a croissant near the radiator.

Around 5 PM, the dog looked up when the deadbolt spun. My father appeared in the doorway, sweaty and drained. He needed a shower and nap, he told Jane. The dog rose to lick his face.

"You can stay for the night," she offered, but she reminded him that the nature of their relationship had changed. She was pissed that he didn't trust her when he hung up two days ago. She insisted upon return of the keys. But within the hour, Jane would succumb to old patterns. While lathering his shoulders she asked if he would speak to the Masturbators that night and endorse her Veterans Day plan. "The target is Standard Oil, but I think Lester and Robin need to hear from you that it's OK to do this on the same day as the MOBE rally."

Sam agreed, and she joined him in the bath.

However, later with Sam, Robin, and Sharon viewing Jane's map at Lester's, it became apparent that Jane had withheld a vital piece of information: she decided to bomb not just 30 Rock but also the General Motors skyscraper in Midtown and the Chase Manhattan Bank tower in the financial district, *simultaneously*.

"This is really something," gasped Sam. "Who's your team?"

Lester shouted, "She's using Pat and David, the two most exposed people. It's a suicide plan. And what about the MOBE?" Lester aimed his next words right at Jane: "A bombing on the day of the rally will damage their credibility. They want to show that we can demonstrate *peacefully*."

Sam sneered, "And how many more villages get torched in Vietnam while they demonstrate peacefully? I love it, Jane."

Lester poked: "Then maybe *you* should do it?"

My father faced the wannabe Rasta, his awkward nest of salt and pepper dreads completely mismatched to his 1950s sexist attitude. "Robin and I are committed tomorrow," Sam said quietly, and announced their plan to bomb the courthouse at 100 Centre Street.

"Right on," came responses from Sharon and Robin, sprawled on the couch.

Lester also nodded in approval, "You're gonna jam up the Panther Twenty-One trial? Right on, Sam! Right *fucking* on."

Jane was surprised as well. Why hadn't Sam told her earlier when they were fucking? "This is interesting, very interesting." She whirled to Lester. "And why exactly *isn't* Sam's courthouse action interfering with the MOBE?"

Sharon rolled her eyes, tired of Jane's competitiveness, but Sam stood up for his protégé, who had finally arrived. "No, Jane is right. Robin and I can push Centre Street to Wednesday. Tuesday is for Jane."

———————

Shortly after sunset, Demmerle opened his apartment door to meet Sam. After a half-hour of Sam trying to recruit him into a Midwest militia, the informant asked as casually as he could, "Who's running that group? And how many people are we talking about? There might be conflicts. I'm blowing up some shit next week. Brooklyn Bridge. Other stuff too. I gotta know if this is for real."

"About thirty others is all I can say."

"And the *Rat* coverage. How are you pulling that off?"

"We have people everywhere. I'm doing the Armory the night after tomorrow, as a decoy. You can be the lookout."

"Decoy?"

After a heavy pause Sam spoke: "In or out?"

Demmerle nodded, surrendering to Sam's gut check.

"A'right," said Sam, "I'll pick you up here tomorrow at 8:30."

With the slam of the door, Demmerle surmised that one of Sam's "people" at *Rat* had to be the woman who was all over Sam at Woodstock. Demmerle had remembered her from the Panther rally in Oakland in June. She talked like an English professor and went on and on about she was the "star reporter" for the underground paper. He could not remember her name but did remember the name of her bestie. She was hard to ignore when she bounced into the Yippie storefront to sell *Rat*'s advertising in her bright orange sleeveless knit and no bra.

Meanwhile, uptown at the FBI's New York Office, Anderson had still not completely let go of his Rap Brown theory and was now following Swearingen's lead in trying to establish links between Brown, Melville, and the Whitehall bombing. He pulled the same 167s as Swearingen's team and discovered that Whitehall had been named as a target at the Revolutionary Contingent, Demmerle's sophomore assignment. When Demmerle called in, Anderson asked his informant about who he saw at RC meetings a year earlier. He was disappointed to learn that Rap Brown had never attended any. "There were no Blacks at RC meetings, just White kids," Demmerle confirmed. However, there was good news. Demmerle said there was a man who talked quite a bit about blowing up Whitehall and was also "tight with the *Rat* chick." His file showed that he worked for the *Guardian* around the same time as Melville and had a thick 167 showing links to subversive groups all over the Village—David Hughey.

Anderson told Demmerle that if "Sam" reappeared he was to do whatever was asked of him. Demmerle, a short man, cautioned that "Sam" was six foot one and muscle bound. "You gotta send some backup."

The anxious agent offered his informant an increase in his CI status and pay and assured that he would station agents around his block starting tomorrow.

The next day, Monday, November 10, around 8:15 AM, Sam left McCurdy by bike to case the Manhattan Criminal Courthouse on 100 Centre Street. Moments later, Anderson's surveillance team, disguised as vagrants, took positions all along a two-block perimeter around Demmerle's apartment. They hoped to catch Sam returning. Instead, around 9 AM, among the numerous residents exiting the Russian Orthodox neighborhood en route to their jobs, they documented three midtwenties Caucasians, two females and one male (later identified as David, Jane, and Pat), entering the building around the corner at 67 East Second Street.

This morning was Jane's first time in McCurdy. She was stunned to see the rows of rifles and ammunition. "Over here," Pat said, drawing Jane's and David's attention. Resting behind a crate of grenades, David found three devices wired and ready to go—Sam's supportive gift to Jane, like Valentine flowers from an ex.

David produced a headband to hold back his hair, armed the devices, gave one to Jane and one to Pat, and kept one for himself. "That's it."

The three returned to Fourth Street, changed into their bomb clothes, and independently left the East Village, walking right past both of Anderson's surveillance teams. In my last Swearingen interview, I asked him how this could happen. His response explained several mysteries. "The Intelligence Division just gathers intelligence. In most cases they do not have arrest warrants. And their focus at this point was Sam." Thus, on November 10, 1969, at 2:38 PM, two surveillance teams, one in a white sedan and one in a vacant storefront, allowed three bombers to walk right out of their sight.

Pat headed for the financial district. She strolled through the nearly empty lobby of 1 Chase Manhattan Plaza with its lone guard collecting holiday pay. With a breezy smile, she entered the elevator, then got off on the sixteenth floor, where she placed a Bloomingdale's bag inside an open heating duct in the women's bathroom.

Jane and David took the IRT and got off the train at 47–50 Rockefeller Center around 3:15 PM. The streets were unusually quiet for a Monday.

They parted with an awkward kiss and David headed toward the General Motors building on Fifty-Ninth Street. As he crossed the outdoor plaza at

Rockefeller Center, which had transitioned into a skating rink in October, he took note of the families gliding in circles and second-guessed his wiring.

At the same time, Jane lingered in the catacombs of the 47–50 Rockefeller Center subway station in her Jackie O bomb clothes. Its passageways were lined with high-end retail outlets that, as a young girl, she and her mother had patronized. Moments later she was exiting the elevator, the sounds of city traffic from thirty floors down barely audible.

Around 4:30 that afternoon, Jane would be seen entering the McBurney YMCA on West Fourteenth Street wearing street clothes and sitting at a community work desk. A typewriter ribbon recovered by the NYPD would show that the same press release was typed at least five times at the desk where she sat. So far, save for *Rat*, none of the underground papers had published her explanations. This time she was thinking bigger by sending it directly to wire services AP and UPI.

At 11 PM, Jane, Pat, and David gathered on the rooftop along with Lester, Robin, and Sharon, where five months earlier the collective had been born. They tuned a portable radio to WBAI. Shortly after 1 AM (November 11), the jock announced that explosions had ripped through Midtown Manhattan and the financial district like a Soviet attack. Police were barricading blocks. Subway service had been suspended. Seven floors below, distant sirens materialized seemingly from all directions raging through some of Amerika's richest real estate.

They toasted Sam, who they presumed had left for Milwaukee. It was a great night for the revolution.

While this went on, my father scampered across town to see his best girl. Since he would be leaving the city that was his home, probably forever, he would try one last time to convince Jane to come with him.

Heading south on Avenue A, he remembered that Jane claimed there were FBI agents in a white car around the corner. He broke into an adjacent tenement and dashed over the interconnecting rooftop and down the stairs. When she answered to his knock on the door, he radiated: "You're amazing." Adrenaline pumping, they made intense love for the last time, and in their afterglow, Sam made his most earnest pitch to wait out the winter in Milwaukee, hoping that by then the intensity of the attacks would have blown over.

She shook her head. "I have to be at *Rat* tomorrow."

His six-foot-one frame enveloped her five-foot-two body. The embrace felt so good to them both. He didn't want to let go, and she didn't want to think about tomorrow.

Jane woke alone at 7 AM feeling reborn. The concave space in her mattress was the last trace of the man who made her. She fed and walked John Keats and picked up the *New York Times* at a newsstand, anxious to read about her work. On the front page she expected to see a feature story about the triple bombing; instead, it was business as usual, with a picture of Nixon announcing a new trade policy. She eventually found the bombing article squeezed into a scant few paragraphs in the bottom right-hand corner. It continued on page 20, reduced to a three-column box no bigger than the shoe ad next to it. She crushed the paper into a ball.

Next, Jane walked ten blocks north to *Rat*, greeting Jeff Shero with an innocent "Good morning."

"Have you heard?!" the normally mellow editor-in-chief screamed with his Texas accent. He waved (Jane's) Mad Bomber communiqué that he found in the morning mail while explaining excitedly to her wide eyes that "squares were gorging themselves at some piggy ball on the top floor of the RCA building." They had to walk down sixty floors because the bomb blew out all the elevators. In ballroom dresses and tuxedos?

Jane forced a smile, trying to deflect her terror. She had felt sure the building would be empty due to the long holiday weekend. But she had missed an ad for a Veterans Day formal.

A staffer shouted, "And one pig down."

Jane gasped, her lips starting to dry. "A cop was in the building?"

"Night watchman. He was responding to the called-in warning and was looking for the bomb. Moron could've been killed. Next time!"

Others chanted, "Right on!"

Jane would later learn from the *Times* that ammonia in the cleaning closet where the bomb had been placed had transported the explosion. It was by sheer luck that she was not, at that moment, a cop killer.

While Jane was rethinking her life, at around 9 AM Swearingen stood in front of Cement Head, Anderson, and the three Joes, reminding the room that he had predicted Chase, Standard Oil, and General Motors *and* profiled Melville almost two months ago. The homeroom teacher was being ignored by the cool kids.

Anderson took the floor. Talking fast to control the meeting, he preached that David Hughey and his girlfriend Patricia Swinton were undoubtedly key players. "My CI mentioned Swinton by name. She works for *Rat*. Hughey does deliveries for *Rat* and conspired to blow up Whitehall at RC meetings in '68. He also worked with Melville at the *Guardian*. Melville has strong ties to the Alpert woman, who the NYPD confirmed opens *Rat*'s morning mail."

"Good work, Joe," said Malone, talking past the only agent in the room not named Joe. Then he turned to Sullivan: "We should arrest all three of them tonight, right after we get Melville at the armory."

Swearingen cleared his froggy throat. "Um, at what armory do you intend to arrest Melville?" There were three in Manhattan. Demmerle had presumed there was only one and never asked Sam which one was the target.

Malone, who needed arm-twisting to give Swearingen just twenty men for his Melville-*Rat* theory two months ago, did not waste a second signing the authorization for three hundred agents under Sullivan to stake out numerous potential targets throughout Manhattan. His next call was to the Associated Press. He hated the liberal media but ordered donuts and coffee to be waiting for the photographers and reporters outside the building for the perp walk. Tonight was the night the New York Office would make Hoover proud.

Jane met David at her place that night and celebrated the triple action with a bowl of his best hash and a bottle of wine. Still peeved about the lack of media coverage, she spat, "The *Times* is a shit paper." David consoled her and confessed that he and Pat had had their final fight that morning and he was looking forward to working with just Jane from here on. Perhaps they hoped that with the thrill of the attacks and Sam splitting town, nature would take its course and they would finally find each other in the throes of revolutionary romance. At 10:15 PM they toasted their achievements and moved closer for their first kiss as comrades and lovers.

WBAI broke the moment with news of another explosion—the courthouse on 100 Centre Street. "The destruction will interrupt the trial of multiple Black Panthers for several months," said the announcer. The couple smiled, praising Sam, not knowing that at that very moment, one mile north, he was being handcuffed in front of the Federal Armory on East Twenty-Sixth Street. Jane and David would find out in a moment when a loud knock and a voice called from the hallway, "FBI, Miss Alpert. Please open the door."

They spun in reflex, searching for an escape route. Through the window they saw a line of police cars on Avenue A. Jane took her last breath of free air. Gazing at David, tears of tension welling, she twisted open the deadbolt. Cops flooded the tiny flat, leading the couple out in handcuffs. A second team followed and bagged everything in sight.

John Keats watched quietly from his spot by the radiator.

"You should be careful with that," Sam said, pointing to his tear gas pen. "Don't release the spring. Just carefully unscrew the capsule."

The agent followed his instructions, taking great care with the weapon they found on him.

My father was frightened but was comforted only by the fact that the agents in the squad car and now in the interview room seemed more afraid of him than he of them. He and Demmerle had been thrown very hard against the stone wall at the federal armory. "OK, OK, you got me," Sam said, trying to deflect their aggression. As he rounded Twenty-Sixth Street, he could see that the army trucks, which earlier in the day were parked on the armory side of the street, had all been moved to the residential side. He knew this could not be a coincidence. The pigs must have moved the trucks earlier in the evening near the homes so that they could claim they caught him in the act of trying to bomb civilians. It also meant he and Crazy George were surrounded.

That was an hour earlier. Since then, he had been strip searched, finger-printed, strip searched a second time, and escorted into a small room at FBI headquarters where he sat looking at a young, well-dressed agent toying with his weapon.

Outside the room, a second agent, Henry Byers, anxious to get in, passed Swearingen, who was asked to watch through the mirror. Swearingen did not like what he saw.

Byers had no previous knowledge of the case but was being groomed as the next head of the New York Office. To this end, he was handed the most prestigious interrogation of the year as Swearingen was told to wait outside. On top of that, SAC Joe Sullivan had violated protocols by bringing the suspects directly into interrogation, instead of to the US Commissioner's office, for an identity hearing. Swearingen was stewing. *We're not supposed to present a circus sideshow for the press. If Melville and Alpert hire Kunstler, the whole case will be tossed on the FBI's conduct alone.*

Byers had little interest in Swearingen's theories. He sat half cheeked on the table, and said, "Sam, my name is Henry Byers. Can I get you some coffee?"

"Yes, thank you."

"Sam, you gave us quite a time. You had this office jumping for months. Marine Midland was good, but the courthouse, that was brilliant, right past security. You know, that guy may die."

"What guy?"

"The guard at the courthouse. He may lose an arm."

"I'd like to see a lawyer."

"It's pretty late. He probably won't be reachable until the morning," said Byers. "Maybe there's someone else you'd like to call?"

Sam shook his head as Byers leaned across the table and toyed with Sam's revolver. "He's gonna lose that arm, for sure. Maybe his life." In his court testimony months later, Byers would admit that this was a ruse. No one had been hurt. But my father couldn't know this at the time. Exhausted, he closed his eyes. In the darkness of his thoughts, he heard Byers state his epitaph. "You got away with it for a long time, Sam, but you were bound to kill someone eventually."

The other agent, still obsessed with Sam's weapons, interjected, "This is strictly off the record Sam. Did you intend to use the gun?"

Sam laughed bitterly. "No. I'm not even sure it will fire. It's very old. I've never fired a gun."

"Why were you carrying it?"

"I don't know. I'd never use it."

A third agent entered with urgency. "They're here."

The agents handcuffed Sam and led him out of the room. Passing the front desk, Sam noticed a familiar back: Jane. Behind her was David, stern and scowling. In a minute, they were out of sight. Between his involvement with Rap Brown, the Black Panthers, and Ivan Lopez and having built bombs for half-a-dozen other cells, my father wondered, *How many were in custody?*

He turned to Byers. "You know I acted alone."

"What's that, Sam?"

"I'll give a statement. I acted alone."

21 | REWARDS FOR THE WICKED

WHEN THE NYPD BROKE INTO MCCURDY the next morning, the police found the massive supply of assault weapons—but not a single stick of dynamite. Sam had brought the last of it to Robin's house the night before. By contrast, in Jane's apartment they found a soldering wire, flux, and a marked-up map of Midtown.

Ironically, this evidence against Jane was bad news for prosecutors. Getting a unanimous guilty verdict in 1969 from an all-male jury meant convincing them that a twenty-two-year-old Ivy League woman was the architect of eight terror bombings. Swearingen summed it up bitterly in my last interview with him: "In 1969 how many women even knew how to use a soldering gun?" Instead, the DA and the federal prosecutor focused their trial strategy around my father, whose disaffected reputation fit the stereotype of a mad bomber.

Pat, Ivan, Gil, John, and Lester had each heard of Sam's and Jane's capture on WBAI, thanks to Cement Head's donuts-and-coffee press junket. They skipped town that night. Pat would remain underground until her capture in 1975. Since our first meeting, she would assist me over the years with fact-checking when I uncovered another piece of the puzzle. To this day she remains proud of her contributions toward wounding the "enemy of the people."

As for others in the collective, they are less proud. As the 1970s evolved into a more decadent era, the women remained vigilant while the male Masturbators retreated back into the mainstream and the comfort of their families. None have publicly spoken of their involvement in these events. Gil left the East Village and used family land in the Catskills to open a Transcendental Meditation retreat. In a self-published book about Zen, he reduced his participation in the Melville Collective to a reckless dalliance with "terrorists" in his youth. Lester fled to Jamaica, avoiding a charge. He never returned to the United States, and I never learned what became of him. Ivan reinvented himself. Jane told me over one of our coffee-house meetings that through family connections, he managed to cover up his involvement with what would become one of the most militant Puerto Rican radical groups, Movimiento Independentista Revolucionario en Armas (MIRA), and became a journalist. She would not reveal his name to me but said, "If you follow network news, you've probably seen him." John Cohen fled to a family home in the Berkshires, appointing himself as a go-between to radicals in underground. He would visit Sam frequently in Attica.

While the men retreated, Sharon did not. With an insatiable passion for freeing Sam, she led the Crazies in a fundraising binge, addressing audiences at every art house, movie theater, and street show in Lower Manhattan. She convinced Jeff Shero to run a regular series in *Rat* for months, under the head-line FREE SAM MELVILLE. Circulation boomed and for the first time surpassed the *East Village Other*, making Shero the most talked-about editor in the New York underground press. But it did not last.

A few months later, Morgan, feeling Shero was exploiting his female volunteers, organized a takeover of *Rat* via an activist group she and Jane founded, called WITCH (Women's International Terrorist Conspiracy from Hell). They renamed the paper *Women's LibeRATion*, ushered Shero and all male volunteers out on the street, and anointed Jane with the official title she always craved: Star Reporter. The paper's voice grew substantially more acute, particularly in its militant focus on discrimination of women. Following the arrest of half a dozen of the paper's volunteers, *Rat* closed its doors perma-nently in 1970, but not before Sharon managed to leverage its popularity to raise the $50,000 for Sam's bail.

But when Sharon showed up in court to present the bond for Sam, the judge raised his amount to a staggering $100,000. His lawyer pled for clemency, claiming that my father had a young son that he was supporting. However, the FBI showed that my father had not seen me in more than a year.

Just one of many "Free Sam Melville" posters pasted all over the East Village to raise his $100,000 bail. *Author's collection*

Through sheer force of will, Sharon managed again to raise the entire amount from her well of wealthy leftists. But this time my father refused to take the money. He was quoted in the *New York Times* as he announced to a packed courtroom, "It would be racist for me to be free on bail when the Panther Twenty-One suspects were being held without any," once again choosing his principles over his freedom or his son. Sadly for me, the judge agreed with my father. Sam almost escaped from the Federal House of Detention by tying up a guard. He was remanded and would never walk city streets again.

Elsewhere in the movement, the romantic cachet of Sam and Jane's story lit a cultural fuse. In December 1969, the Weathermen held the last of its national "war council" meetings in Flint, Michigan. Organizer Bernardine Dohrn told delegates that they need to stop being afraid, follow the East Village model, and begin an "armed struggle." She announced that they would henceforth be referring to themselves as the Weather Underground.

In January 1970, only three months since the arrests, the spark of the Melville Collective inspired weekly destruction by Marxist groups across

America. In March 1970 the Revolutionary Force 9 committed what the FBI called "Melville-esque" bombings of three Manhattan skyscrapers. No one was injured.

Not all attacks were without casualties. On March 6, 1970, at 18 West Eleventh Street, less than a quarter mile from Robin Palmer's apartment at the residence of Cathy Wilkerson, members of Weather accidentally blew themselves and her father's townhouse to bits while assembling bombs they intended to plant at a military formal dance at Fort Dix, New Jersey.

In this volatile climate, with daily time bombs in courthouses, office buildings, ROTC centers, and police precincts creating New Left folk heroes, prosecutors were apprehensive about getting a conviction for the Mad Bomber who popularized the trend—particularly if a trial would expose a long and humbling examination of FBI incompetence and Red Squad's entrapment methods. Weighing this against the diminishing chances of a conviction, the system blinked with a sweetheart deal: 18 years (instead of 130) in state prison if David, my father, and Jane all pled to what the FBI wanted so desperately to prove: a conspiracy. The promise was that with good behavior, they would all be out in five.

It was a miracle offer, furnished via Hoover's desperation for Congress to grant the Bureau emergency powers. But then came the Jane problem. She had amassed quite a following by speaking at rallies, often with Morgan. She was not interested.

With Jane on a roll, Sam and David had little ammunition in persuading her to take any deal involving jail time. It took several weeks of pressure by Jane's attorney, along with impassioned pleas by both of her ex-lovers, until she finally agreed. When she did, everything seemed to be heading toward a (relatively) happy ending. Sam would get his freedom in five years, I would get my father back, and the FBI would get its nicely packaged conspiracy to present to Congress. That is, until Jane's bail continuance hearing on April 5, where she swore that if her release was extended so she could satisfy her public appearance commitments, she would return in two weeks, accept the plea, and surrender. Her parents vouched for her integrity, representing that the $25,000 bond they posted was their life savings. Morgan also organized a petition to free Jane. The judge had always loved Morgan's performances as Dagmar Hansen in the 1949–1956 TV comedy *Mama* and granted the extension. But minutes after he banged his gavel and set Jane free, Jane Alpert disappeared.

Sam and David's plea bargains were immediately revoked.

With Jane in the wind, on May 4, 1970 (the same day as the massacre at Kent State), my father accepted the best offer his lawyers claimed he was going to get. He pled guilty to bombing the Federal Building and the Whitehall Induction Center—ironically, two bombs he did not deploy. Despite pleading to only the federal charges, the deal was for eighteen years in state prison. (When I interviewed Sam's lawyer, he claimed he could not remember why and refused to check his records.) He agreed but he had a condition: his conviction would allow David to plead down to a lesser charge. David ultimately pled to "guilt due to mental defect" and received a sentence of three years in a federal psychiatric facility.

Once in prison, my father became convinced that pleading guilty had been a mistake. He was considering firing his lawyer, withdrawing his plea, and going to trial. In the next month the prison uprising at Attica broke.

Shortly after my father's memorial at an East Village church crowded with activists and Black Panthers and with an FBI van stationed out front, Abbie Hoffman went into hiding. My father's death haunted Hoffman for years. He grew ever more paranoid while underground, repeating to his brother and confidants, "If I end up in prison, I would be assassinated, just like Sam Melville."

Over the months and years that followed, several key players managed to find ways to not only profit but also prosper off my father's capture and his demise. Christmas bonuses for 1969 saw FBI Director J. Edgar Hoover award Robert "Cement Head" Malone a $5,000 bonus for the arrest of the Melville Collective (approximately $35,000 in today's economy). Sullivan and Anderson each received $1,000. Swearingen, without whom the FBI wouldn't have had a case, received only $200 under the condition that he accept yet another distant transfer three thousand miles away, to Los Angeles, where he was tasked with hunting down West Coast Weathermen, of which by all accounts there were few. He accepted the assignment happily. His methodology of comparing personality traits and motivations to form profiles would be adopted as standard FBI procedure, although he would never receive acknowledgement for this.

Hoover himself got a nice gift from Nixon. While a mostly Democratic Congress refused to declare the Panthers, the Yippies, or the Weather Underground as "enemy combatants," in December 1970, after Sam's very public arrest, Nixon made it known through back channels that there would be no official inquiries into COINTELPRO or the methods Red Squad used to quash the New Left. Over the next decade this policy would furnish bundles of FBI promotions as CIs claimed to have heard and done things that were actually authored by their handlers. FBI agents I talked to claimed that this model was referred to in the New York Office as "doing a Demmerle."

Demmerle managed to prosper off my father as well. While he had still not received the bonus he was promised for bringing my father in, Marine Midland Bank did agree to pay him a $25,000 reward for providing information leading to the arrest of the persons responsible for bombing their building. Trapped in a cell, just one hundred feet from the man he betrayed, he was scared for his life, since a *New York Times* reporter outed him as an informant. He let Anderson know that he would not be a good witness unless his situation improved. The FBI moved him into a hotel on the condition that he testify to a conspiracy that connected Pat, David, and Jane to Mad Bomber Melville. He would have to claim under oath that Melville confessed their names to him.

He agreed.

After the Attica massacre and my father's very public memorial, Demmerle tried to reintegrate himself into the East Village counterculture. But the public outing made the informant useless to law enforcement, and the activists who once were his friends now chased the imposter down St. Mark's Place. Socially homeless, to counteract the books written by Hoffman and Rubin lambasting him, Demmerle attempted to market his own memoir. To attract the liberal press, Demmerle revised his narrative into something of a confession, claiming that his actions went past the role of informant and more deeply into that of provocateur. The FBI didn't agree. Done with the social climbing factory worker, they declined to grant him the necessary permissions. His memoir was never published. He changed his last name to DeMerl, remarried, and settled in Austin, Texas, where he became a local artist. He died of cancer there in 2008, surrounded by friends but estranged from the wife and child he abandoned to help the FBI.

But by far the biggest profiteer off the Sam Melville saga was Jane.

Her first attempt to have a meaningful voice from the underground was *Mother Right*, Jane's feminist manifesto published in *Ms.* It was not exactly a hit. They didn't edit any of its deeply misandrist passages nor its condescending eulogy for the victims of Attica. It brought Jane attention, but not the kind she had hoped for. Shortly after publication, Weather shut its doors, and John had to organize fundraisers so that Jane could stay underground. (One was the fundraiser that Robin took me to when I was twelve.) Feeling the weight of her misstep, out of allies, and tiring of life on the run, in 1974 Jane surrendered to the FBI. Whatever she told them must have been good. They offered her one of the lightest federal sentences ever given a political bomber: a mere eighteen months for the bombings themselves and only an additional nine months for jumping bail and evading justice for nearly five years. She would serve even less.

By 1977 Jane was released from prison but was a pariah to the left. She and her mentor had hit rocky times, but Morgan still pipelined her copyediting jobs for *Ms.* (rumors alleged a brief affair) and advocated to the publisher William Morrow and Company on behalf of Jane's second attempt to be relevant, her tell-all memoir, *Growing Up Underground*. Morgan felt it was important treatise on chauvinism of the radical left, which by then was in steep decline.

Morrow paid Jane $25,000 for her story (about $100,000 today). However, learning from her mistake of criticizing movement men who were still active, Jane narrowed her general animus to mostly my deceased father, who could offer no rebuttal.

The caricature Jane had crafted for *Mother Right* was transformed from the victim, "half-dragged" into participating in bombings, to an *empowered sister*, one who overcame domination by my father, weaponized her sexuality, and led the collective in a successful attack on the Vietnam War machine. In the final pages, she sees the hypocrisy of the movement and, grown strong through penance, turns state's evidence and returns to mainstream life.

A 1980 review of her book in *Rolling Stone* sympathized with Jane's atonement. Many of their readers by this point had morphed from Woodstock '69 to NASDAQ '79. However, to those who still saw the Melville bombings as a bonfire of their noble youth, the result seemed repugnant. Jane got a book deal. Sam got a bullet at Attica.

22 | FINK'S BAG-O-MARBLES

THE DOOR READ Jane Alpert and Associates, but stepping inside the tiny suite for the first time, I saw only one desk.

The questions that remained for me in 1989 were not those that could be answered by FBI agents or former coconspirators. They had to be answered by Jane herself. I knew she would need some kind of collateral, so I had her contract in my bag.

She welcomed me, and we commiserated for a few minutes about my mother's disastrous birthday dinner at the Plaza earlier that month. Maybe she thought she could mother me into signing over my father's story. "I have a question," I said.

"Yes?"

"I have wondered why, if as you say, you loved him, did you write such nasty things in *Ms.*?"

She got quiet. No doubt she had had to defend this choice before. Was it really because my father "cheated" on her or didn't take her seriously or used her for stability while he planned revolutionary acts? That's certainly reason to be furious. But to destroy his reputation after death? Surely even Jane was not that petty.

As it would turn out, Jane's motives were not really those of a scorned woman at all. "I have many conflicting feelings about your father," she said with a distant gaze. "That article in *Ms.* exploited the negative ones."

I began racking my brain trying to remember the opportunities when she had exploited her *positive* feelings. Would history remember my father differently if the *Guardian* had wanted to publish her thoughts, instead of *Ms.*? Or if Morgan had not become Jane's rabbi? What did the real Jane Alpert feel? Was there a real Jane Alpert, or just various ones for hire? What about the profile in *Letters from Attica* and her memoir? In both, she bashed my father without a sponsor to exploit her and deflected any responsibility for the collective's capture. She threw movement men under the bus when she knew all along that it was both the chivalrous attitude of men of the era and the sexist attitude of law enforcement that resulted in her tender treatment. In fact, in the deepest of ironies, Jane owed the whole of her liberty to sexism. Did she feel sorry that she'd manifested such profound hypocrisy or that her freedom was built on the back of my father's reputation and the denial of his place in history? Of his life?

I pulled the contract out of my bag and asked the one question that had hooked me when I was eleven. "Why did you dedicate your profile in *Letters from Attica* to me, personally? 'To Jocko Melville'?"

"I thought in time you would be the only person who would care to know those personal things about him." She knew I did not want to wait years while I sued the government for documents. I looked down at the contract. *I'll get it over with*, I thought. *I'll learn the truth. Right now. Today.* But it would be a truth that she would once again own—this time probably forever.

Maybe it was Sam's ghost I heard at that moment, finally answering my many calls for clarity. It whispered that the contract was a lie and that I had gotten all the half-truths I was ever going to get from Mother Right, as well as the radicals.

"I'm sorry. I can't sign this."

I could not get a read on her blank look. She knew it probably meant the end for us. Holding a deep stare that had worked well on so many, her last words to me were "I wish I could adopt you," and like the day we met, she asked permission for a hug.

After a brief one, I left her office. It would mean two more decades of painstaking research, but I did not care. My father deserved a better historian than Jane Alpert and Associates.

It was the start of a fresh decade for the rest of the world. The Reagan era was ending and the Clinton era was around the corner. But my Christmas of 1989 and New Year of 1990 came and went with little joy exchanged. Mom and I were still not talking, so I spent the holidays at the home of Jill's parents in Livingston, New Jersey. They treated me like family, even though they hated my obsession with my father. Jill's dad had been a rebel in the '60s. He participated in the counterculture before Madison Avenue got hold of him, before a mortgage and a daughter.

"I spoke with Simon & Schuster," I announced over the Chanukah candles. "I told them I didn't think I could write this book."

I knew they would be happy. I had been so focused on finding my dead father that I had ignored the living hope for a normal life that was right in front of me. I had missed one of Jill's exhibitions at FIT to hunt down an Attica lead in Vermont, and instead of our anniversary dinner, I had prioritized meeting a former Weatherman who had a number for David Hughey. So Jill's mom looked relieved I had given up, and she made a wry joke. "Well, it will be nice to have a chair in your living room where you don't have to move a stack of clippings before you can sit on it."

The truth was far less romantic. I just could not gather the facts I wanted to properly tell a publishable story, and Judith Regan had also moved on to other conquests. In addition, it seemed to me that, with terrorism on the rise, the last thing the world needed was a book about an all-but-forgotten '60s bomber.

When we got home from the weekend, I began to box up my research and put it in storage. The next week, when the ball at Times Square dropped, I convinced myself that my New Year's resolution was that I would free myself from my lineage, free myself to now create new memories with Jill. I didn't realize there was still a malignant cell. It came in the form of a letter from attorney Elizabeth M. Fink, representing the Attica Brothers. "Attica is All of Us," Fink's flier read. It was an invitation to a fundraiser for the upcoming civil trial for the class action of inmates killed or injured in the prison uprising. After twenty years of litigation, Fink had finally secured a date for a trial: November 1, 1991.

Good luck with that, I thought. Rioting prisoners suing for injuries they sustained when the state attempted to rescue the guards they took as hostages? It reminded me of a story I'd read about a burglar who sued the owner of the house he was robbing because his hand got severed in an anti-intruder booby trap. Then again, the burglar won that suit.

Although I hid the flier so Jill would not see it, like "The Tell-Tale Heart," it beckoned to me each day, until I showed it to her and begged for one last indulgence. She choked on her breakfast of coffee and probiotics. "You sat in my parents' living room and swore that this was the end of it."

"I know, I know. But these were the people who knew him in the final days and hours of his life. I'm curious about what he did, knowing he would probably die. Did he mention me . . . my mother . . . anyone?"

"You think murderers and drug dealers are going to have some grand insight into your father while he was running from a cop's bullet?"

She had a way of boiling down my most complex needs to absurdities. Like my mother—and, in the end, don't all boys marry their mother?

"I've tried to be supportive of this, Josh, you know that. But it's time I told you what I think: radicals are not heroes. They are people who don't have the patience to work within a system. They can't wait for progress, so they blow shit up. And from what I've seen, hippies are idiots. Destroy innocent lives to stop a war or oust a president? Why? Don't all wars end and all presidencies? But they think that it's OK to blow shit up because you can't make an omelet without breaking eggs? The children they fuck up are the eggs! You're better than that."

I thought she was overreacting. I thought she knew that I had come to a milestone in understanding my father—an angry loner, mad at *his* father, mad at the world, and caught up in a time when anger at both was sexy. For all this, I had forgiven him. Even though I didn't agree with his choices, I'd come to admire him. But, looking at Fink's flier, I realized my forgiveness came with a personal price. If my father was worthy of my forgiveness, that also meant that if he was murdered, I had a duty to seek his justice. "I just want to check it out. Just one more night."

I returned from a late-night recording session later that week to find the house empty. There was no note, but I could just tell that her spirit, so full of life and smiles, had left. Along with it went my best chance at a family. *Should I try to get her back?*

It was as if I had her parents' number in one hand and the Attica flier in the other, and I needed to let go of one. I knew the right choice. But like my grandfather, who chose politics over his son, and Sam, who did likewise, I couldn't seem to break the chain.

My father figures were gone. And only one remained: Sam's killer.

I was one of about five White faces in the packed Harlem church hosting the Attica Brothers fundraiser. One of the others was David Rothenberg, president of the Fortune Society. He was one of the outside "Observers" brought into the prison to oversee the negotiations between inmate leaders and the governor. He had never spoken directly to my father but told me I should be proud to be his son. Rothenberg was comforting. However, I was getting a bit tired of hearing how proud I should be from people who didn't know him or what it was like to live with his crimes.

"How should I feel," I responded, "about a man who wanted to save the world and gave up his only child to do it?" (When I would interview Rothenberg for this project almost two decades later, he would tell me that what I said still haunted him.)

Another White face was William Kunstler. As Richie Havens sang "Lives in the Balance" from the stage, Kunstler's massive hands engulfed mine. "We had worked all night long on the prisoner demands, me and the other Observers. About 3 AM, as we were being escorted out, I saw your father was in a line of men who were guarding the hostages. I walked over to him and said in a very quiet voice, 'We have many mutual friends.' I embraced him and said that I hoped we would meet again someday. And I'll never forget this because he wouldn't break ranks as he said, 'I hope so too.' But it felt like he knew that we would not." Kunstler finished with a heavy pause and abruptly changed to a lighter subject, "How is Larry working out?" I realized then, after connecting the memories of my several interactions with him, that one didn't have real conversations with Kunstler. He talked, and you sort of kept up.

"Larry is fine," I said. "But the government still won't send me the files."

"It takes time. He's a good man." Then he ushered me over to a group of older White people. "Now I would like you to meet a good *woman*." It was forty-six-year-old Elizabeth Fink.

Everything about Fink was a protest. Her attire was a flowing layered black dress that resembled the robes of a Reform rabbi. It concealed a short, Rubenesque frame that I presumed was the result of a multitude of counter-culture indulgences. Her head was super round, like an overinflated beach ball. "*Yeaaah*, nice to finally meet you," she said offhandedly. She started many replies with a superfluous "*Yeaaah*," leaning on the extra-long *a* with her Brooklyn brogue. Larry had told me that in civil rights circles her abrasive demeanor was a significant asset. She maintained the moral high ground with passionate arguments that got defendants off death row or gained them amnesty, new trials, or reduced charges.

But I had a hunch that with the Attica case, her style might not be a strength. The state had already settled on paltry amounts with the widows of the Attica guards taken as hostages—some as low as $1,500. Fink was asking for $2.3 billion for the prisoners. Add to this the fact that this case would not be tried in liberal Lower Manhattan, where she had a home-court advantage. She needed to persuade a blue-collar Buffalo jury that Attica felons were *victims* of a racist system that pushed them to a desperate act. She needed to show, as she taught me that night, that "Attica was not 'a riot.' It was a rebellion."

It took effort for me take her seriously. A belligerent hair on her double chin bobbed to the rhythm of her words like a conductor's baton. "Are you coming to Buffalo for the trial?" it asked with insistence.

"I would like to, but cash is tight right now. My girlfriend and I split up, and I need to find a roommate."

"I'm renting a big house for the [Attica] Brothers. You can stay with us. Come up during the week we call the scumbag warden to the stand."

I was flattered. "I'll see if I can swing it." Then I asked her if, like Kunstler, she truly felt that there was a conspiracy to kill my father.

"Yeaah. There were forty inmates, including your father, housed in Five Company."

Five Company was a cell block, described by the state's report on Attica (McKay) as "an unusual concentration of a new breed of inmates: young, politically active, avowedly defiant in thought and rhetoric."

"It was in Five Company that inmates were heard discussing a takeover the night before," Fink explained like she was rehearsing her opening statement, "It was Five Company that first broke the ranks. And it was Five Company that composed most of the so-called inmate ringleaders. And seven of the twenty-nine prisoners killed—which included your father—were members of Five Company."

I did not follow her logic. There were over a thousand prisoners scrambling in a large recreation yard when the shooting started. They were not standing in one place or organized by cell block. I rebutted, "Seven dead, by hundreds of troopers firing into a yard of over a thousand inmates? That does not seem suspicious."

She nodded as if I my analysis was reasonable. Then she got close enough for me to smell what she had eaten. "Let's say a bag contains 1,241 red marbles and only 40 blue marbles. You reach in and pull out 29 in a handful. What do you think are the odds that you randomly grabbed seven blue marbles from that group of 40 in a bag with over 1,200?"

"I don't know. It's probably like five hundred to one. But that's not proof."

She chuckled, "You're just a little off by a couple of zeros." Then, she jabbed her thick digit at my chest. "You want proof? Come to Buffalo."

When I got home, I checked my calendar. I had studio gigs I would need to cancel. It would cost me more than I could spare while I was still saving for Dad's FBI files. Asking Mom for the cash was out of the question. She would want to come along.

Was Buffalo worth it? Fink's bag-o-marbles schtick was keeping me up. So, I dialed my best friend Brian at 1 AM. "What are the actual odds?" I asked him. "Are they, like, more than a thousand to one?" Brian was a mathlete and a chess master. He noted the variables, clicked his calculator, and delivered the answer that would have me packing. "There is no way it's a coincidence," he said.

The odds were 62,978 to 1.

PART IV

WHITE MAN'S RULES

Written by Sam to my mother:

dear ruth,
i wrote jocko what i felt was a sincere letter which i hope helps him,
and you. i don't put much credence in schools or their reports but i'm
glad you sent them just the same. he's a bright boy and won't have
any trouble in that respect.

it's hopeless to anticipate getting bail release no matter how hard
people work. this country is approaching a computerized fascism that
must make examples of any who refuse to obey its commandments of
war and racism. i only regret they will probably deny me a death by
firing squad.

Sam Melville
The Tombs, 1970

Written to John Cohen:

i still have much unchecked fury but when i see so many black men
in circumstances far worse than mine i try to relate to that and come
out okay. One thing is certain: in spite of the high racial tension (or
perhaps because of it) when i emerge to whatever sunlight is left in this
world i will not be a honky anymore.

Sam Melville
Attica 1971

23 | THE ATTICA BROTHERS

WHEN SAM WAS A TEENAGER, his hometown outside Buffalo was the base for the mighty brands US Steel and Wurlitzer Organ. However, by December 1991 the region had become like the ghost my father was. As my Amtrak train passed near the blighted towns of North Tonawanda and Attica, it was not hard for me to imagine his final days filled with loneliness.

"I was invited personally by the lead counsel," I bragged to Allen, a sixtyish African American stranger who sat across from me. I exaggerated a bit to fill the void of the six-hour ride, adding that my role was to "assist the inmate litigation team."

"Attica. I remember that," he said, wistfully. "It was like, ten years ago, right?"

"1971."

"Twenty years . . ." He held his solemn look. "Wow. Why now? Who cares anymore?"

I tightened my collar to protest both his question and the chill in the car. "Well, people who lost their fathers." He apologized and sat back to get comfortable, surmising that my answer to his next question would require his full attention. "Why did it take so long?"

In 1971, few Americans outside liberal circles cared much about twenty-nine dead felons. However, the bodies of the prison guards who had been taken as hostages were another matter. Autopsies revealed that troopers had been killed by friendly fire from a regiment of snipers Governor Rockefeller claimed was necessary because inmates had been heavily armed. So when a citizens' investigation (McKay) revealed that the prisoners had no firearms, civil rights lawyers filed a $30 million wrongful death class-action lawsuit on behalf of the wounded and dead inmates.

A new investigation was formed—this time, controlled by Rockefeller's office. In less than a year it was dissolved when preliminary findings alarmed Rockefeller. They were inching toward the same conclusions as McKay: state troopers had behaved "unprofessionally."

Another investigation was formed. And then another. By 1977, there had been four official investigations into Attica: the McKay Commission, the Goldman Panel, the Meyer Commission, and the Scotti Commission—all with similar results.

By 1979, the inmate litigants, who became known as the Attica Brothers, were gaining traction, and it seemed as if Rockefeller, a blue-blood billionaire, would stand trial. Then Rockefeller found an ally. The presiding judge, John Elfvin, ruled that the governor could not be tried until all criminal charges against the riot's twenty-odd ringleaders and the civil suits by the families of the hostages were settled.

About ten years later, in 1988 (around the same time that I began this project), courts had cleared their dockets of Attica cases. By then, Rockefeller had passed away from a heart attack in the company of his young mistress. A month after the funeral, Judge Elfvin granted the Rockefeller family trust "qualified immunity," deciding that under New York law, the governor's executive order to take back the prison with force was not in and of itself a license for his employees—the state troopers—to overstep their duties.

The judge had hoped that without Rockefeller's money as a target, the wind would weaken from the sails of the Attica Brothers. But he underestimated Elizabeth Fink. She had made a career of taking cops to court, and in a classic Brooklyn move, upped the demand to $2.3 billion. Elfvin's return volley was to throw out "wrongful death" as the cause of action and rule that the inmates could only argue "wanton disregard for human life." This charge carried a far higher standard of proof. Fink would now have to prove that troopers *intended* to kill inmates, not merely that the deaths and injuries were the result of troopers being unprofessional. Elfvin also disallowed any troopers to be named in the complaint. Only their superiors could. The final defendants were pared down to four bureaucrats, three of whom had not even gone into the prison during the assault: the Attica warden, Vincent Mancusi;

his vice warden, Karl Pfeil; the New York State commissioner of correctional services, Russell Oswald; and the New York State police major who organized the assault, John Monahan.

Only two were still alive in December 1991.

I concluded my summary to Allen by declaring into Amtrak's cold cabin air, "Now the families of inmates will finally get some justice." My point dissolved as quickly as my breath. Allen leaned in. "Do you know what locals call that prison? The Factory. It was built during the Depression and supplied jobs to the entire area. High-priced lawyers and their egos, that's what this is really all about." He cracked a sly smile. "Justice? Win or lose, there ain't no justice. Not for no Black man in no prison up here."

I turned from him and looked out the window at the speeding scenery. The world outside was now a white blanket of snow covering vacant factories with broken windows and vandalized grounds. Twenty years of urban decay had pushed everyone up here to choose a side: reparations for criminals versus validation for the only remaining evergreen institution. There was no room for a centrist view.

"What's this trip about for *you*?" Allen asked.

"I want to know what my father was doing in that yard for four days." For years I had scanned photos of the Attica's D Yard. I'd seen a sea of faces, felons each, mostly sitting and waiting for a resolution while troopers hovered on the rooftops with rifles. It was like photos of immigrants entering Ellis Island: long looks of blank sorrow as they submitted to the fate of an impersonal system. Was my father in there, sitting among them? Waiting passively wasn't something the man I had come to know by this point would do. "I want the truth about his role in the uprising and his death. I want the facts that each side is ignoring."

Allen reminded me that he had lived upstate since he was a child. "People here are pretty simple. On weekends, the women shop and cook. The fathers and sons hunt and fish. If their boys can shoot straight, they join the state troopers or become guards, just like their daddies. And it's never spoken, but the message to their sons is clear: your first sign of a new friend at Attica is the color of his skin."

My train pulled into Buffalo Station about 4 PM. An hour of crawling through a blizzard with a map balanced on the dash of my Rent-a-Wreck proved useless in finding the courthouse.

I pulled up to a phone booth poking through three feet of snow, pried open the bifold door, and jammed in the frozen metal buttons to dial Liz Fink. "Hey, Josh, the day is over," Fink barked. "Everyone is back at the bunker," her cheeky name for the 1931 Victorian home she had rented for her estimated three-month stay. Its eight bedrooms housed her legal team. She had promised one of the bedrooms to me for my weeklong visit.

Fink answered my knock on the large oak door with a gregarious grin. "Welcome to hell!" she said as I shivered on the porch. She immediately reneged on her offer. "Yeaah, the house is full, Josh. I'm really, really sorry. I can't let you stay." She had reserved a room for me at the Motel 8, the preferred residence of Buffalo's junkies and prostitutes. "But why don't you come in for dinner?"

Inside, she introduced me to Mike Deutsch, her second chair. His long beard and classic Ashkenazi features reminded me of the famous profile shot of Sigmund Freud. Her third chair, Joe Heath, had a pasty complexion, big blue eyes, and a dense blond ponytail. Their faces were buried in paperwork and they offered only a casual nod as a greeting.

Also in the bunker were two ex-inmate leaders. Everyone addressed fifty-eight-year-old Frank Smith as "Big Black," or just "Black." He stood over six feet and was the inmate head of security in Attica's D Yard during the uprising. By this time, he was a private investigator. "You look like your dad. Anyone ever tell you that?"

"Yes, here and there." I never got acclimated to these comparisons. My father was over six feet tall and almost completely bald by the time he arrived at Attica. I was five foot seven and had shoulder-length curls appropriate to the music industry.

The other Attica leader in residency was forty-seven-year-old Akil Al-Jundi. Akil had a tight Afro and intense, uneven eyes framed by jagged scars. He was shot by troopers during the assault, leaving holes in his face and hands that took several operations to close. "It's great to see you again, Josh," he said, bringing me back to a lunch we had about a year ago. Standing between the two men who had endured unimaginable episodes of racism, I never felt Whiter.

During dinner, everyone ate quietly. When plates were clean, Fink's team scurried to the sanctuary of their rooms or to the TV lounge without a word

In Liz Fink's kitchen with Attica leaders at the 1991 civil trial in Buffalo. Left to right: Akil Al-Jundi, me, Herbert Blyden, and Jomo Omowale. *Author's collection*

to me. Heath was the exception. He saw me by the door putting on my coat and said, in his smooth South Carolina accent, the most welcoming comment I had heard that night: "How 'bout a tour?"

"Thank you. I'd like that."

Heath began by telling me that their Victorian *bunker* had become the subject of recent controversy in the *Buffalo News*. Months earlier, Black and Akil had arrived ahead of everyone else. They parked a dented, rusting station wagon on its gentrified block and carried boxes and a fax machine inside. Neighbors phoned authorities. One speculated that George Clinton might be playing at the college. It was of no comfort that the visitors turned out to be Attica ex-cons who had become Fink's assistants, nor that the owner of the Victorian sided with the inmates and, to spite his pro-state neighbors, granted them a six-month sweetheart lease.

Heath ended our tour in the library, which Fink had turned into her evidence locker. I listened as he gazed sorrowfully at dozens of large photos of inmates gunned down during the assault. It was horrific. Bodies were punctured over and over like pincushions. *These were not rich kids getting back at their parents, like the Weatherman or the Yippies.* Many of these men had children. At that moment, Attica became about more than just *my* absent father.

Heath cleared his throat. "So overt was the racism at Attica that during the summer, guards would dump two wheelbarrows of ice into the yard so that inmates could take a few cubes back to their cells."

"Why two wheelbarrows?" I asked, not getting it.

"Well . . . a guard would dump the first wheelbarrow and yell, 'White ice.' A few minutes later, a second guard would do the same and yell, 'Black ice.'"

"What about the Latinos?"

Heath shrugged. "Exactly." Then, he shoved the pictures in a folder and tossed them on the table as if they were worthless. I asked, "Will you be using those to impeach the warden tomorrow?"

"No. Elfvin decided that visual evidence of brutalities would prejudice the jury."

To my layman's view, these photos clearly fulfilled the burden-of-proof for wanton disregard for human life. I thought perhaps the judge was disallowing them due to journalistic bias. "What paper took them?"

Heath laughed. "The state took them," he said with thorny irony. "Y'see, the troopers didn't see D Yard as a 'civil rights massacre.' To them, it was a crime scene. They took these photos minutes after the assault, hoping to document all kinds of weapons they claimed the inmates had made. But they didn't find any."

The folder slid off the top of the pile and was absorbed into a dozen others. I asked, "The McKay report said my father's body was found behind a barricade of sandbags near the center of the prison—are there any photos of that?"

Heath had never heard of or seen any sandbag barricade, even after looking at hundreds of photos for close to a decade. He spread his hands over the pile and came up with one folder tagged in magic marker: TIMES SQUARE. Inside were many eight-by-tens of the front, back, and sides of the prison's epicenter, known by that nickname. One eight-by-ten was a contact sheet with four sequential photos of the ground around Times Square. However, in each, the border cut off the very spot where both the McKay report and Robin said my father's body should have been. My lips tensed. "Why would they crop out his body—especially if they wanted to document the Molotov cocktails they claim he was throwing?"

Heath's tone went as flat and dry as the Sahara: "Maybe they didn't want to memorialize the fact that his body wasn't there—or that he had no weapons." His grim glare would not release me. Heath added that there were also conflicting reports by the Bureau of Criminal Investigation (BCI) cop who shot my father. "I got Tobia's statements here somewhere," he said, as if I should already have known the shooter's name.

Time slowed for me as Heath rifled through a box labeled BCI STATEMENTS. I already knew that eleven such BCI inspectors were assigned to observe the assault and document whether or not passions got the best of the six-hundred-trooper assault team. As it would turn out, the BCI did not find even one such instance. This was a running joke in the Attica Brothers camp: expecting eleven BCI inspectors to report accurately on six hundred fellow troopers they lived and fished with was absurd.

Heath finally gave up. "They must have been misplaced. I'll keep looking tomorrow."

"Can I try?"

Heath looked around nervously. "Technically, you're not even supposed to be in here." This was odd since there was not even a door to the study. "Well," he added in a whisper, "I'll keep looking, and I'll see you tomorrow in court."

I nodded, content that the trip upstate was already paying dividends. I had the name of Dad's killer: Tobia.

En route to the front door, I passed the remaining two bedrooms. They were empty. Whatever Fink's reason for not wanting me to stay in the bunker, it had little to do with the house being "full."

By the next morning, the sun had melted last night's snow, and the streets became rivers. This would be my first challenge to being on time to Judge Elfvin's downtown court.

John Elfvin, a big shot in the Western District, had a courtroom with high ceilings and Old World decorative plaster. He had caught the Attica case right after his appointment by President Gerald Ford in 1974. Fink would imply to me that it was not a coincidence that such a new judge got such a big case. A graduate of Cornell, he had an undergraduate degree not in anything related to law but in electrical engineering; rather than spend a single day working for the state, he earned his legal bones in private practice. (He would retire in 1998 after a sexual harassment charge from his clerk.)

At 10 AM, I pushed open the large door to his courtroom and heard the testimony of defendant Vincent Mancusi, Attica's former warden. He was a shriveled prune of a man, eighty-three at the time, with lots of "I don't knows" and "I can't remembers" sliding from his thin lips. Elfvin had granted Deutsch a small procedural mulligan: to treat Mancusi as a hostile witness on direct examination. The activist civil litigator was working it hard, indulging a nervous habit of twisting a pinch of hair from his Sigmund Freud beard as he fired question after question. Mancusi denied everything, including hearing any of the one thousand shots fired less than a football field away from his office window on September 13, 1971.

I scanned the room and saw the back of both Fink's and Black's heads at the plaintiff's table. Sitting next to them was Heath and three others who would become key to my trip.

The first was a woman with a blanket of straight, long brown hair. I would soon learn that the mane belonged to Fink's paralegal (more on her later). To the left of her was Herbert X. Blyden, the best known of the inmate leaders who survived the assault. He had made a career on the Attica lecture circuit but earned his seat at the plaintiff's table because he had broken away from Fink and the Attica Brothers to represent himself. It had caused noticeable tension. His head shook an outraged *no* in reaction to Warden Mancusi proudly testifying that he had commissioned a monthly *Muslim Report* listing prison trouble-makers. "Like him," Mancusi punctuated by pointing a frail finger at Blyden.

The *Muslim Report* warned Albany of the growing concern over the Black militants who were making "unreasonable" demands. Most of the complaints came from inmates in Five Company, the "troublemakers" of the prison. Mancusi's report was passed up the command chain to Governor Rockefeller. To the governor, many African names in the report bled together: Akil Al-Jundi, Jomo Omowale, and all the X's: Herbert X, Richard X, etc. However, the governor could not miss the one prescriptively White name.

"Is that the same Melville who—?" the governor asked his adviser, coun-cilman (and later mayor of New York) Ed Koch.

"Yes, sir, the Mad Bomber," replied Koch, "that meshuga hippie who blew up Standard Oil."

The jury would never get to see any Muslim reports or learn of how maddening seeing my father's name would be to Rockefeller. Elfvin had denied them into evidence.

Left of Blyden, the back of the third head had greased black hair; that head belonged to Jerry Rosenberg, age fifty-four. Rosenberg was a Lenny Bruce type and a celebrity convict. He had earned a law degree, using the prison library, and held the distinction of being the only jailhouse lawyer to have ever argued in front of the US Supreme Court. He was doing life for a double cop killing he was charged with when he was just twenty-five. An armed US marshal sat by his side. Like Blyden, Rosenberg was also dissatisfied with Fink and was representing himself. The ex-warden's wriggling finger focused next on him. "We put smart-ass Jews in the hole for weeks when they helped scum with appeals."

Rosenberg chuckled and took notes.

At his advanced age, Mancusi may have been unconcerned with his overt bigotry. He knew his town and, thus, the jury. However, his attorney, Richard Moot, was thinking about the public record and stood. "Your honor, my client's answer should be stricken, and it should be noted that all of Mr. Deutsch's questions are irrelevant."

Rosenberg sprang up and countered with vaudevillian sarcasm: "Your honor, counsel's objections are *Moot* points."

The gallery laughed.

I took the laughter as a cue to release the goliath brass door. Its squeak triggered Fink to turn. Seeing me, she whispered to her long-haired paralegal, who in turn whispered to Blyden and Rosenberg, who all turned in unison to watch the son of Mad Bomber Melville slide into the back row of the gallery. As Deutsch continued his direct examination of Mancusi, Fink walked to me and whispered. "I have a picture of your father—at Attica. Do you want to see it?"

"Yes, please," I whispered.

"It's not pretty."

"I *want* to see it."

She returned to the table, and soon I noticed an eight-by-ten manila folder passed from her to the paralegal (who I would soon learn was the buffer between Fink and her dissenters, Blyden and Rosenberg). The paralegal passed it to Rosenberg, who inserted a note and passed the envelope to a bailiff, who brought it to me.

I stared at the string sealing it shut. Who really needs to sit alone among strangers and see a picture of their father's corpse?

I did.

Dad lay on a gurney propped up against a railing. His torso was covered by a blanket that conspicuously hid the fatal wound in his shoulder. His face looked as if he were asleep, except it was gaunt with death. In magic marker, an obscure code was written on a cardboard plaque balanced on his chest: P-13. This image was the first photo I had ever seen of my father in which I was not a child on his knee. Tears began to well.

I dug out Rosenberg's note, wondering what the Attica leader had to tell me.

Joshua,

Me and Herb [Blyden] want you to know that your dad was a great and loyal man to the cause and his friends. Nothing can bring him back. But payback is coming to these motherfuckers, and soon the world will know!

—Jerry the Jew Rosenberg

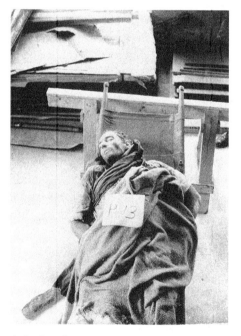

Author's collection

24 | UPRISING

JERRY ROSENBERG AWOKE SHORTLY BEFORE 9 AM on September 9, 1971, to the sounds of smashing cans and shouting. Prisoners were running full speed past his cell. A familiar face paused at his door as it slid open. "Jerry, we just took over the joint."

"Who's *we*? Is it a race riot?"

"No, no. It's everybody!"

He shoved his legs into his gray prison chinos.

In his authorized biography, *Doing Life*, Rosenberg wrote that he looked down from the mezzanine to the first floor where he saw hundreds of rampaging inmates opening whole tiers with master keys and acetylene torches. The loud hum of a motor caused him to stretch his neck over the railing, where he saw a three-ton forklift moving toward the hallway to the metal shop. Hanging off the forklift like a tank commander was a man he recognized as Mad Bomber Melville. Rosenberg would tell me when I interviewed him, "The sight of Sam riding a forklift meant that this was the big one."

Before his first pat-down in Attica, my father had developed a reputation in the New York penal system as difficult and dangerous. He'd already had a turbulent stint in three previous prisons, assaulting a guard in the Federal House of Detention, from which he nearly escaped, and leading a prison work strike in the Tombs, the aptly grim nickname for the Manhattan House of Detention. Plans to blow out a wall with explosives made from cleaning fluids had been found in his cell in Sing Sing. All this earned him the prison nickname the Bomber and assured that a maximum-security facility would be his destiny. At thirty-six, my father walked through the gate of the high concrete walls of Attica. Fellow prisoner William Coons described Sam, with his war on petty regulations, as a "swell guy" who would "give you the shirt of his back but he won't wear the right one to the mess hall."

Just one week before the uprising, my father stood, hands in his pockets, with other inmates of Five Company for the morning count. Every inmate knew that this was strictly forbidden; you were supposed to keep your arms in front of your body, with palms visible. But daybreak temperatures even in warmer months could drop below forty, and the members of Five Company always made a point of making a point.

For the swaggering, overweight corrections officer (CO) Tommy Boyle, their protest was his opportunity to teach them who was in charge. On this morning, it was Blyden, doing ten years for armed robbery, who drew the hack's attention. "Hands out, Mohammed!" Boyle snarled into Blyden's face, pointing the business end of his "nigger stick" lassoed to his wrist (a common term used by Attica COs). Blyden stood six inches over the hack, with a knife scar across his light brown cheek as a trophy from a fight at his former prison. Blyden eyed the wooden tip an inch from his nose. He held his

Sam's mug shot upon entering Attica, 1970. *Author's collection*

temper and turned his palms up, thinking of the reckoning that was around the corner.

Next in line was my father, recently released from a long stint in solitary, where he had already spent one out of every of three of his days at Attica. Today, his hands were in his pocket, shielding the sores on his knuckles earned from close-fisted pushups on its cement floors. Boyle thought of jettisoning them with a jab in his gut, but among the Brothers, Sam had achieved saint-hood. Eyeing the line of Black inmates, Boyle recalled when he had witnessed my father interrupt a game of hoops between two teams of Black Panthers by commandeering their ball with racist sarcasm, "We're playing White man's rules today, guys." It was well known that my father had bestowed his bail on the Panther Twenty-One Defense Fund, and this was after he blew up the courthouse hosting their trial.

Panthers loved the Bomber. And Panthers controlled the yard.

Boyle moved on. But my father did not.

"Hey, Boyle! Why don't you tell me to get my hands out of my pockets? Aren't I in your fuckin' army?"

"I don't respond to coon lovers."

My father ripped a fist from his pocket to balk a right hook. Boyle flinched, lost balance, and landed back first on a picnic table. Chess pieces scattered, along with his pride.

Fifty-seven-year-old Warden Mancusi was running out of ways to pun-ish the Bomber. A month earlier, he had canceled the English class my father taught. This action would turn out to be the Warden's first serious mistake. Sam's students were members of the Latino faction, the Young Lords, who revered him. Word spread, and the Lords organized a two-day work strike in the prison laundry, bottlenecking production. Mancusi grew frustrated with the man who was forging ties between the race-centered factions in his prison.

Solitary was also proving pointless—my father liked it. Sam's longest stretch in the punitive segregation building (HBZ, or Housing Block Z) was for "demanding human treatment" in the mess hall. The protest cost my father three weeks of sunlight. After each stint, Mancusi had him rotated to a differ-ent cell block, hoping to weaken his influence. Within a year, the warden had run out of road and made his most dire mistake: sticking my father in Five Company. Others already in the subsection of C Block were key organizers of recent uprisings at the Queens House of Detention and the Tombs, and the large all-out uprising in Auburn Correctional Facility. Ironically, Mancusi's intent to isolate "troublemakers" would result in consolidating a dream team of prison insurrection specialists.

Blyden, who had organized a work strike with my father at the Tombs two years earlier, was already waiting for the Bomber. He was head of the Attica inmate grievance committee, a full-time vocation that was yielding scant results due in large part to the prisoners' lack of unity. Black, White, and Latino factions hated each other. Blyden saw an opportunity with Sam and invited him into the elite Muslim subsect, the Five Percenters. My father would become its only White member, sending a strong message.

Mancusi would come to realize the stupidity of pairing my father with Blyden and Five Company in less than a month when the phone on his desk rang at 8:45 AM on Thursday, September 9. It was a panicked guard calling from Times Square; inmates had broken ranks, and the Bomber was leading a pack toward the steel door of the metal shop. According to prisoners' testimony published in the McKay report, my father wrapped a towel around his fist and punched through its small plate-glass window, reached inside, and unfastened the lock. The prisoners rushed in. "Tools, equipment, the table saw," my father yelled. "Whatever you can grab. Let's do it!"

Ed Cunningham, a portly veteran CO known for taking pleasure in beating inmates with his hunting buddy Tommy Boyle, saw Sam rush toward him. He reached instinctively for his stick until Sam grabbed his wrist. "Cunningham. We've been waiting a long time for you."

By 9 AM, nineteen minutes into the uprising, the prisoners controlled two of the four recreational yards, Times Square, all four catwalks, the tunnels, the prison commissary, the infirmary, the metal shop, and the power station.

The bulk of the inmates exited into D Yard, where Richard X. Clark, a lean, muscular twenty-five-year-old Five Company member and Five Percenter, commanded a company of Elijah Muslim prisoners. The Muslims stood out from other inmates, having fashioned their own uniform of professional-looking white collared shirts and gray slacks. "I want a wall of white 'n' gray, right now!! Do it!" Clark shouted like a drill sergeant.

Muslims swiftly formed a human net at the receiving end of a gauntlet composed of dozens of inmates armed with sports gear. The gauntlet stretched across D Yard's baseball field; the men who composed it pummeled captured guards rushing through. With arms covering their heads they hurried into a human net of Clark's Muslims, who ushered the bleeding hacks into a corner of Times Square. Once they were cornered, a pride of Black Panthers armed with bats and gardening tools told them to strip. Guards became prisoners, cooperating with their captors, which was more comfortable than looking at each other half naked and humiliated.

My father came upon this scene with a dozen or so captured COs from the metal shop. At his side was Don Noble, a bony young Panther with a perpetual scowl, serving life for murder. Noble noticed Boyle, his most hated guard, in Clark's custody and charged forward, threatening him with the tines of a rake. Boyle's eyes found his friend Cunningham, who was bloodied and held firmly by the Bomber's grip. When Clark ordered his Muslims to stand down so Panthers could deliver some payback, my father and Noble remained. Clark had been a leader in the Auburn insurrection a year earlier. There, the state reneged on its promises in exchange for the nonviolent return of control. Beatings followed for months. Every hack now in Clark's custody probably felt that this time Clark was determined to have leverage in the form of flesh.

My father saw a problem: "I'm not sure about keeping pigs in the corner," he whispered to Clark, and pointed toward the rooftops where uniforms were gathering with binoculars and rifles. "We need to advertise."

Noble overheard and got between them. "Advertise?! What the fuck you mean, advertise? These ain't no fuckin' White man's rules today, Bomber! The Black man rules today, y'dig?"

Clark snapped back at the hot-headed Panther, "No, he's right. We need these pigs! Ain't no use going to the chair over some White devil that ain't worth your spit!"

A fifty-gallon oil barrel containing a water/gasoline mixture was positioned over the pitcher's mound in the center of the yard. The blindfolded COs were then placed next to their new toilet. Clark picked fifty Muslims to form a circle, linked arm-in-arm to protect the same people who had, time and again, beat them. This was the last ground almost half of the fifty-three hostages would ever sit upon.

Cunningham, still full of vinegar, maneuvered himself closer to the perimeter and spoke under his breath to my father. "I'm just wondering, Melville, how you planning on gettin' outta this?"

My father summoned his trademark irony. "I'm already in this shithole for good, Cunningham. You're a state employee. 'How are *you* getting out?' is the question."

As the hostage area was forming, Rosenberg swam through the sea of scrambling inmates to find Roger Champen. "Champ" was the other renowned jailhouse lawyer at Attica. A former drug addict, he was serving twenty years for robbery, yet, with no formal training in law, he had made successful arguments for inmate appeals and managed to remain unaffiliated with any of the Black factions: Muslims, Five Percenters, or Panthers. As D Yard was deteriorating into a convention to settle scores between rival groups, Champ and Rosenberg saw an opportunity for something greater. If they could just assemble some leadership.

Rosenberg spotted my father through the crowd and waved him over. "Bomber, who are the big cats in Five?"

My father looked out over the sea of a thousand bandannas and Afros. Champ handed him a megaphone, and Sam called out names: "Brother Akil . . . Brother Clark . . . Brother Blyden . . . Brother Crowley . . . Brother Hicks . . . Brother Noble . . . please come forward!" The spark of the first inmate government was forming.

According to Blyden's testimony, it was my father who first recommended that Blyden, Champ, and Rosenberg head up a group they had decided to call "Spokespersons," the inmates who would communicate with the outside. (The term "leaders" was avoided because "inmate leaders" at Auburn were the focus of reprisals and extended sentences.) Akil insisted, "Bomber should be a Spokesperson," citing my father's political notoriety. Robin Palmer was standing next to him; when recalling this scene to me later, he claimed that my father declined, preferring instead to assemble a team to reenter the cell blocks to retrieve blankets, mattresses, and food from the commissary. Blyden sided with Akil. "Guards are in there shooting at anything. Besides, we got to have more than just brothers at the table, or we get nowhere with the Man."

My father acquiesced, took his place with the Spokespersons, and handed the bullhorn back to Champ.

As they formed picnic tables into a makeshift boardroom, Clark voiced a need to maintain order and, if necessary, hand out punishments. Inmates due for release within the next month would very likely sabotage the uprising. Others were trying to kill the hostages, their only bargaining chip. "Look around, man," Clark said to Blyden. "This shit is out of control."

Clark wanted to organize a core of Muslims to act as D Yard cops. This time, Noble's objection won out. "We can't have no Koran-quoting motherfuckers keepin' this shit tight," the Panther yelled. "That's fine for guarding the piggies in the middle. Not f' niggas with shanks." Noble wanted his more ruthless Panthers to have marshal authority. They argued for several minutes until they agreed upon on a neutral captain—the most imposing yet unaffiliated inmate in the yard: Frank "Big Black" Smith, serving a dime for armed robbery. Black assembled a regiment of somewhere between fifty and two hundred men (accounts vary), composed equally of Panthers and Muslims, and several Young Lords to keep order and dole out instant justice to interlopers. When it became clear that the inmates chosen as guards consisted almost entirely of African Americans, Black asked my father to organize a grouping of fifty or so White inmates to add to the mix. The multiracial group wrapped strips of cloth around their arms, transcending the color of their skin via colored armbands, the colors of which designated their function: night patrol would be white bands, green would be for escorting officials in and out of the prison, and purple would be the D yard cops who would dole out punishments for counterinsurrectionists. They became known as Purple Bands.

The Spokespersons and Purple Bands made up what the McKay report would later attempt to identify as "the ringleaders":

- Herbert X. Blyden, 32, ten years for robbery. Muslim.
- Jerry "the Jew" Rosenberg, 32, life for felony murder. Agnostic.
- Sam "the Bomber" Melville, 37, eighteen years for felony arson. Atheist.
- Richard "Champ" Champen, 38, twenty years for robbery. Agnostic.
- Frank "Big Black" Smith, 38, fifteen years for robbery. Unaffiliated.
- Richard X. Clark, 25, four years for attempted robbery. Muslim.
- Akil Al-Jundi 37, twenty years for manslaughter. Panther.
- Don Noble, 26, fifteen years for drug possession/murder. Panther.

There were several others.

As mayhem continued around them, the dozen or so determined men took seats around the picnic tables to decide the fate of over twelve hundred others. Black, White, and Latino leaders began to work together in a whirlwind of racist tension. It was an unheard-of miracle for Attica. Their first decision was unanimous and easy. They wanted to bypass Warden Mancusi and demand to talk to Russell Oswald—the prison commissioner himself, who claimed that his administration would be the leader in reform.

Russell Oswald had finished walking his pedigreed Airedale terrier by 7 AM on the morning of the uprising. At 9:15, after his second cup of coffee, his assistant marched into his office with word from Warden Mancusi: Attica's prisoners were holding hostages in D Yard. Instead of panicking, he was energized. When Oswald took office at the beginning of the year, he inherited the multiple lawsuits filed against Auburn Correctional Facility. Inmates claimed that since the inmate uprising last year, Auburn had become militarized, with daily civil rights abuses. Oswald felt Auburn was a lost cause that would tarnish his tenure but saw Attica as his opportunity to show that he had the right stuff to become New York's next law-and-order governor, after Rockefeller ran for president in '72. He asked his secretary to have the jet readied to take him from Albany to the Buffalo airport and a town car to shuttle him and his team to Attica.

Four months earlier, in May, Oswald had summoned Mancusi to Albany. He asked the warden in front of his subordinate, Vice Warden Karl Pfeil (the third and only other living defendant in the '91 civil trial), "What's wrong with giving the inmates more than one roll of toilet paper a month and more than one shower every ten days?"

"The state is on the verge of bankruptcy," Mancusi jeered, and positioned himself as an advocate for the common man. "You want to let the animals tell you how to spend tax dollars? This is just more Black bullshit, Russ." Pfeil allegedly supported his boss with a stereotype bandied by other Attica guards: "Mr. Oswald, Muslims don't even believe in toilet paper."

On the morning of the uprising, it was Mancusi and Pfeil's provincial views that would inspire Oswald to call one of the most politically savvy strategists he had met through Rockefeller, Councilman Ed Koch. Koch had experience with prison unrest. He had negotiated a peaceful surrender at the Tombs work strike last year with my father as a prisoner liaison. His first recommendation to Oswald was to determine if Mad Bomber Melville was loose in the yard. He stressed that my father was a dangerous and resourceful arsonist; he had a talent for disruption and nullifying the engineered institutional divide of the races. "He was the inmate I spoke with at the Tombs, even though the Blacks ran the prison." Determining Melville's degree of involvement would be a key if they plan on retaking the prison peacefully or otherwise.

Oswald already knew about my father from an essay he had written to his defense attorney several months back. "An Anatomy of the Laundry" was an analysis of economic inmate abuse at Attica. The national minimum wage at the time was $1.60 an hour, but Mancusi paid laundry workers only 45 cents *a day* and kept commissary staples like soap and toilet paper at inflated prices, some over three times their normal civilian retail price.

> Because of the Pig-sanctioned Right to capitalize on the needs of other inmates, and the accompanying fear of losing their lucrative Jobs, our brothers who work in the Laundry have become docile slaves, House Niggers, and therefore, an impediment to our Liberation. . . .
> Let's [quit and] force the Pig to bring in those unionized laundries. . . .
> Brother-Man, now is the time to act! . . .
> JUST HOLD BACK AND MAKE THIS COOKIE CRUMBLE !!!!!!!
> PEACE & POWER
> YOUR (SLAVE) LAUNDRY MAN
> RIGHT ON ! ! ! ! ! RIGHT ON ! ! ! ! ! RIGHT ON ! ! ! ! !

Had "Anatomy" remained a private communication, it might have been forgotten as just any other inmate gripe letter. (The complete "An Anatomy of the Laundry" can be found in the appendix.) But Sam asked his lawyer to distribute copies to other radical attorneys. By mid-June the essay had made it three thousand miles to San Quentin and into the hands of renowned Black activist George Jackson. Jackson then organized a work strike in San Quentin State Prison, which in turn triggered more demands from Five Company at Attica:

- Ceasing the censorship of mail
- More newspapers and books (a constant prison complaint)
- The right to have an attorney present during interrogations

Sam's gripe letter was about to balloon into a work strike that would cripple the entire institution and create a model for reform that could go viral.

In June, Oswald ordered Mancusi to tweak some of Attica's harsher rules in hopes of calming things down. Prisoners would now get more than one hour of lights at night, wages were raised slightly, penalties involving visiting rights were stopped, and, most important (and key to understanding the uprising), inmates were now allowed to gather in groups larger than three.

But rather than be pacified, Five Company took this as a sign of the system cracking. Solidarity increased. As it did, Mancusi sanctioned more beatdowns and cell raids. By August, they had risen from several a month to several a day. Four weeks before the uprising, my father described the mood at Attica in a letter to one of his corevolutionaries.

August 12, 1971
Poder hermano!
I can't tell u what a change has come over the brothers in Attica. So much more awareness and growing consciousness of themselves as potential revolutionaries. Reading, questioning, rapping all the time. Still bigotry and racism, black, white and brown, but u can feel it beginning to crumble in the knowledge so many are gaining that we must build solidarity against our common oppressor—the system of exploitation of each other and alienation from each other.

Among the problems we face is how to form revolutionary aware-ness relating to our prison condition vis-a-vis the street and at the same time avoid the obvious classification of prison reformers. Socialists in the past faced a parallel situation in the building of trade unions. When the working-class movement gained the strength to demand bargain-ing power with the capitalists, the unions were bought out w/ a few larger crumbs from the banquet table that the workers had built but could not sit at.

The example is not exactly the answer of course, but the basic problem is: how to avoid the pitfalls of economism, that is, settling for simple reforms, however "far-reaching," as opposed to revolutionary structural change. When u come right down to it of course, there's only one revolutionary change as far as the prison system in Amerika is concerned. But until the day comes when enough of our brothers and sisters realize what that one revolutionary change is, we must always be certain our demands will exceed what the pigs are able to grant.

Keep in touch my strong Latino brother.

Sam

By August's end, Oswald was convinced he could no longer confront the Attica problem remotely. In an end-run around Mancusi, he used inmate attorneys to arrange a private sit-down with Blyden, my father, and others in Five Company. However, growing unrest in other parts of the US penal system would plague Oswald's plan. On August 21, as George Jackson was being escorted back to his San Quentin cell, he pulled a tiny pistol hidden in his Afro and ordered a guard to open the tier. Inmates overpowered several COs and took them as hostages. What happened next became something of a riddle. Several of the guards and inmates were found dead in Jackson's cell. Jackson himself was also shot and killed, allegedly while trying to escape. Jackson's death made national news, and Five Company saw its mysterious circumstances as a state-sanctioned murder.

Six days later, Five Company organized a 450-inmate vigil that panicked Mancusi: all of C Block entered the mess hall wearing black armbands. They sat at attention, backs straight, staring into space and refused to eat. The deafening silence made headlines from the radical presses to the *New York Times.*

In response, Mancusi sent the vigil's organizers (which included my father) to solitary, and in preparation for an uprising, he reached out to the governor's private police force, the Bureau of Criminal Investigation. He asked the BCI to put together dossiers of Attica's most dangerous—the Bomber, a Buffalo local, in particular.

While the warden was preparing for an uprising, my father used his isolation to complete the third and final issue of his underground newsletter, the *Iced Pig.* Copied by hand and smuggled across the cellblocks, the *Iced Pig* brought awareness about Jackson's murder, and for the first time in his radical career, my father shed his pacifist beliefs and advocated for *physical* violence as an appropriate response.

U r beautiful brothers! Strength and Solidarity r the greatest weapons to gain dignity. Strength and Solidarity is what u showed on the 27th. As if one man, there was silence and fasting at the noon mess in memory of our revolutionary brother George Jackson. Many brothers wore black arm bands defying the pigs' barbaric dress code.

On the day of Jackson's funeral, the Weatherpeople bombed 3 offices of the California Corrections Dept. Unfortunately, no one was hurt. Get it together Weatherfolk!

My father emerged from his final stint in HBZ on September 4, five days before the uprising. According to the McKay report, he would caucus with Five Company that night. The topic of discussion was how Oswald had never shown up for his second promise of a meeting. Varying stories on why Oswald was a no-show have survived the decades. One says there never was a meeting planned, only a rumor of one. Another claims that Mancusi manipulated Oswald into leaving the prison compound by telling him that his wife was hospitalized, triggering his hasty exit. But it was moot. All that mattered to Five Company now was that it had been stood up a second time by someone at the top of the prison administration food chain, and, with nowhere left to go, it was time to implement their final solution.

On Thursday, September 9, at 8:45 AM, Five Company took a cue from Jackson's playbook and used the lone CO escorting them from the mess hall as their opportunity. My father, along with Blyden, Noble, Clark, and Tommy Hicks stalled the march back to their cells near Times Square. The CO cracked his stick on the cement floor and yelled, "Keep moving. Back in line." Hicks did the opposite. "You know what's going down, motherfucker." He struck the guard on the head. Blood stained the floor. The moment was upon them. And Five Company scattered like pool balls.

My father sprinted through the narrow tunnel of Attica, pulling the heated echoes of forty felons in his wake. His first instinct was to lead them to the heart of Ahab's profit center—the metal shop.

25 | A SURPRISE ALLY

"THIS WHOLE DAMN MESS WAS OSWALD," Mancusi shouted from the witness stand. "He thought he was Dr. Doolittle and could talk to the animals."

I was still grieving over my father's body in the P-13 photo when the warden called him an animal. *He* was the animal. He had been a twenty-year veteran of the prison system, yet he was deflecting the blame of the bloodiest prison upheaval in US history onto his deceased codefendant, who had been in office for only six months.

"I didn't know what was happening after that. I just locked myself in the office," Mancusi said. "I got the call from Times Square and I never left—not even to use the bathroom." This was his plausible deniability, but then the warden went on to contradict himself: "I only heard about things on my two-way radio."

Fink's cocounsel Deutsch spun and objected with his finger in the air like a Baptist preacher, "Your honor, the testimony of the radio was already ruled against as a vehicle of hearsay because no log was accurately kept of the transmissions." Judge Elfvin looked at Mancusi, cornered by Deutsch's redirect, and called a recess.

It was at this point that the third head at the plaintiff's table, the one with a blanket of brown hair, turned to me. This was Fink's personal paralegal, forty-one-year-old Sharon Fischer. Fate would have an interesting agenda for this second Sharon germane to this story and me—one that started awkwardly.

She rose quickly, as if she had been counting the minutes to leave her seat. Her plumage whipped around her body like Batman's cape. Coupled with wide-rimmed glasses and intense eyes, the still-burning zeal of a radical was evident. The voice, however, didn't match. It was a high-pitched, upstate twang that reminded me of a cartoon character. "Oh Joshua, it is such an honor to have you stay with my husband and me. You bet." Sharon bobbed enthusiastically with a wide grin as we walked out. "I've wanted to meet you forever. I have a dedicated Sam Melville shelf in my personal library."

"No kidding."

Fink knew I was interested in Sam's history, and Sharon was a local gene-alogist by profession. So instead of staying at the Motel 8, Fink proposed I move to Sharon's guest room.

The Motel 8 had cardboard pillows, and the septic tank was not working due to the snow. But I would have preferred it to Sharon's, because she lived more than ten miles away from both the courthouse and Fink's bunker with its evidence room—my real goal.

"Oh, your dad was such a hero," she continued without pause. "You must be so proud."

"Yes. Thank you," I said flatly. Was she just another radical who was so enamored with him that putting politics over his family was acceptable?

"What do you do?" she asked, pushing past my disinterest in the exchange. I was looking past her, eyeing Rosenberg as marshals escorted him down the hall. I wanted to speak with a man who was a crucial figure in D Yard. He is barely mentioned in the 470-page McKay report, nor were the two other White inmates (Peter Butler and Skip Broome) who were instrumental at the negotiat-ing table. *Why did the state only want to focus on Blacks as the "ringleaders?"*

I was so naive.

"I'm a record producer," I half-answered.

"Sam was a musician. Did you know that?"

Of course I knew that.

Blyden was moving in the same direction as Rosenberg, descending down-stairs to the ready rooms. I was about to escape Sharon's shower of praise, but Fink blocked me. "We don't talk to the other camp." She meant Blyden and Rosenberg. She hooked her arm into mine and spun me, waddling down the opposite stairway.

"Has Sam's name come up in the trial yet?" I asked.

"Yeah," Fink grumbled. "The defense tried to use his name to prejudice the jury in the opening statements." When we entered the plaintiff's ready room, she pointed to a three-foot-high stack of transcripts and indicated that I was free to review its thousands of pages.

"Oh! Just so you know," Fink added, "Robin Palmer will not be testifying."

I had asked her about Robin at dinner last night, and she had vacillated. Today she was emphatic. "Yeah, Robin changed his story too many times. Makes for a bad witness, and he is now a right-wing reactionary. . . . And once a porn actor."

I shared her frustration with Robin, but this was disappointing. Robin would have probably been the only witness who would lay a foundation for Dad's murder into evidence, and with the conflicting versions he had told me, Sharon, Jane, and others over the years, I wanted to subject his facts to Fink's vetting talents. "Couldn't you at least depose him?"

"It's complicated. If I depose him, the other side gets to see that testimony, and we don't really know which version he's going to tell. Plus, I don't want to sidetrack the trial with a distraction of how one inmate died."

One inmate? As if Dad was just like any other at Attica? I kept my cool, remembering that there were over a thousand others in the class of Attica Brothers.

Everyone settled into chairs, and Fink turned to business. I had still convinced myself that I was part of the team. I took notes, pretending that at some point I would be asked for my opinion. When Fink paused for a breath, I looked at Deutsch and interjected, "Mike, I don't get why you objected to Mancusi's testimony about the presence of the radio in his office. Isn't the radio proof that he must've heard shots coming from the yard? They must've been broadcast when troopers used it to communicate."

Deutsch's eyebrows raised. "Good point."

I couldn't tell if he was taking me seriously.

After the recess, Fink and company went back to the courtroom. I hung back to sort through the stacks of transcripts Fink invited me to read. It didn't take long to find what she was referencing: defense lawyer Josh Effron's opening statement.

> Everyone in Attica was a convicted felon. Some had more than one conviction on their record. Some had convictions for serious, violent crimes. Some had killed policemen. Some were general murderers. One was known as the Mad Bomber, a man by the name of

Sam Melville, who was convicted of setting a number of bombs that exploded, that killed and maimed. . . . Guardsmen on the roof could see the trenches he dug. You could see the foxholes. You could see the barricades he built and Molotov cocktails.

Fink objected:

Your honor, I'd like to ask for a mistrial. You specifically stated that the defendants not speak about specific crimes that certain inmates committed. Mr. Effron just made a reference to Sam Melville. Not only did Mr. Effron violate the court's order, he totally misrepresented what Mr. Melville was in jail for. Mr. Melville considered himself to be a political prisoner. He was an engineer, and he made quite sure, in all of his bombings, not to hurt anyone. And so it is not fair to his memory or to the evidence. We would ask you to correct the record for the jury.

Fink had worked for years to get to this point, but she was willing to go back to square one with a mistrial just from the mere mention of Sam Melville.

Judge Elfvin replied, "Denied! Please! Sit down."

And so, it went. Effron went on to claim that my father built a rocket launcher and manufactured hundreds of Molotov cocktail bombs. Fink tried to rehabilitate. She said in her opening rebuttal that the rocket launcher was a "sculpture" and that the bombs were duds that contained only noncombustible cottonseed oil.

Why would Dad make fake bombs and a dummy rocket launcher? I had seen the rocket launcher in photos. It looked like a B-movie prop.

But Effron's opening statements revealed the defense's endgame: to use Mad Bomber Melville as the prime example for why extreme force was necessary. I'm sure my father enjoyed that from his grave. But it was bad for the case; juries don't easily unhear the word *bomb*—especially in 1991, when terrorism was on the rise. To win her case, Fink would have to keep Sam Melville out of her Attica story. In her head was probably the fact that she had invited the Bomber's truth-seeking son to sleep in a bedroom twenty feet from her evidence locker.

Clock parts, and the general design of devices used by my father for attacks in New York and Chicago, were also used to make the rocket launcher in D Yard. *Author's collection*

One of the only shots that shows the rocket launcher with people standing close for scale. Sam's trench can be seen at left, and the sandbag barricade where he was shot is at far middle left. *Author's collection*

As Sharon drove me to her house that evening, she was making good on her promise for a tour of Sam's hometown, North Tonawanda. We passed the venues that were the tapestry of his youth: the music store, where he probably bought his first guitar; his high school, which likely nurtured his love of history and music; the one movie theater, where he probably took his dates. None of it spoke to me. I couldn't extract any insight into how he would evolve into a bomb-throwing radical. Then I noticed several Marine Midland banks, the bank Jane Alpert claimed in her book that my father bombed "randomly." Several were spaced along the main artery.

"Marine Midland seems to be everywhere," I told Sharon.

She smiled. "Tonawanda is their corporate headquarters."

Over dinner I mentioned that there seemed to be a strange vibe I was getting from Fink and the lawyers. "I thought Liz wanted my help. She asked me to come upstate. But I feel like I'm in the way." Sharon offered general gossip rather than a direct answer. She claimed that the close quarters had begun to take its toll on the team; several at this point were speaking to each other only for professional purposes, and they argued over how political to make the trial. "The cause is all that's holding them together," she concluded. "They're even rude to me."

I found it impossible to be rude to Sharon. She had been working ten hours a day for no pay. She had donated furniture when Fink rented the empty Victorian. Her earnest spirit, sweet eyes, and smile, not to mention her dedication, were telegraphed in her every expression. Yet, Sharon's version of the dynamics of the legal team included an antidote, when passion got the best of her and she chastised one lawyer who had "misplaced" critical evidence. Fink bullied her with a penetrating Brooklyn accent that could inspire birds to flee their nests. "'You don't tell my colleagues how they screwed up,' she yelled at me. 'That's my job.'"

Sharon was trying to stay calm as she sawed at her meatloaf. "Like all the film footage taken by the state, you can see the troopers blasting away at unarmed inmates. The jury gets to see none of that because the lawyers couldn't find the fucking file on the day of the evidence deadline." Then, she added as an aside, "You should ask Liz about that film. There's some of your father. I can't bring it up to her again. She'll chew my head off."

Had Dad's death been caught on film?

"Joe Heath couldn't find the reports made by the guy who shot my father. He was rather cavalier about it, like, as if misplaced evidence was routine. The 'Tobia statements' I think he called them."

"They misplaced Tobia!"

Sharon pushed back her chair and stood. "Oh my God, it's the only statement where we can prove a trooper lied his pathetic ass off! Fink subpoenaed that pig fucker to testify, and he showed up here last week." Sharon was now on fire. "It was hysterical. Tobia thought *I* was Liz Fink and he stormed up to me like John Wayne with his pudgy face and yelled, 'I didn't do anything wrong that day!' And he called me a cunt. So, I said to him, 'I'm not Liz Fink.' And I pointed down the hall. So, Tobia storms up to her and yells the same thing in her face, only this time he added 'fat cunt.'"

"You think they knew each other," I asked Sharon, trying to stay on point, "Tobia and my father?"

"Yes. Most likely. They both grew up in Tonawanda, there are only a few places to hang out, and they were the same age."

This was too big a coincidence for me to ignore. Then Sharon said, "His office is right down the street from the courthouse."

"He's still in Buffalo? I'd like to speak with him."

"He probably wouldn't have the guts to face you. He's now a prominent attorney. A fixer for the Buffalo Bills."

Those outside of New York State might not realize how devastating this news was. "The Bills" were not just a football team, they were Buffalo's proudest institution. If they lost a playoff game on Sunday, it was acceptable to call in sick for work on Monday. Linebackers and quarterbacks were local gods. Ticket brokers wielded significant power to those who would do any favor for fifty-yard-line seats. And I just learned that the state trooper who bragged that he fatally shot my father was the NFL team's lawyer.

26 | TROUBLE AT THE FACTORY

VINCENT TOBIA WAS STILL EATING his steak-and-egg breakfast at 2 PM on September 9, 1971. His wife answered the phone to the urgent voice of his BCI unit leader, Ed Stillwell. She handed the receiver to her husband. "Ed needs you at Attica."

Thirty-two-year-old Tobia was a ten-year state trooper veteran with political aspirations. BCI inspector was his most recent promotion—the equivalent of making detective for a city cop. Tobia could not resist the hard cases that curried favor with higher-ups. Today was his lucky day. "Vin, there's trouble at the Factory," said Stillwell. "They grabbed at least a couplea dozen COs, including Cunningham and Boyle."

Tobia had been to the wedding of at least one Attica guard and hunted on occasion with another. However, he held his poker face in front of his boy, a skill he perfected from growing up in the blue-collar Buffalo neighborhood of Lovejoy (only a stone's throw from Tonawanda), where his after-school activities were hustling pool and amateur boxing. He had promised this Thursday afternoon to his adopted toddler, Vince Jr., but he had slept in and now Stillwell's call took priority.

"I'm out the door, Ed." He grabbed his .38 and kissed the forehead of his three-year-old with a promise to reschedule their quality time for tomorrow, unaware that he would have to break that date as well.

By 4 PM, sufficient state troopers had gathered in the prison parking lot to take back the institution by force. But instead of readying for an assault, they stood aimlessly. Tobia joined his BCI unit and reported to Stillwell, who

234

looked unhappy. "Oswald is telling us to stand down. He wants to negotiate. We're still waiting on CS [gas], so I don't see the harm."

"Are communications set up?"

"You're not gonna believe this." Stillwell poured his third cup of coffee since lunch. "He's been in and out of there several times already. Each time he comes out the demands get longer. I think they're up to about seventeen, including removal of Mancusi as warden." He added an aside about what must have seemed like the most ridiculous of them: "And transportation to a nonimperialist country."

"I see," Tobia said, seeing no humor in the comment. He checked his service revolver, figuring he'd be using it later.

Stillwell told him to report to Hank Williams, the head of the state police. He had personnel files from the FBI of inmate ringleaders. One grew up right near him.

The next morning, Friday, September 10, sleep-deprived troopers were awakened at 6 AM and ordered by Oswald to gather in the Attica parking lot. Their mission: to assemble thirteen hundred cheese-and-egg sandwiches for the inmates. Instead of arresting prisoners, the troopers would be catering for them. The sandwiches were left in the tunnel between the prisoner-controlled areas and the outside world. The Spokespersons dubbed the tunnel "the DMZ" (demilitarized zone) and some just called it "No-Man's-Land."

Upon opening his eyes, one of the first things Sam noticed was that hostages, who had slept on the ground and were covered with dirt, were being allowed to exercise by walking within the circle. Inmates taunted them with obscenities from the other side of the human ring of Muslims.

Sam met Robin at the food line. Robin was anxious for intel. News had spread that much of the prison had been recaptured as they slept and that the only ground that inmates now held was D Yard, the kitchen, and the power station.

Sam volunteered the minimum: "A lot of brothers didn't make it into the yard." What he didn't share was that of the thousand that did make it, it was not clear how many prisoners were participating in the uprising willingly.

"What about our demands?" asked Robin.

Working with the Spokespersons for a tighter list had yielded the opposite. By midnight, Oswald and his crew of advisers had left D Yard exhausted. "They're growing," Sam explained wearily.

"Oh yeah, man. Good," Robin was proud to have authored one. "I told them, I said we need transportation for any inmate that wants to go to a nonimperialist country."

"Hmm. Good thinking." The only demand Sam cared about was the one advanced by Rosenberg: a letter from a judge providing that no reprisals or extended sentences would be levied against the prisoners for the uprising.

When I asked Robin for more vignettes, he inadvertently revealed something key about his relationship with my father at this time. "Your dad was pretty tight-lipped about everything that day."

Why would that be? I thought. Perhaps it was because, despite a close relationship with the informant Demmerle, Robin had miraculously avoided arrest. He was captured six months after Sam for an unrelated attempted bombing of his own, and instead of being sent to Sing Sing, with similar radicals, Robin was given a mere five-year sentence and, although he had no violent crimes in his history, was sent three hundred miles north to the same maximum security prison as his associate, who was also currently among the most feared revolutionaries in the country.

Robin said my father was less concerned with the progress of the Spokespersons than he was with the conditions of the inmates. "He was just thinking about the Brothers, how everyone was holding up." For security purposes, Big Black had not allowed Sam (or anyone) back inside the prison to get provisions. This included access to the toilets. After a night of 1,200 inmates celebrating their freedom, D Yard was now a messy patchwork of soiled sheets, and with Oswald's cheese sandwiches and coffee working their path, by noon, a solution to waste would become dire. According to Robin, my father (a plumbing designer by trade) saw a more practical use of his expertise than sitting at the tables playing a fruitless game of Model UN.

He found Clark and Noble, and the three men climbed up on the catwalk for an elevated view of the yard. "If we can't use the state's shitters, we'll make our own." Sam pointed to a spot by Times Square. He would take a team of the inmates the Purple Bands claimed were causing trouble and keep them busy by having them dig a latrine.

It would be his last plumbing job. In less than two days, the latrine would become his grave.

Oswald wanted it on record that he was working with the Spokespersons toward a peaceful surrender. According to his memoir, *Attica: My Story*, he and his attorneys worked past midnight Thursday to produce the no-reprisal document he had promised. Shortly before noon on Friday, September 10, they finally got to Attica with the paper in hand.

Overcaffeinated from an all-nighter and determined to memorialize his marquee moment, he trekked through the Attica parking lot and chose two cameramen from among the several TV crews. As a train of reporters trailed him to the prison entrance, he proclaimed that with his no-reprisals document, signed by a judge, the uprising would end that day. However, like most things at Attica, an intent to broker peace would result in the opposite.

Oswald and company were patted down in No-Man's-Land by Green Bands wearing pillowcases with slits cut for eyeholes. Satisfied that Oswald and company were not armed, they escorted them through the tunnel. Once in D Yard, the commissioner asked one cameraman to set up at the negotiating table. The other was granted access by Black to roam the yard. The eager cameramen wasted no time getting shots of inmates and directing them to repeat testimonials for more dramatic retakes, getting B-roll (secondary) footage of several pointing in the air, miming happy, angry, and surprised reactions to things that would be added later. The inmates cooperated, confident the liberal press was on their side.

Meanwhile, at the table, things were not going well for the commissioner. The no-reprisals letter, it turned out upon close examination by Rosenberg and my father, was only for crimes committed during the initial hours of the uprising. Rosenberg told me, "Your father thought it was worthless." He and Champ agreed. Rosenberg shouted at Oswald, claiming that each day the uprising progressed was potentially a new felony. As the camera focused on Rosenberg, he tore the paper in front of Oswald's face. This action was the cue for the hundreds of angry inmates to boo in unison. They could be heard by the troopers, looking down from Attica's rooftops, guns ready, and the five hundred others in the parking lot waiting for their turn to "negotiate."

The commissioner was escorted off the stage and through the tunnel by Noble and his command of hooded Panthers.

Once through No Man's Land and outside, anxious reporters crowded Oswald and demanded that he explain the ruckus. "This is far worse than Auburn or the Tombs," Oswald claimed. But the reporters pressed: "What about the hostages? Are they OK?" and Oswald, still punchy from lack of sleep and embittered by rejection, told them something that would derail all hope of peace.

By 5 PM in D Yard, there was a noticeable difference from the conditions of the day before. Tents were arranged in quadrants; Sam's instructions for a six-by-ten ditch for waste was completed near Times Square; Muslim guards and Purple Bands were running the yard with precision; threats against hostages abated; they were given more food, cigarettes, and medical attention; those severely injured had been released into No-Man's-Land; and mattresses were distributed to the ones who remained, so no one needed to sleep on the ground any longer. There was a small acoustic band playing songs in one corner of the yard, and people would get to lie under the stars for the first time in years—for some, decades.

Sam approached Blyden, and along with Noble, Akil, and Clark, they once again climbed onto the catwalk, proud that they had achieved more in half a day than a year of petitions.

Thinking of the news cameras that were in the yard earlier, Blyden seemed satisfied. "When the world sees this, *this* is how we win this shit."

At 6 PM, inmates gathered around a nineteen-inch black-and-white TV positioned like a *gohonzon* in the corner of the yard. Attica was the only story. They cheered at the sight of themselves, proud and righteous, fists thrust toward the sky, with shouts of unity and speaking articulately about Attica's horrid conditions. The next image was of the Spokespersons: strong, proud Black men, demanding better treatment, capped by an angle on Rosenberg, ripping up Oswald's "worthless" peace offering amid the furor of the mob.

The inmates cheered at their TV image, but their ovations abated with a sharp edit to the hostages: looking like Middle America's White fathers and uncles, bound and blindfolded, blood contrasting with their pasty skin. Following this shot came the hammer: Oswald, angry and trying to salvage his media moment, responded in frustration to reporters pressuring him after his hasty exit. "We have information that the hostages have been tortured and *mutilated*."

Food and trash hit the nineteen-inch screen. Blyden and others seized the stage and led a mass chant: "Attica, Attica, all or nothing! Attica, Attica, all or nothing!"

And my father knew: fame, once tasted, would become a demanding mistress.

———————

By the next day, Saturday, September 11, talks with Oswald had apparently broken down. While yesterday peaceful surrender was discussed in collegiate tones, last night's TV broadcast, with Oswald's claim of "mutilations," soured the mood. Today, squaring off with the prison commissioner in his eighth and final visit into the yard was the charismatic L. D. Barkley. He was the new face of the uprising, his aggressive and intellectual rhetoric channeling Malcolm X.

With my father standing behind him, cameras trained on Barkley, who leaned close to Oswald, cutting him off frequently, accusing the commissioner of lying to the press. Oswald insisted that his comments were taken out of context: "I had been misinformed by your people."

"*Our* people," Barkley yelled. "You mean *your* snitches."

Another Spokesperson yelled, "We gonna deal with them, make no mistake. And we gonna deal with you too."

Oswald's bulging eyes dodged as he faced mounting accusations of his treachery.

"His lies are a crime against humanity," yelled someone near the table.

Suddenly, an inmate wearing a football helmet grabbed the mic from Barkley's hand and pointed to Attica's scapegoat. "Why don't we keep the big piggy? We got him. We don't have to let him go nowhere! I say we keep him until they turn the water back on."

Blyden stood fast. "No! We granted him safe passage"—as if promises still applied.

Oswald might not even have known what was next, exit or execution. As Clark waved his hand and Sam, Black, and a unit of Muslims formed a wall around the commissioner, he rose with the momentum. Suddenly, the air filled with the shouting of Barkley, who recovered the mic and preached to the world through the TV cameras. "These men lie to us, and they expect our trust. We will no longer deal with Oswald and his goon squad of liars. Only the Observers!" The name referred to a team of congressmen and journalists brought in the previous night to broker a surrender.

As Oswald was being shoved to the exit, Sam rested a desperate hand on the commissioner's retreating shoulder. "More chefs in the kitchen will only make this worse. You have to get Rockefeller to come."

"You radicals always presume that one person has the power to do anything," Oswald shouted as the current of Muslims pushed him through the tunnel into No-Man's-Land.

Sam shouted, "*Make* the power, man. We're out of time." But Oswald was gone and Sam knew it was only a matter of a day or so till trigger-happy troopers would start taking potshots from the rooftops. Noble joined Sam, watching their last hope of peace vanish into the tunnel. "Well, Bomber, it's official now," said Noble. "Definitely ain't no White man's rules today."

27 | "THEIR THROATS WERE SLASHED"

ON MY THIRD DAY IN BUFFALO, Shawn arrived. He was about four years my junior, attending law school in Buffalo with plans of becoming a state's attorney. His father was L. D. Barkley.

In 1971, Shawn's father was on parole for forging a signature on a $180 check when he was pulled over. He had no driver's license—a minor parole violation. He was sent to the already overcrowded Attica. There, under the guidance of Blyden, Barkley became radicalized. He had been at Attica for less than six months when the rebellion broke out. Barkley became the most recognized face of the uprising for those watching the nightly news. His sound bites had defined the struggle. "We are men. . . . We are not beasts, and will not be beaten as such." When the prison was retaken, Shawn's father was shot and died on September 13. He was twenty-one years old.

Shawn was articulate and better educated than me, and he had an angry edge I recognized. I was thrilled to meet someone from similar circumstances. However, like Pat's daughter Jenny, Shawn was also detached from his father's history.

Sharon introduced us and launched seamlessly into a briefing on how Judge Elfvin had been stacking the deck. Between her breaths, I asked him a dozen questions until the intensity of the situation had him yearning for escape in the form of looking for a bathroom. "There's one over there," I said. "I'll go with you."

While we were washing our hands, I suggested he and I make a joint entrance in court that afternoon. "Our presence will show the judge that real families are dealing with loss on the prisoners' side, not just the side of the hostages." Shawn looked skeptical. I pressed, "Don't you want to know the truth about how your father died?" And I remembered his father's poetic words: "When you are the anvil, you bend. When you are the hammer, you strike."

"It doesn't matter," Shawn said casually. "He wasn't a real father to me."

———————

Karl Pfeil, Attica's vice warden, was in the witness box when Shawn and I entered. Sharon turned, tears welling, when she saw her two prodigal sons. She nudged Blyden and Rosenberg. Fink turned with them, her expression unreadably flat at the sight of us.

We took our seats, and within minutes, a note written by Blyden was passed back through the gallery into Shawn's hands. We each took a corner of the page:

> Dec. 21, 1991—Brother Herbert X. Blyden + Legal Advisor: the Hon. Jerry the Jew Rosenberg
>
> In Religious terms, Joshua has great significance—Biblical and Metaphysical! Shawn has that Irish/Black Liberation ring to it: IRA, the struggle for freedom, Justice and Equality in Ireland. This Struggle, be it Black or White or indifferent, must be carried no matter where warriors encounter oppression/repression/recession.
>
> Jesus, Mary, Joseph, and Sam + LD would shudder in their graves at this treatment of young Warriors, for whom they died! Joshua was a fisher of men much as Jesus was! Go out into the wilderness, head held high and stand tall and proud amongst the Neo-sports people (football, etc.) in this game of sport and play.

I didn't understand the part about the football. In fact, most of it seemed too inside for me. I said to Shawn, "You should keep it." But Shawn shook his head. "It's cool, man. *You* keep it." He released the note, never breaking focus on the proceedings. Fink rose from her table and walked back to us. "I have some film of your dads together. Come by the house tonight," she whispered.

She was looking at Shawn, but I answered for both of us: "What time?"

"After dinner," and she swaggered back to her table.

I spied Shawn, wondering if I had stepped over the line again. He smiled at me for the first time. "I'll come."

The testimony of Karl Pfeil suddenly became contentious. Deutsch was getting terse as he took the vice warden through the events of twenty years ago in testimony that would prove key to the verdict. "Mister Pfeil, you were ordered to return to your house on the evening of Sunday, September 12, 1971, the night before the retaking of the prison, is that true?"

"Yes."

"This was because, after lingering outside, you had grown combative in front of fellow guards."

"I wasn't happy with the way the governor was handling the situation."

The next morning, with news that the prison had been retaken by force and several hostages were dead, he rushed to the Attica morgue.

"Even though you were ordered to stay home?" Deutsch pressed.

"Yes."

"And what did you see?"

Pfeil discovered the bloody body of his close friend Ed Cunningham. He stumbled out of the morgue, tears welling, and blurted to fellow hacks and waiting journalists that it was true, his best friend had been "mutilated by the inmates," adding that he saw Cunningham's "throat was slashed wide open." Headlines would use his words that afternoon, thus setting the national mood about the justification of force to retake the prison.

Deutsch showed Pfeil a morgue photo of Cunningham's body, riddled with bullet holes. "Do you see any mutilation in this picture, Mr. Pfeil?"

Pfeil started to squirm. "No."

"Is the throat cut, as you said it was, sir?"

"No."

"If the throat wasn't cut, how come you reported that they were?"

"I don't know."

One theory was that in order to identify the bodies, the hostages' blindfolds were pulled down under their chins. The bandanas became soaked with blood that had found its way toward the low point of the neck.

After decades of reliving the trauma, Pfeil might have realized this and today, with the pressure of a full room of family and reporters, only now asked himself psychically what damage his single act of panic had caused. How much hate did he generate? How many bad decisions had cascaded because his loyalty could not permit him to accept that his best friend had been killed not by vengeful inmates but by someone who might be dating his sister or with whom he shared a daily ride to work? Would he ever know who it was? Maybe he knew already and had been carrying the secret for twenty years. He began to sob.

Deutsch asked Elfvin if the jury could see the photo to verify that Cunningham's throat had *not* been cut. Elfvin did not even look up. "Denied. This is upsetting the witness." He called a recess.

28 | KUNSTLER AND THE OBSERVERS

BY FRIDAY NIGHT, SEPTEMBER 10, the town of Attica, only five miles from the prison, was experiencing its own version of a takeover. Vigils of locals who had presumed their loved ones were dead abounded. Rumors that busloads of Black militants were on their way from Harlem to expand the riot into the town's streets had residents panicking, and bars and stores were besieged by media teams. Like Vietnam, suddenly every American would learn Attica's name and location.

In this chaos, a brigade of high-profile prisoner sympathizers nicknamed "the Observers" was being escorted into the yard. The Spokespersons submitted close to one hundred candidates, but only thirty or so dropped everything to journey to the prison. They included Assemblyman Arthur Eve; activist David Rothenberg; Clarence Jones, editor and part owner of the *Amsterdam News*; and Tom Wicker of the *New York Times*. However, Don Noble suggested the two men who would turn out to be the most pivotal: Bobby Seale (the Black Panther Party national leader) and the Panthers' well-known radical lawyer, Bill Kunstler.

At 10 PM, almost thirty or so Observers emerged through the tunnel of No-Man's-Land into D Yard, with cheers from inmates as if they were liberating Allied forces. A cluster of news cameras entered with them, setting up a broadcast cocoon around the picnic tables. The Observers took seats and introduced themselves to a captive crowd. Several inmates were invited to address them via the loudspeaker system. The hundreds of state troopers outside the walls heard it all—hardened felons lamenting at length the harsh life at Attica. Their room and board were paid for with the tax dollars of every trooper listening. Eleven o'clock, midnight, 1 AM, 2 AM—a cavalcade of orators blurred one into the next until even Kunstler begged for a break. "Tomorrow, there will be more of us," Kunstler said into the mic. "Bobby Seale told me he is on his way. But right now, I want to see the hostages."

At 2 AM, my father wandered the yard, ignoring the glow from the flood-lights illuminating the negotiating table like a night game at a sports arena. He was going to check in with Clark at the hostage circle before trying to get some rest in his tent. As Sam neared the hostages, huddled like mourners in the rain, Cunningham, sniffling from cold, called to him: "Hey Bomber, a bunch of us wanted to know what's the cheering about."

"Kunstler. A lawyer." Sam looked at the forehead of the veteran guard he hated. His head bandage was leaking blood. Sam summoned the inmate medic to redress it.

Suddenly a double line of Purple Bands was shaping a path through the patchwork of blankets and campfires. Sam nodded in salute to Blyden and Clark as they cleared the way for Kunstler like an earl. He entered the hostage circle. His talks with the hacks were brief, just enough to establish that they were well cared for.

"As you can see," said Blyden, "no one is mutilated."

Kunstler seemed satisfied and upon exiting the circle noticed my father, whom he had met briefly on the way in. "You should be at the table," Kunstler proclaimed. "Your voice is important, Sam. They respect you."

"I don't see the point of it, other than that it's keeping everyone calm. Rockefeller is not going to budge."

"We may never get amnesty, but we have to hold out. The integrity of the other twenty-eight-point proposal rests on it."

Sam took a breath. *Had it gotten up to twenty-eight points? And amnesty? For taking over a prison?*

"Bill, today I look up and see twice as many pigs on the roof as I did yesterday. Tomorrow there will be even more. So just remember, we're not Abbie and Jerry. We're not gonna call a lawyer and quote the Constitution. We're gonna stand our ground, and in the end, a lot of us are probably not coming out of here."

At a rare loss for a comeback, Kunstler sighed. "I understand." He was wavering over whether or not inmate leaders should accept the state's proposal—without amnesty.

My father locked his arms with two other inmates to complete the human wall protecting the only thing keeping them alive. Kunstler hugged him. "I hope we meet again." Without breaking ranks, my father replied, "Whatever happens, tell everyone that people here are as together as I once hoped they could be on the outside."

"I will," said Kunstler.

Off in the distance, almost as if the crowd was responding to Sam and Kunstler's conversation, a chant began.

"*Attica, Attica! All or nothing!*"

Cameras trained on the crowd. Their floodlights scanned like watchtower beacons looking for tonight's Pulitzer-worthy clip to use as a soft out to a commercial.

"*Attica, Attica! All or nothing!*"

29 | RAIDING FINK'S BUNKER

DESPITE ALL THE CONTROVERSY, the biggest newspaper in the area, the *Buffalo News*, had sent only one staff writer to cover the 1991 trial. Dan Herbeck, an upstart at the paper, was assigned to write a paltry one-column daily update. Attica centrists were in good hands with Herbeck (who in coming years would coauthor the authoritative book on Timothy McVeigh, *American Terrorist*). Instead of waxing partisan politics, Herbeck sought human-interest stories. He was excited to learn from Sharon that the son of infamous Buffalo local Sam Melville was in town.

Outside the courtroom, Herbeck intercepted Shawn, Sharon, and me coming back after recess. He whispered a few words to Sharon and then went inside. Sharon turned, showing us all her teeth. "Oh my, Dan wants to do an article about the two of you."

Hoping that this might stir Tobia, I agreed.

In a small room reserved for the press, Herbeck began with the basics: what we did for work, how our lives were progressing, etc. Shawn talked about law school. I talked about my brief encounter with a few bigwigs in music but omitted how poorly this translated into a decent living or mended my shattered personal life.

Herbeck asked us how we felt watching the people responsible for the deaths of our fathers. The scene felt cliché, like I was watching a movie about me but starring an actor I hated. So I said something quotable: "What's really on trial here is the attitude of New York State—that the inmates' lives were expendable." I added that I wanted Tobia, who was certain to read the piece, to know that he had nothing to fear from me and that I wanted only to talk with him.

By now, Shawn had completely withdrawn. "I don't really have a story to tell." He didn't want his name to appear. I pressed, indulging my absurd lack of boundaries: "This is an opportunity to make a statement."

But he was vehement. "No, man, this is *your* thing, not mine."

That night, Shawn and I drove to Fink's bunker in hopes that she would keep her promise to screen the Attica retaking videos made by the BCI. Shawn was quiet for the ride—still blistered, I presumed, about the interview.

Blyden was at the door when we arrived. He set aside his hatred of Fink, and in anticipation of seeing the son of his murdered protégé, he brought several other disaffected Attica Brothers. They ushered Shawn into the kitchen for a joyful reunion. I tried to mingle and take advantage of rare access to Blyden but felt like an ex at a wedding. I managed to ask him how he remembered my father. "Sam was a righteous brother. A righteous brother. Loyal to the cause. I remember hearing his voice on the bullhorn: 'Will Herb Blyden come to the front?' When I got there, he said, 'Our lives are at stake.' He told me, 'And it is vital that we get the blocks together.'"

I listened to Blyden but lost interest in his often-repeated Attica apocrypha. "What about the other days? Can you tell me what my father was doing?"

"Well, just like the rest of us, he was waiting for the troopers to come over the wall."

My father, waiting? Blyden, waiting? Clearly, the Attica leader was not interested in budging off his homogenized version—at least not while at Fink's house. Akil, on the other hand, was spying our exchange and not looking happy about it.

I left the kitchen and walked the house in search of Fink. I learned that she was out to dinner with Black. I discovered Deutsch in the TV room watching a basketball game, with video cassettes labeled ATTICA 9/13/71 piled in stacks next to the VCR. I pointed to them. "Liz said I could get a viewing."

"Yes, of course. Right after the game"—which was in its third quarter.

I left him and wandered past the open archway to the evidence room. With everyone occupied, I contemplated a breach of trust, but the game was winding down. "How's now?" I asked Deutsch.

"Yes, as soon as the game is over," he repeated as if the previous exchange had never happened. I tilted my head in confusion. The final minutes were crawling. In a moment, Deutsch switched to another network and the start of a fresh game.

I decided it was time to adopt my father's Marxist view of property.

Fink had consolidated a significant amount of Sam Melville documents into a spot in the corner of the evidence room. I found the autopsy folder. Atop its several pages was an eight-by-ten black-and-white photo of Dad lying on a table. Most unnerving was our resemblance. I finally saw it in the shape of our bodies and his peaceful face.

The camera showed several small entry wounds in his upper left shoulder, only a couple of inches apart, like the result of a shotgun blast. Why hadn't Fink given me this instead of the cryptic P-13 photo with his wound covered by a blanket?

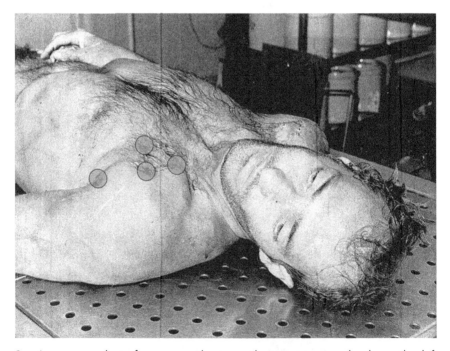

Sam's morgue photo focuses on the several entrance wounds above the left shoulder (which I've circled here), each about the size of a quarter and each no more than four inches apart. *Author's collection*

I shoved it in my bag.

In another folder hidden under the radiator, I unearthed a series of ballistic reports and a large map of Attica. Markings P-1, P-2, P-3, etc., all the way up to P-29 were handwritten in pen around various areas of D Yard. A spot marked P-13 was right near Times Square. Yesterday I had asked Joe Heath what the P-13 marker on Dad's body meant. He said, "When the BCI found bodies of guards they toe-tagged them by name. But when they found inmate bodies, they just labeled them P-1, P-2, P-3 . . . etc." Fink was planning to use this map to show the callousness of the defendants. Elfvin wouldn't admit it.

I shoved it in my bag.

Finally, I found a file marked Tobia. Inside were the "misplaced" kill reports. Three different ones described the incident in conflicting detail. I was about to start comparing them when I heard the front door.

Fink and Black were in the entryway. When I emerged to meet them, she noticed my long face and halfheartedly apologized for Deutsch not letting me watch the assault videos as she promised. She said I could come back the day after tomorrow. "Mike, there are no games on Sunday, are there?"

"No," he responded flatly.

But I was returning to New York Sunday morning. I knew that for hard-working attorneys, weekends were for anything but Attica. I also knew that if I left Buffalo without seeing the film, I would never have the chance again. "How about tomorrow?"

"Whatever, sure," Fink tossed, and she ditched me to join Shawn's homecoming in the kitchen. She brushed past Akil, still lingering in the archway. The man with more facial scars than words chose this moment to come menacingly close to me. "What is it you're trying to learn, exactly?"

"My father spent three days in that yard. And I can't seem to find one Brother who wants to help me understand what the hell he did in all that time."

Akil nodded sadly and rubbernecked to see if anyone was lurking. "Do you know why history sides with Spartacus and not the Romans?"

"Spartacus? I only know about the Kubrick movie."

"And the Zealots at Masada. You know about them, right?"

I nodded.

"They were thieves and radicals also. They knew Rome would crush them," he said as he ushered me out on the porch where it was seventeen degrees. "But their sacrifice made history."

"OK, why? Why is that?"

"Because solidarity is contagious. Time remembers. And battles like Attica are not won in days. They are won in decades. Your Dad saw . . . we *all* saw, that if we gave up, there would be promotions for Oswald, for Mancusi—perhaps a presidency for Rockefeller. And that, to us, was worse than death. And I remember your father's last words to me that day."

30 | SEPTEMBER 13, 9:05 AM

THE PLAN TO RETAKE THE PRISON ON MONDAY, September 13, was originally conceived by Major Monahan as an assault with no further warning to prisoners. Monahan thought that the element of surprise would minimize hostage casualties. He could not have been more wrong.

Two days earlier, on Saturday, September 11, Sam walked through No-Man's-Land along with Clark and Black, carrying the morning rations. He thought, *How long would troopers tolerate making our meals? Oswald would soon cut them off—probably tonight, or indeed by tomorrow morning.* Hard decisions had to be made. Sam asked Clark—one of the few Attica leaders with military training—for a word in private, along with Black, Noble, and Akil.

"How do you see them coming at us?"

Clark had already given this a great deal of thought. "Two assault teams. Rubber bullets. They come across catwalks A and C and push us toward the center."

Sam agreed. "The teams would need to converge at Times Square. What if we cut off access?"

Akil added, "We still control the metal shop"—where inmates made gym lockers for 70 cents a day that the state sold for hundreds of dollars.

Sam nodded. "We put lockers at all four intersects. I can draw current from the main," energizing the blockade. "If they cannot go forward, they will try to climb down."

"Then what?" Black asked.

Sam pointed to Times Square and the latrine he had supervised. "Expand it in both directions. Parallel the catwalks. Fill it with gas. If they try to post ladders, we toss in torches."

The idea was to create a trench of flames, blocking troopers descending from the catwalks. Sam looked directly at Black, knowing this would need his OK. "We'll need every milk bottle and jar from the commissary and oil barrels from the power factory."

Jars and fuel—everyone understood. But all of this would require a lot of very visible manpower. Black asked, "How to plan to pull this off without the pigs seeing?"

"I think they should see. We're serious. They have to know that."

Clark looked concerned. "Yeah. *They* gonna get serious too."

Sam nodded solemnly and uttered the words that Akil would tell me twenty years later. "The only real choice we may get is how we end this."

Two details of inmates set to work. Sam led several dozen to salvage the lockers from the metal shop. Another battalion of inmates started expanding the latrine, while Sam and Robin ran wire from the breaker board to the fences.

Around 6 PM, rooftop troopers watched the Mad Bomber use brute strength to roll a fifty-five-gallon oil drum across D Yard like a Hebrew pushing a pyramid brick across the desert. Behind him, a line of inmates followed with bags of flour, sand, and fertilizer and armfuls of empty ketchup, milk, and peanut butter containers. Sam cracked open the oil barrel to discover bad news. The barrel contained cooking oil, which was not combustible. "Crap," Robin frowned. "Looks like we used all the gas for the latrine."

Sam nodded but started to hand out ladles to a line of waiting men and motioned for them to ration the cooking oil into jars.

By Saturday evening, the yard had gone through its final transformation. While yesterday had brought the order and comfort of a campsite, tonight inmates would go to sleep in a military installation. The latrine was now a rabid L-shaped scar along the perimeter, as if a meteor had made a right turn while scorching the earth. Barricades made from sandbags protected stockpiles of bottle bombs placed at entrances to the yard and under the large windows looking into the tunnels. When troopers marched through, inmates would force a retreat by showering them in Molotov cocktails.

Just some of the hundreds of dud Molotov cocktails made from coffee and peanut butter jars. Inmates used noncombustible cooking oil for an accelerant. *Author's collection*

At first light on Sunday, November 12, Sam could see several rows of Muslims bending toward the ground. After prayers, at about 8 AM, inmates gathered around the TV for news on their last hope of a peaceful resolution: Bobby Seale.

As Seale was being processed through security, Blyden, Clark, and Champ met one of Oswald's lawyers in No-Man's-Land. The news was not good. A CO named Quinn, who had been injured during the first hour of the uprising, died of his injuries in a nearby hospital. It was Attica's first on-the-record casualty. Champ was somber when he briefed the Spokespersons. "This means now every one of us could be charged with felony murder."

Rosenberg shook his head. "But to put twelve hundred of us up on charges for one death? Not gonna happen."

Blyden got loud. "You willing to take that risk?"

"Nah, man. No way," said Noble, giving Blyden a knowing look.

The two men were thinking about something that the Observers and the press would not know until weeks later. It was not merely one death of one guard they would be charged with. During the past two days, Purple Bands had cut the throats of snitches trying to pass a note to a local TV reporter during his visit into D Yard. Blyden grabbed the reporter's notebook and brought the inmates before an ad hoc tribunal. The reporter was released, but the treacherous inmates were sentenced to death on the spot. Their bodies were currently stored out of camera range. Amnesty, the twenty-eighth and final demand, began to look like the only one worth holding out for.

Rosenberg remained optimistic. "Let's see what Bobby says."

It was two hours before Seale was cleared, briefed, and led into the yard by Purple Bands. He was accompanied by the last of the remaining Observers: Kunstler, Tom Wicker, and Clarence Jones. In the ready room, some were pressuring Seale to endorse the state's compromise: to give in to the inmate's twenty-seven of the twenty-eight points but let the prisoners take their chances *without* amnesty. If Seale gave a thumbs-up, the uprising would end that afternoon.

However, when he took the same stage as L. D. Barkley, Blyden, and many other Attica inmates over the past three days, instead of psalms of revolution or a plea for life, in his defining moment Seale addressed the one thousand anxious and desperate men by saying that before he could endorse the state's proposal, he'd have to check with the Black Panther Party's Central Committee and "get back to them." The Observers gaped in disbelief. Reporters would speculate in columns for days that perhaps the more militant Spokespersons had persuaded Seale that blood was nobler than compromise.

Seale capped his speech with a raised fist and "Power to the people!"—the trademark climax that had roused thunderous applause many times in his career. But today only sporadic claps could be heard, echoing off Attica's stone.

Sam whispered to himself, "I guess that's that."

Clarence Jones turned to the Bomber. "You don't think there's a chance the state will back off?"

"In Ohio, the National Guard killed four students just for having a sit-in. The system is at war. And Attica is the front line."

As Seale walked defiantly off the podium, passing Sam with a nod, Jones rushed to take his place. A relative unknown in the yard, and armed only with my father's words echoing in his mind, Jones grabbed the mic and urged the inmates to accept the state's proposal. "They cannot possibly prosecute everyone for one death. Please, people," he said into the PA. He was booed as he passed the mic to Blyden, whispering to his face, "Talk some sense, Herb, for God's sake!"

But, instead, Blyden put the mic close to his lips and shouted, "*Amnesty, amnesty!*" Big Black stood next to him with the latest draft of Oswald's proposal. He held it above his head. And, like Rosenberg two days before, angled toward a news camera and violently tore it in half. The yard chanted, "*Amnesty, amnesty!*"

Sam felt a tingle. The turkey shoot was coming. He grabbed a pencil. As the remaining Observers passed him on their final exit from the yard, Sam stuffed his last written words into Jones's pocket.

"Who was the note to?" I asked Akil as I shivered on Fink's porch. Was it to me? To Mom? To Jane?

Akil got close. The vapor from his breath enshrined us in his next words: "It was to revolutionaries listening all over the world."

> Power to the people!
> We are strong.
> We are together.
> We are growing.
> We love you all.
> Ho Ho Ho Chi Minh.
> Please inform our next of kin.

At about 2 AM on the morning of September 13, Sam watched police place additional video cameras on the rooftops. Come daybreak they would document something important, something worth putting up cameras at multiple angles. He approached Black for permission to go inside the prison one last time. In his cell were some poetry books and a clean shirt. Black nodded. There seemed little point in maintaining security anymore.

The empty halls of the prison carried the sounds of liberated inmates celebrating their last night of freedom, and maybe of life itself. All cell doors were open and their contents, with the sum of Attica's hearts and minds, scattered through the tiers. Sam's books and magazines, which he'd curated for almost two years into a personal library of Marx, Lenin, and Che Guevara, had been ransacked into confetti. His guitar lay under his cot. It had a split in the neck. It would never play the same. He tuned it the best he could and played one of his favorite songs, "Blowin' in the Wind." The song he played for Jane that won her heart.

What caught his eye next was the one thing that had somehow survived the chaos: his travel-sized magnetic chessboard. He had stashed it in a tight corner under his toilet. Arranged on its ten-by-ten board was our game. Only three moves in, I'd brought my queen out. *Always keep your most powerful piece in reserve*, my father had tried to teach me on one of our rare Saturdays. He meant to remind me of that in his response later in the week. With an eighteen-year sentence, he thought there would always be time to finish a game of chess with his nine-year-old son.

He put the game aside, sat on the edge of the cot, guitar cradled between his legs, and sang the song he'd written for me when I was three:

> You've heard, of course, of the zebra,
> And perhaps the duck-billed platypus.
> But have you heard of the unicorn?
> The unicorn with just one horn.
> He's a mythological character,
> Found in most Latin literature.
> He's quite a fabulous invention
> And should it be your intention,
> You can search the land and the seven seas,
> You can look and look for as long as you please,
> But you'll never, never, never, ever
> find a unicorn.

The last verse trailed into the darkness. He picked the queen off the board and placed it in his pocket. It was time for war.

Starting from child's pose, at 6 AM on September 13, my father bent his body into the last yoga moves he would ever do. He took a deep breath through his nose, appreciating the pungent combination of urine and gas in the nearby trench because it meant he was still alive. The hard rain had finally come around 3 AM. The dawn revealed that many tents had not lasted. Inmates were soaked, the ground was mud, sandbag barricades had sunk, and tension was high.

At 8 AM, Blyden gathered in the tunnel with the people who would define his place in history. Rosenberg suggested again that they surrender and take their chances with no amnesty. He was shouted down. Quiet nods and silent prayers soaked up the air for a full minute until Black broke the peace. "OK. I think it's time to show the Man we mean business."

The vote in the yard that came next was mere ceremony. It would have been impossible to know how many of the 1,281 inmates were in favor of accepting the state's terms. It didn't matter. The decision, already made by the handful of Spokespersons, was presented as a fait accompli. "We are MEN!" Blyden screamed into the mic. The inmates responded with cheers. Then Blyden ushered Barkley to the mic and Barkley orated their eulogy. "We do not want to rule. We only want to live. But we have come to the conclusion, after close study . . . after much suffering . . . after much consideration . . . that if we cannot live as people, then we can at least try to die like men?"

"YES!!!" resounded the cry of a thousand slaves.

Next, Clark and Noble suggested a decentralization of the hostages in order to make a rescue attempt impossible. "We need to scatter them: the walls, the latrine, the catwalks."

Eight of the fifty-three hostages were blindfolded and paired with what the McKay report would call "executioners." For this job, it was agreed that Muslims were too charitable. They would be swapped out for Purple Bands and a few volunteers.

Like couples doing the waltz, each pair shimmied across the yard up the ladders and onto the catwalk near Times Square. There they would stand, shanks to their throats, daring the state to blink for what must have seemed like an eternity.

Major Monahan (the fourth defendant in the civil suit) observed from the roof and radioed down to group commanders. Assault teams formed. The helicopter powered up. Seventy sharpshooters took positions on the rooftops lining the perimeter of the yard, tweaking their scopes.

At the front gate, 470 troopers stood in a double line, waiting to receive gas masks and shotguns. No rubber bullets were handed out. No first-aid stations were set up. No records were made as to which weapons were assigned to which troopers. The BCI group commander assembled his elite corps, which included Tobia, Stillwell, and nine other inspectors. "You are only to observe," the group commander ordered. "You will not be issued a weapon. However, under no circumstances are you to allow a weapon to fall into the hands of the enemy."

Tobia merged with A Company and weaved through the prison halls and up to the catwalk leading to Times Square. Sam's blockade of electrified filing cabinets would be in their way soon. The unit stopped at the threshold between shelter and the gray daylight, ears pressed to their walkie-talkies, waiting for the "go" or "no go."

Sam climbed onto the catwalk to check his work. Ten feet away, he saw "executioners" and their dance partners growing fatigued. One pulled a crate from the barricade and allowed his hostage, Ed Cunningham, to sit and offered him a cigarette. His hands bound, the shivering guard gummed its soggy end. Sam stepped up to the guard he often thought about killing and reached into his pocket for a lighter he would use to ignite the Molotov cocktails waiting for him in the bunker directly below them. "You should consider quitting if we get out of this."

The guard's sagging face uttered his last words. "I'm gonna consider a lot of things."

They had been standing for close to a half hour, waiting. For what? Oswald? Troopers? No one knew. Sam checked the filing cabinets blocking access to Times Square. Tapping one with a wrench to test the flow of current he saw no sparks. The power had been cut.

Suddenly, the sound of a helicopter became obvious. Sharpshooters rose in formation on the roofs. On the catwalks, troopers pushed forward, fitting gas masks and pointing weapons.

The helicopter appeared from over the wall, circling like a bird of prey, the distorted voice from its megaphone blaring, "Lay down your weapons and you will not be harmed. Report to the nearest trooper with your hands raised over your head." Before anyone could respond, a pendulum hanging from the chopper jettisoned two thin streams of gas, spreading over the yard like a lover's arms.

Sam looked over the side of the catwalk for his barricade of fertilizer bags ten feet below. Robin called up to him. "Holy shit, they're here already." Sam grabbed the ledge and leaped down to join him.

Within seconds, the tear gas reached Times Square, and the second it did he heard the sprawl of rapid gunfire. Monahan's snipers instantly killed seven of the eight hostages and most of the "executioners." Screams raced across Sam's ears from above, along with the crash of his stacked cabinets. Within seconds the yard was a fog, thick as a London autumn. Rockefeller had brought out his most vicious queen, far more savage than Sam or anyone had anticipated. And she was capturing every piece on the board.

The bodies of both hostages and "executioners" laid out for identification on A Catwalk. *Author's collection*

31 | THREE TRUTHS THAT TELL A LIE

I SLAMMED THE LATCH ON THE DOOR to Sharon's guest room. Alone for the first time with the files I liberated, I pieced together the last seconds of my father's life.

There were three Tobia kill reports, one typed, two handwritten. In each, the BCI inspector claimed that he was standing on B Catwalk, about sixty feet away from Times Square, when an "unknown trooper" approached and asked him to hang on to a shotgun that was abandoned by another trooper. Although all three statements deviated as to why Tobia fired on my father, the detail that Tobia fired a weapon that he was asked to secure by an unnamed trooper was the one worth repeating in each.

The first report, time-stamped within twenty-four hours of the shooting stated the following:

> I saw him take a knife from his pocket and run to a ditch which was located nearby which contained hostages which were prison guards. As he stabbed all of the guards, I fired the shotgun, striking him. He then ran back behind the barricade.

In this version, Dad had the superhuman strength to withstand the thick pepper gas that immobilized about a thousand inmates, mustered the endurance to stab several guards (presumably while the others passively watched), and then withstood a shotgun blast to the chest as he ran back about fifty yards to hide behind the barricade. Absurd as this was, it might have held up were it not later revealed that no hostages were stabbed and no knife was found.

In round two, dated several days later and after the media got hold of the autopsies, "Tobia" (or whoever wrote this) had replaced the knife with a bomb:

> He had in his possession an unknown quantity of Molotov cocktails and was attempting to throw them. I yelled at him to desist from doing this, but he continued to do so and kept running from behind the sandbags to the front of the barricade and returning behind the barricade. As he attempted to throw a Molotov cocktail, I fired one shot in his direction, and he subsequently appeared to fall behind the barricade.

My understanding of acoustics from being an audio engineer came in handy here. There is no way my father could have heard Tobia shouting to him from sixty feet away with helicopters overhead. And according to the McKay report, the cocktails of "unknown quantity" that Tobia alleges were in Dad's "possession" would turn out to be only a few empty ketchup bottles and some rags. That begged the question of whether Tobia assumed that investigators reading this report were so dumb as to think my "dangerous" father would bluff an armed trooper with an empty condiment jar?

Finally, one year later, the McKay Commission report was published and rumors spread that findings of the second, newly formed Goldman Panel would impeach statements made by troopers for the McKay report. Now troopers might lose their pensions for perjuring themselves—or worse.

By this point, public sympathy toward the inmates had elevated, and Tobia (or his ghostwriter) was asked to author *another* statement. He revised his role to that of a trooper concerned for my father's safety—just before he shot him in the chest:

> There was a roof or some kind of metal overhang which prevented me from seeing what he was doing when he was out of the bunker. I lifted my gas mask and shouted to him to "Stop." I put my gas mask back on and then motioned with my hand for the inmate to stay down.

How benevolent.

All this contradicted the various versions I heard from Robin (who was not mentioned in any of the statements) and the testimony of others—most notably Richard Clark. In his book *Brothers of Attica*, Clark claimed he saw my father in custody *after* the assault. Another inmate, Peter Hoey, testified that he saw my father shot "from above" in the act of surrendering. One state trooper told a filmmaker he saw a White prisoner in the area where Sam's body was found, shot for no apparent reason while his hands were raised, minutes after the assault had ended.

Regardless, at that moment, I was willing to decide that all of them were emotionally compromised if I could at least make some scientific sense of Tobia's testimony. I didn't want my father to be a victim, hunted like an animal. Even suicide by cop was something I could normalize over thinking that the government was out to murder my father and was watching my family, watching me. My whole worldview, at that moment, depended on how far away Tobia was standing when he fired.

Was it really—as he claimed—sixty feet?

A single projectile could easily kill from the sixty-foot distance, if Tobia used a single slug and not buckshot. Then Dad's death could be a "good shoot."

I looked at Tobia's handwritten, unsigned statement, dated the day after the assault and before real facts came to light. In it he claimed, "I cannot remember if the shotgun I used had buckshot or a slug." This was an odd detail to specify, because no other kill reports written that day bothered noting this distinction, and Tobia, being in the BCI, would have known that this detail was germane to the obligatory ballistic tests to come. I had liberated those reports from Fink, along with the photo Fink had tried to keep from me—the one of Dad lying on a coroner's slab with the lens trained on his upper-left torso. It showed three or four small entry wounds, not one. They were about three inches apart, and none of the holes in his chest were bigger than a quarter. The state's pathologist report (written by Richard Abbott, who would confirm this in a videotaped interview I did with him in 2016) claimed that a single slug would have left only one hole the size of an apple.

I scanned the ballistic report. According to it, buckshot used that day had a diffusion of five to eight inches when fired from more than thirty feet. But the diffusion of Dad's wounds was only four inches. And according to the state itself, the distance needed for buckshot with a diffusion of only four inches was less than fifteen feet.

Tobia lied about his distance. Dad was murdered at point-blank range.

And something else came to mind: if Robin was being truthful about being right next to Dad when he was shot, he would surely have known his death was an unequivocal assassination. I understood why Tobia lied. But why did Robin?

This contact sheet was one of many turned over by the state as part of discovery in the 1991 civil trial. The arrows (added by me) show the location of my father's bunker where he was shot. In each shot, his body is just out of frame. Since the goal of these photos was to document weapons, to justify the overwhelming use of state force, I had to wonder why the state redacted its prime example: the body of Mad Bomber Melville, allegedly with a homemade bomb in his hand.
Author's collection

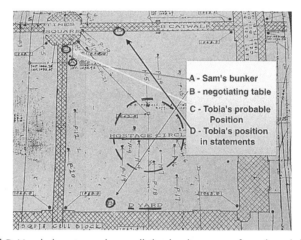

The map of D Yard showing where all the bodies were found and the "hostage circle." The numbers P-1, P-2, etc. show where each dead prisoner was found. My father was P-13 (A). I marked up this map as part of my early analysis. The arrows show the difference between where Sam's killer claims to have been standing when he fired and where he had to actually be standing, based on the evidence. I found this in Liz Fink's evidence room. *Author's collection*

The only known photo of Sam's barricade. Out of thousands of photos taken of D Yard after the assault, this is the only one that clearly shows its exact location. I found it in a discarded file in Fink's evidence room in 1991. The markings (added by me) show the location where the state trooper fired, standing near Times Square, about twenty feet directly above his target. *Author's collection*

I awoke the next morning late for my screening of Fink's Attica tapes.

Liz answered the door to the bunker, and before even hello, she barked, "How did you like the papers?"

Had she noticed the missing reports from the evidence room? No. She held up the *Buffalo News*. She meant my interview with Dan Herbeck, published in the Saturday morning edition. I shrugged. "I haven't seen it."

"Where's Shawn?"

"I called him, but he wasn't interested in seeing the tapes."

"Yeaah, well, we have some good news," she said, tossing the paper and changing the subject. "The defense is ordering the transcripts from Mancusi."

"Why is that good news?"

"Generally, when one side orders the transcripts of a witness, it means they're gearing up for an appeal, which means they think they're going to lose."

"I guess Mike really tore him up on the stand."

"Well, the warden's testimony was absurd—that he didn't know any shooting was going on! Who's gonna believe that? Especially when he had a two-way radio sitting right next to him."

"Yes, the radio," I said, and smiled at Mike Deutsch sitting on the couch. He returned the smile and moved over so I could join him.

The first tape was of the negotiating table, taken by news cameras two days before the assault. There was my father, standing behind L. D. Barkley, who was shouting into Oswald's face. Time had frozen my father. Except for an 8mm wedding film, this was the only moving image I had ever seen of him. He was the thriving young man that Jane, John, Robin, and the New Left fell in love with.

The second tape opened with troopers wearing safety-orange rain ponchos and gas masks descending into the yard like robot clones from a science-fiction apocalypse. They flanked out onto B and D Catwalks, 12-gauge shotguns firing indiscriminately into the lingering clouds of tear gas. You could see inmates throwing jars that smashed into walls. But none exploded. Then, they were mowed down by a line of ponchos. Although the tape had no sound, I could imagine the echoes of gunfire segueing into the wails of agony.

After eight minutes, almost as suddenly as it began, the shots stopped.

From there, my mind took over, blending my fantasies with those of Robin Palmer's recantations on my couch when I was twelve. I imagined that I saw my father peek over the top of the barricade. The gas cloud was starting to lift. Under its horizon, my father saw what looked like the morning after

Woodstock: rain-soaked garbage and debris everywhere, bodies that could have been asleep were it not for the blood widening around them. He had survived, and he knew what that meant: a life filled with endless beatings in HBZ. The unity he had helped create would vanish as investigators would turn brothers against each other by offering deals for testimony.

It was over, all of it: his fight, the revolution, everything. He reached into his pocket for his queen from our chess game: empty. He dug deeper. It must've slipped out when he lit Cunningham's cigarette and now lay on the catwalk under the guard's corpse.

"Well, at least we tried," he said to Robin, as he saw the rifleman on the catwalks moving into formation. And giving in to finality of it all, he stood.

A pop from the shotgun of a faceless policeman ripped past their ears. Robin whipped around to see the man he admired unconscious, crumpled in the corner, barely breathing. Blood was seeping through his shirt. Robin looked around for a medic who was not there. Next came a cold muzzle pressing against the back of his skull and the voice of the faceless policemen: "Down on the fucking ground, motherfucker. Right now. Do it! Do it, or so help me God, I'll blow your fuckin' head off."

Robin kissed the mud, his emotions mixed that he himself wasn't the target. In a few moments, he would be naked, along with a thousand others, marching back to slavery. But he would be alive.

I hid my rage from Fink, who was sitting next to me. She had no place in my thoughts. They were the words I was never able to say:

My Dad's picking me up.

Can we build this together, Dad?

How will I know when she likes me, Dad?

I love you and I'd really like you to meet my dad.

It's a boy, Dad.

Do you want to grab a drink, Dad?

I'll take care of you, Dad.

Dad, I'm really going to miss you

My father and me, 1963. *Author's collection*

32 | THE VERDICT

AFTER FOUR WEEKS, THE JURY CAME in around mid-January 1992: they found only one of four defendants "responsible": Karl Pfeil, the vice warden, who was Ed Cunningham's good friend. The man who, in his moment of extreme grief, started rumors that "throats were cut," which inspired the days of bloody reprisals. One responsible defendant meant only inmates who were affected by Pfeil's actions—which were in the wake of the assault—would get a settlement. Since my father and twenty-eight other inmates were shot and killed *during* the assault, their estates would receive nothing.

The phone rang. My machine picked up and Mom's voice followed its beep. "I want you to know something." We had not spoken in weeks. I braced myself. "I'm sorry I gave you such a hard time about going to Buffalo. And sorry that I've been so hard on you about this . . . journey. I get now that you must do it without me. I'm sad about that, but I understand. And I want you to know that I'm going to help you. With the money . . . if you need it . . . for the trip, or whatever."

I picked up the receiver. "Mom?"

"Oh, you're home. I was leaving a message."

"Yeah, I heard. I'm glad to be back, and I heard you. Thank you."

"Oh . . . well . . . you're welcome. I love you, you know."

"I know."

There was a long awkward pause, which she broke. "What did you find?"

"As soon as I figure it all out, I'll tell you. But there's something I'd like to share with you, if you like. It's what David Hughey told me."

"That's one of the radicals?" She mulled it over and finally said, "Sure." Maybe at this point she was finally ready to entertain some perspective from the "crazed hippies."

I pulled out a transcript of my phone conversation from several months back. David was the most empathetic of the radicals I had tracked down in the Melville Collective. "I asked him, 'Do you think Sam wanted to die?' and he said, 'When Sam and I were being held in the Federal House of Detention before the trial, there was a book he began reading—*On Life After Death* [by Elisabeth Kübler-Ross]. This book is about preparing for death and preparing the spirit for the afterlife. It had a huge influence on him.' And then I asked David, 'You're saying he wanted to die?' and David said, 'Not in the traditional sense. Not like someone who takes their own life. I'm saying he knew he *would* die. Sam was very affectionate, loved people and animals. He put himself in an unlivable situation when he abandoned you. He had to be self-destructive after making that choice. I believe this because his character was totally incongruent with him abandoning his son. The only way out of the situation was self-destruction.'"

She took a deep breath. "Oh my God." I could tell she was sobbing. "He was the most amazing man, your father. There was no other like him. And you were eleven. I couldn't think of a way to say this amazing man abandoned you. So, I told you what I told you. I'm very, very sorry."

I bent forward, still conflicted as I was when she first told me, realizing now that I had to live with the fact that my father vanishing from history was just as painful as his vanishing from my life. His true path was always toward the revolution and ultimately toward that yard; our tenuous bond as father and son was now the last remaining proof of his tenure on earth.

"He let go of me, but I couldn't let go of him." I asked my mother, "Why is that?"

"Because you are stronger," she replied.

Before we ended our first supportive conversation in almost three years, she painted a picture of Sam's funeral—not the spectacle covered in the *New York Times* but the one that happened after Kunstler and the Panthers had gone, after the FBI vans had pulled away and the East Village continued its path of revolution. This funeral took place by a glade in Harriman State Park, near the Appalachian Trail where we camped when I was a child. Mom held the small cardboard box containing my father's cremated remains. His boyhood friends from the Bronx were the only people in attendance—no lawyers, no radicals, no cops. No me.

Each took a turn saying something heartfelt. One had a pocketknife and carved an inscription on the tree under which the ashes would be buried. In a quick discussion about what he should engrave, someone suggested a single word:

SPARTACUS

Sam, moments after his death, fallen behind his sandbag barricade. *Author's collection*

33 | BEAUTIFUL THINGS

ONE LIFE'S ALBUM CAME OUT IN JULY 1992. It sold over four million units, earning the group, the producer, and me by association a Grammy. My goal when I entered music was to have one platinum record award before I was thirty. Thanks to One Life, I had four. But it was hard for me to enjoy the moment knowing the corrupt role I played and what my father might think.

Through my first brush with success I began partying with rising singers, actresses, and movie producers. They were all stylish, provocative, and exciting. But I was as done with glamour as I was with the '60s and Attica. What I yearned for now was someone conventional with whom to build a nest, someone who would take me far away from the heartache of social change and break the chain started by three generations of rebellion.

In 1995 I accepted a blind date set up by a friend I hardly knew. Like my mother was to Sam, this woman and I were political opposites. She was a Republican on the partner track for the accounting firm Deloitte Touche. She didn't have a headshot or demo. She'd never participated in a protest. What she did have was three other suitors that week, all millionaires. Meanwhile, as a record producer still on the come all I could offer her was a nine-dollar all-you-can-eat sushi bar and, for sizzle, the story of my father.

On our second date I showed her the half-finished book proposal I tried to write for Simon & Schuster. She sat on my couch and read the entire fifty pages while I picked at my cuticles wondering if this was a stupid move.

Three years later, she became my wife and the mother of our two beautiful children, both delivered via natural home births. She gave me my dream of having a family and the chance to prove that men are not destined to follow in the patterns of their fathers.

But every time a new chapter about Attica was revealed in a movie or documentary, my wife would see my disappointment as my father's contributions were ignored. The pattern began for me long before I met her, when I was sixteen. ABC produced a TV movie called *Attica* starring Charles Durning as Oswald. I watched with great interest, but I could find no trace of Dad. Mom said his role was given to other characters. The Hollywood term for this is *compositing*, combining two or more real persons into one fictional character. My father was composited into several other actors, all of them Black. The main one was played by Morgan Freeman. Mom explained to me that this was probably done because a White man defending Black prisoners was "too complex" for a TV audience in 1980.

A decade later, apparently not much had changed about TV audiences. The year after the '91 trial, Hollywood again focused on America's biggest prison uprising. HBO produced *Against the Wall*, a more politically layered but no less monochrome version of the event. Samuel L. Jackson played a composite of my father, Richard Clark, and Don Noble. The elaborate counterassaults my father staged were composited into a nameless Caucasian hippie, tripping on acid. His one line was "Far out, man." Just like the 1980s movie, Jerry Rosenberg was not present, nor was any White or Latin leader.

Over the years since, several documentaries and books about Attica were produced. They all used Fink as a go-to consultant. She directed them to the inmates that worked for her and their families as sources for interviews. She never directed anyone to me.

By 2010, when the case against the state was concluded, Fink's race-centric narrative had become the most public understanding of the event. And neither she nor the state, for that matter, had any interest in moving off the interpretation that Attica was anything more than a conflict between redneck authorities and angry Black felons. No mention of the social justice politics, nor the personal vengeance of Rockefeller; nor of the White or Latino inmates (who also suffered reprisals) who had come together in a whirlwind of racial tension; nor the widows of the all-White hostages killed by friendly fire of all-White troopers. They were brushed under the rug by the spectacle of Fink's moral victory against the mighty State of New York. I was confused by this, because when Fink was raising money for the Attica Brothers legal fund, her fliers and newsletters had a banner that read, ATTICA IS ALL OF US.

When tightening up my research for this project, a friend sent me a link to a recording between Nixon and Rockefeller on the day of the retaking. Their exchange told me that this agenda may have ended with Fink but had started at the top:

> ROCKEFELLER: Mr. President, the prison is secure.
> NIXON: Good, good. Was it as we thought? Was it the Blacks who did this?
> ROCKEFELLER: Yes, it was the Blacks. They organized this, the Blacks.
> NIXON: But, we got them, right? The ringleaders?
> ROCKEFELLER: Yes.
> NIXON: And the hostages? They're safe?
> ROCKEFELLER: Most yes. A few, uh, ten I think, didn't make it out.
> NIXON: Ten?
> ROCKEFELLER: Maybe eleven.
> NIXON: Eleven?! Jesus! Well . . . that's not too bad.
> ROCKEFELLER: That's life.

The Quaker president never inquired about inmates.

I had no trouble understanding why the state wanted to polarize Attica. By 1971 New York was just returning to normal from the radical actions authored by the Black Panther Party, the Yippies, the Weather Underground, and many other New Left groups connected to my father. The last thing a Republican administration wanted to do was admit that to truncate the endless campaigns of hard-left activity they had to use a prison riot as cover to assassinate one of the movement's most effective activists. But I could not help but laugh as I reflected on the irony that Fink had found common ground with, of all people, Nixon. How sad for her Attica clients of *all* races who sacrificed so much to make a bigger point. And how sad for my father, whose contributions at Attica had been erased because he was an inconvenient truth.

My father wouldn't have cared. Beautiful things don't seek attention. His war was against racial inequity, so of reassigning his contributions at Attica to the Brothers, my father would have approved.

But I didn't. My father had been stolen a second time. This time by America's lust for reduction and Fink's single-minded victory. And I think Sam would have agreed with me that this polarized oversimplification of the Attica story has been a major contributor to our culture's ease at ignoring the evils of mass incarceration. Even the most conservative among us would have to admit that if the majority of US inmates were Caucasian instead of African, mass incarceration would be as big a campaign issue as immigration or reproductive rights. Instead, by 1997 Attica had been distilled down to a spear of sarcasm to throw at your boss when you are asked to work late and you imitate Al Pacino in *Dog Day Afternoon*, wagging your finger: "Attica, Attica!"

Every couple years, my wife would ask when I'd get around to writing a truth about the uprising that only a handful seemed to know. I was too frightened. After the Oklahoma City bombing in '95, all bombers were "terrorists," regardless of their motives or methods. Instead, to appease my father's ghost, which still appeared when I faced difficult decisions, I focused my attempt at activism on the injustice with which I had firsthand experience: how recording artists are ripped off by the music industry. I thought the world might want to know why many Grammy-winning acts filed for bankruptcy. However, the FBI had taught me that the Melville name would quite probably continue to undermine my efforts. I could envision wholesale rejections by publishers that were veiled reasoning for "We cannot publish a book by the son of the Mad Bomber."

So I created a nom de plume.

Miraculously, my first book, written under my fake name, sold through three printings in less than a year. There would be a second book. A year later, a third. Then a fourth and a fifth. It was not long until the alter ego I created to dodge the FBI became a music industry brand.

This other version of me was much more like Sam: outspoken and vigilant about the rights of others, many things that "Josh" was not programmed or allowed to be. Soon, my alter ego was asked to lecture at Harvard Law, UCLA, NYU, and over a dozen other music business programs that had begun to use my books. I was appearing on TV as an expert in artists' rights, debating pompous guests on Fox who advocated for the legitimacy of "sharing music" on Napster. I argued for the rights of creators, which pitted me against Google, Apple, and other Big Data giants who in 1999 were trying to subvert rights to privacy while turning music, film, books, and news into the free toy at the bottom of their cereal box.

And finally, I had become at least some version of my father's son.

It was during my first book tour in 1999, when Sharon Fischer, whom I had stayed in touch with since the '91 trial, sent me the obituary of Vincent Tobia. The man who bragged for years that he shot Mad Bomber Melville had died suddenly of a heart attack at age sixty. Sharon told me the news of the Attica Brothers' victory had finally gotten to him. Tobia spent the last year of his life dodging activists. He once took a swing at a reporter who called him a murderer. According to the obit, cluttered with backhanded compliments describing him as "colorful and combative," Tobia would not make partner at any large firm. And the closest he would come to having an impact on politics was when a Buffalo Bills player was arrested for a DWI or spousal assault. Tobia was the fixer sent to glad-hand cops with seats.

When I interviewed Tobia's good friend and law partner years later, he told me the rest of his story. Only months before Tobia's death, his wife divorced him. After the funeral, his son, from whom he was estranged, sold his father's prized collection of Buffalo Bills championship rings, the most tangible symbol of his father's success. His son used the money to exit the legal profession his father had pressured him into and became a professional fly fisherman.

I had tried to hate Tobia even before I knew his name, but learning about his end, I could not. I had forgiven my father, and it was time to pardon his assassin as well. "The more you can do without, the freer you are" should apply doubly to hate. Tobia was just a working-class cop who'd follow any orders to provide for his family—even murder.

The crimes we commit for our children.

Soon after Tobia's death in 2000, a newsletter from Fink arrived. Nine years of state appeals had gotten to her as well. For the sake of closure, she was accepting their paltry offer of $12 million, the same amount the state offered a decade earlier. Fink spun this as a victory in the press, but to those in the legal trade and to Blyden, Rosenberg, and a dozen other separatists who had successfully sued for higher amounts, the view was depressing.

It would take several more months to negotiate division of the $12 million among the 1,200 litigants in the class, but the first cut was the easiest:

$4 million for fees to Fink and the legal team. The second cut would go to a subclass of thirty or so Attica victims who were beaten in the days *after* the rehousing of prisoners. Coincidentally, many of them were Fink's helpers, and one was now her live-in boyfriend, Frank "Big Black" Smith. He would receive, $150,000, and through other related suits, more than any other Attica victim. Fink had to be pressured by Sharon Fischer and the *Buffalo News* into carving out a portion for the twenty-nine dead. In the end, she acquiesced, and their estates would get a mere $25,000 each.

The balance and vast majority of 1,281 litigants, who were in the yard, injured or not, participating or not, would receive an even more paltry $7,500 each. Unanimous approval from *all* litigants was required.

I asked myself, would my father want me to accept this absurd settlement where the living get more than the dead? I recalled a 1973 letter written to Fischer from civil rights icon Martin Sostre she had shown me. He wrote, "Sam Melville was the only real political prisoner at Attica." Didn't my father deserve more? Maybe. But the answer to whether I wanted to stall the settlement over pride weighed on me. For several days I consulted my father's ghost until the answer seemed obvious. Attica victims had waited decades for validation and closure. It was time to give it to them. However, I had one condition: I wanted to testify at the settlement hearing. I wanted to give a victim's report, *on the record*, that Sam Melville was *murdered* by the state. And I wanted a separate amount as restitution: one dollar.

Fink was livid. "What good can come of it?!" she yelled at me over the phone. But from a PR perspective, she needed the thumbs-up from the son of one of the most famous Attica casualties. And I too needed closure. And so, once again, in the year 2000, I found myself in an upstate New York courtroom. This time was on the witness stand, where, in a twenty-five-minute statement, I entered into evidence the facts that proved my father was assassinated. I concluded with the eulogy that history had denied him:

> I often wonder what kind of life Sam would have made for himself after Attica. While at Attica, Sam became an educator and spent his time organizing classes and teaching convicts to read and write. In a prison where racial tensions ran high, he managed to cross the boundaries and helped prisoners everywhere stand up for their rights in a time when prisoners were not thought worthy of any.

But, more importantly, had he lived, he probably would have continued in his desire to be an educator. He would have been able to share with his son what it means to stand up for something you believe in. He could have taught me, and the youth of today, what those troubled times were about. He could have held his grandchildren in his arms and witnessed his son's wedding. Instead, I have come to know my father only through the memories of others.

I hope to impress upon this court the tragedy of the murder of a man who took the rap for others, who devoted his incarceration to helping his peers, who protected hostages, and who gave up his freedom to oppose the tragic waste of sixty thousand American lives in Vietnam.

Fink never looked up from her legal pad.

Upon exiting the courtroom, she intercepted me in the hall. "Did you get what you wanted?"

Somehow, I knew it would be the last time I'd ever see her, so I asked, "Why does it always seem like we are at odds?" I was hoping that now that the case was over, she would confess that hiding the truth about my father's role at Attica was just about securing justice for the inmates. But I was in for a surprise. It was not business at all.

"I didn't like your father."

"Did something happen between you two?"

"Well, nothing specific. I worked with him at the *Guardian*." She needed to take a deep breath for the next part. "He was a sexist, and I'm fat."

"He didn't like you because you were fat?"

"Yeaah well, men back then were a bit different than now. We expected them to be sexists. Your father related to women in a sexual way. He had no use for fat girls."

That didn't ring true. Diane Eisner was not model-thin, nor were some of the other lovers I had spoken with. But my response was tempered. "Well . . . I am *not* my father."

The woman who was never short of words, at that moment, had none. She disappeared from my life, removing me from her mailing list. As she made her way toward the exit, a thought came to mind: *All that resentment from being overlooked by a man thirty years ago.*

That sounded familiar.

In 2010, Robin Palmer's voice, now frail from cancer, found me through the telephone. He had sent me his $7,500 share of the Attica settlement. He considered me a son, he said, because of his love for Sam, and we spoke for about an hour. In that conversation, he disclosed his nearly four-decade-old secret.

In 1972, he cooperated when asked to testify for the McKay report and claim that Sam's shooting was random. He said to me, "I couldn't talk about Sam's death because of the Molotov cocktails. My lawyer said you better keep that to yourself or they will indict you for making the bombs. I know you're not happy about that, Josh, but I would not have made it out alive if I didn't say what they asked. I was in fear for my life." He stopped short of admitting that his version of how Dad was shot was a fiction. Maybe by now he had come to believe it, needed to believe it. I couldn't imagine the intense conflicts that he must have been experiencing. I didn't see the need to crush him with what I had learned.

Robin Palmer just weeks before his death in 2010. © Martine Bisagni

His confession to me that day was not a coincidence. He asked if I would come to Ithaca to be by his deathbed. Still angry, I made an excuse about logistics and family obligations. I knew he meant no harm. I knew he had difficult choices. Still, I could not face him. But a week later, when the news of his passing reached me, I was profoundly sad and feeling shame. He was the best of the father figures I had collected, and it was only upon reflection, years later, that I realized how much, in his own way, he loved and watched over me.

Like he would a son.

Robin Palmer died of cancer on October 10, 2010. He was seventy-seven.

So many in this story had passed without fanfare. And because of the lengthy battle, so few of the Attica Brothers enjoyed their victory. Herbert Blyden died of cancer in 1997 at sixty-one, having never received his settlement. Jerry Rosenberg died three years later in a prison hospice in Rochester at the age of seventy-two, having served forty-six years, the longest of any inmate in New York State penal history. I interviewed him only months before he passed. Then, he told me things that never made it into the official record, some of which you have already read. He never got his Attica money either but earned recognition through America's greatest validation: a TV drama about his Supreme Court victory. He was played by Tony Danza.

By 2013 I had a girl, age thirteen, and a boy, age seven. Instead of burdening them with my paternal angst, in somber moments I closed the door to my study and took out my version of a scotch bottle: the large plastic container I labeled P-13. It contained twenty-five years of research. I cannot remember how many times I ran my hands over the yellowed edges of FBI papers and the articles curated by Mom that started it all. I would search for new meaning in old facts, wondering how complete my truth was. Was Jane an informant who proffered the collective to the authorities? It would explain why she never ran and why she fabricated a story that my father was the reason for their arrest. I'll probably never know for sure. And was my father a righteous freedom fighter or just an angry loner who found a fashionable outlet for his rage? I could not decide. I'd cry or shake my head in frustration retelling over and over how I could explain his story to my kids in a way that would help them appreciate their linage. Failing, the box would go back in storage.

Then, one afternoon in 2013, my answer came. The container's guts once again were on the coffee table, but this time my seven-year-old, Jack, was playing *Minecraft* on his iPad only one room away. Beautiful. Bright. *He's never known a world without a Black president.* How could I explain the struggles minorities had to endure barely two generations ago and the insane choices his grandfather and great-grandfather made to make that possible.

"Who's that man?" he said, appearing at my side.

"That's my father."

My daughter also peeked in, knowing I'd never spoken of him.

"He was famous for some remarkable things. Shall I tell you about them?" I didn't want to make the same mistake as my mother—whitewashing the truth.

"You're a writer," my daughter said. "If he was amazing, you should write about him."

And I froze.

How many people over the years had encouraged me? How many times had I scoffed? But looking into my children's eyes, I had a revelation: the reason I could never tell my father's story was because first I had to become a father myself.

I thought about Sam's Marxist mantra, *The more you can do without . . .* , which was embraced by the Boomers. Somehow it seemed tragically incomplete. For if children are not our skin in the game of life, what is? The best way to improve the world is to raise a productive child, and hopefully one who becomes an honest leader.

That is *today's* revolution.

"Good idea," I said to both my kids. "Tomorrow I will start."

Jack climbed on my lap, and his sister sat upright with her perfect dancer's posture and put down her cell phone. My wife and companion of twenty-plus years joined us, with a plate of sandwiches made up of peanut butter, alfalfa sprouts, and hot sauce on oat bread, ready to help with the tough questions. When I was done, the room was quiet. The chain of lies was broken.

"Dad," Jack said, shifting the subject, "can we play some *Minecraft* now?" Jack loves to meet me in the virtual landscape of the computer game where there's no disparity in our size. He usually ends up killing me with a sword, the same way Sam, my giant, let me best him when we wrestled on that red carpet on the Upper West Side.

"OK," I said, "but how about afterward we go have an old-fashioned catch?"

He thought and reconsidered. "No, you're right, Dad. Let's go do that instead."

And within moments, we are playing in the sun.

Joshua Melville
March 18, 2010 · 🔒

Breaking the Chain.

My grandfather never played ball with my father. And my father never played ball with me.

Things can change.

20 Likes 9 Comments

👍 Like   💬 Comment   ↪ Share

ACKNOWLEDGMENTS

THIS IS MY FAVORITE PART. If you are compiling a list of thank-yous, it means that a labor of love (or torture) is done. It also means that your story will have a place in the world and a life of its own. And yet, even after thirty years of research, it is hard for me to call this work complete, just as it is equally as hard to allow something so personal to be published. Stories involving radical bombings and government-sponsored murders present challenges for publishers when they are labeled as nonfiction. So, for taking a chance on this story, I must start by thanking Jerry Pohlen, Devon Freeny, and Cynthia Sherry of Chicago Review Press and Brian Sweany of Recorded Books. I must also thank Doug Grad, best man at my wedding and the person who gave me the idea to write this book in 1987; he has been its industry champion ever since. All our jousting over, well, everything, was worth it.

Next, I must thank Caroline Leavitt, a developmental editor and great author in her own right, whose brutal honesty, coupled with a tender heart, showed me what this story was really about. And Jeff Lyons, who told me to trust my instincts over story-editors-for-hire (including him) and introduced me to Caroline.

It is a treasured friend who is willing to spend a weekend with a writer's early drafts. So, if you appreciated the level of historical detail and honesty of the period, then these people deserve a great deal of collective credit: Ron Kuby, Sharon Fischer, Barry Isaacson, Bruce Kawin, Jeremy Varon, David Viola, Chris Christopher, Sue Ross, Christine Carabetta, Brent Carter, Cara Sadownick, Constantinos Hatzopoulos, Deborah (World Of), Jennifer Kelly, Maya Solovey, Michelle S., Mike Laskow, Monica Dizozza and Jamie Freiberger, Neville and Cindy Johnson, Sasha Odnoralov, Brian Dorfmann, Scott Dacko, Susan Jane Gilman, and Adam Belanoff.

Some of my beta readers were also donors of tributes and services to my crowd-sourcing campaign. Their contributions and talents helped to liberate the many government documents and travel needed for interviews to bring this project to life. They are too many to list; however, I must call out several for their extreme generosity: Adrian Arkin, Bob Israel, Jay Frank, Lew Friedman, Linda C., Mimi Behan, Steve V. Gin, Brian Kallies, Shelia English, Lenora Degan, Laura Lepore, Nancy Marie, Andrea Andresakis, and my oldest friend from literally before birth, Rick Salpeter.

Finally, but most importantly, my family, my mother and my children, who put up with my moods, missed weekends, and frustrations. You were the inspiration for all this work and every breath I take. And along with family, I must include my dog, Buddy, who stayed by my side every day, and whose benevolent eyes gave me the best feedback of all. But mostly, yes *mostly*, my wife of over two decades who encouraged me, supported me, gave me two amazing kids, a life anyone would envy, and helped me find strength when I felt like quitting. You are my greatest friend forever.

Thank you to all who helped me on this journey. I feel very blessed to have you all in my life.

AN ANATOMY
OF THE LAUNDRY

by Sam Melville, written in Attica, 1971

BECAUSE OF THE PIG-SANCTIONED RIGHT to capitalize on the needs of other inmates, and the accompanying fear of losing their lucrative Jobs, our brothers who work in the Laundry have become docile slaves, House Niggers, and therefore, an impediment to our Liberation.

These Laundry slaves, who, for the most part, are some well-meaning and intelligent individuals, have been so thoroughly indoctrinated and duped by this Dog-eat-Dog system that they don't even realize that they have become House Niggers and instruments of their own oppression.

How does the Pig exploit the Laundry slave? How does the Pig profit? Like so: The average wage of a unionized Dry Laundry Worker on the outside is 3.50 per hour, whereas, the average wage of a Laundry slave here is 25¢ per day. The Laundry slave works 3½ hours per day for 25¢; an outside unionized worker would earn $10.50 for the same work. Projected to a monthly basis, the slave gets $5.50, while an outsider gets $231.00. There are 40 slaves in the Laundry for a monthly payroll of $220.00. If the State were forced to pay union wages, the payroll would be $9,240.00. Yearly, it's $2,640.00 as compared to $110,880.00 (Dig). Our active support of this saves the State $108,240.00 annually.

HOW?

The slaves are allowed three Laundry contracts at one carton (33.50) per month. So, the slave's *real* salary is $10.50 per month, plus the $5.50. Who pays this? WE DO! We pay the slave $3.50 for four work days a month, work which he completes in no time at all. The Pig pays the slave $5.00 for 22 days *hard work*! Thus, the State gets 18 more days of labor than we do, for our $3.50, and the State only pays the slave $1.50 more. Now, I ask you, is that ignorant slave with the crease in his pants slick, or is the Pig *slick*? The Pig gets the cash saving, the labor, and the wages paid to the slave as soon as the Commissary opens.

So, you see Brother-Man, we have the power to stop this. No Riots or Violence but just refusing to cooperate in maintaining our own misery just because we want a crease in our pants and don't want to wash our own dirty underwear. Yes, let's force the Pig to bring in those unionized laundries and pay that $110,880.00 a year to run the laundry. By saving $3.50, we can cost him $110,880.00 that he can't afford.

Brother-Man, now is the time to act!

STOP PAYING!

JUST HOLD BACK AND MAKE THIS COOKIE CRUMBLE !!!!!!!

PEACE & POWER

YOUR (SLAVE) LAUNDRY MAN

RIGHT ON ! ! ! ! ! RIGHT ON ! ! ! ! ! RIGHT ON ! ! ! ! !

KEY GROUPS
AND ACRONYMS

BCI: Bureau of Criminal Investigation, a division of the New York State Police.

Black Panther Party (BPP): Militarized African American nationalist group.

Chicago Seven: The seven persons charged with inciting a riot near the Chicago Democratic Convention in 1968.

CLP: Communist Labor Party of America; activist group believing in Marxism as a foundation of government, 1920–1967.

Crazies: Radical East Village protest group.

FBI: Federal Bureau of Investigation; law enforcement agency charged with stopping domestic terrorism.

FLQ: Front de libération du Québec; Canadian pro-Castro, anti-capitalist bombers seeking independence of Quebec from Canada.

FUNY: Free University of New York, also known as Alternate U; warehouse in the East Village that hosted political/radical group meetings and New Left education classes, founded and run by Sharon Krebs.

Guardian: Far-left newspaper.

Melville Collective: A loose affiliation of anti-imperialist radicals responsible for bombings attributed to Sam Melville.

MOBE: National Mobilization Committee to End the War in Vietnam; non-violent protest group.

Motherfuckers (Up Against the Wall Motherfuckers): Radical anticapitalist East Village protest group.

NACLA: North American Congress on Latin America; leftist group founded in 1966 to provide information on trends in Latin America and its relationships to the United States.

Panther Twenty-One: The twenty-one Black Panthers arrested for conspiracy to bomb several NYC police precincts in 1969.

Rat Subterranean News: East Village underground newspaper, 1969–1971.

RC: Revolutionary Contingent; anticapitalist group formed in 1967, centered on teaching survival skills for a coming US revolution.

Red Squad: The New York Police Department's division of undercover agents that infiltrated subversive groups.

SDS: Students for a Democratic Society; activist group cofounded by Tom Hayden in 1961.

SNCC: Student Nonviolent/National Coordinating Committee; radical protest group. Under the leadership of H. Rap Brown, it turned militant in the mid-1960s.

V&R: Veterans and Reservists Against the Vietnam War; early 1960s antiwar protest group composed of ex-military.

WBAI: 99.5 FM in New York City; listener-supported radio station, reporting political news and opinion from a leftist perspective.

Weathermen/Weather Underground: Radical offshoot of SDS.

Yippies: Youth International Party; flamboyant activist group founded by Abbie Hoffman and Jerry Rubin in 1967; popularized the term *guerrilla theater.*

Young Lords: Anticapitalist Puerto Rican nationalist group.

Young Patriots: Predominantly White military left-wing organization that grew out of Students for a Democratic Society and focused on African American poverty.

CHARACTER GUIDE

* Composite character or fictitious name

Akil Al-Jundi: Attica inmate leader.

Jane Alpert: Melville Collective collaborator.

*Joe Anderson: FBI special agent, Intelligence Division.

L. D. Barkley: Attica uprising leader.

*Lester Barns: Melville Collective collaborator.

*Gilbert Bernstein: Melville Collective collaborator.

Herbert Blyden: Attica inmate leader.

H. Rap Brown: SNCC leader, author of *Die Nigger Die*.

*Henry Byers: FBI agent.

Roger "Champ" Champen: Attica inmate leader.

Richard Clark: Attica inmate leader.

John Cohen: Sam's good friend.

George "Prince Crazy" Demmerle: FBI informant.

Mike Deutsch: Attica Justice Committee attorney.

*Diane Eisner: A girlfriend of Sam.

Judge John Elfvin: Attica civil trial judge.

Elizabeth "Liz" Fink: Lead attorney for the Attica Brothers.

Sharon Fischer: Paralegal for the lawyers representing the Attica Brothers.

Bill Grossman: Sam's father.

Helene Grossman: Sam's stepmother.

Joe Heath: Attica Justice Committee lawyer.

Abbie Hoffman: Yippie cofounder.

David Hughey III: Melville Collective collaborator.

*Jill: Josh's girlfriend.

John Keats: Sam and Jane's dog.

Sharon Krebs: Melville Collective collaborator.

William "Bill" Kunstler: Radical attorney.

*Larry: Josh's FOIA attorney.

*Ivan Lopez: Puerto Rican radical collaborator.

John "Cement Head" Malone: New York FBI director, 1965–1972.

Vincent Mancusi: Warden of Attica.

Josh "Jocko" Melville: Son of Sam Melville.

Ruth Melville: Josh's mother, Sam's wife.

Sam Melville: Anti-imperialist radical.

George Metesky: New York's first Mad Bomber.

Robin Morgan: Feminist activist, friend of Jane Alpert.

Don Noble: Black Panther, Attica inmate leader.

Russell Oswald: New York State prison commissioner.

Robin Palmer: Melville Collective collaborator.

Pete Perrota: NYC police detective.

Nelson Rockefeller: Governor of New York State, 1959–1973.

Jerry "the Jew" Rosenberg: Attica inmate leader.

Jerry Rubin: Yippie leader.

Bobby Seale: Black Panther leader.

Albert Seedman: NYC police chief in charge of investigating subversive bombings.

Shawn: L. D. Barkley's son.

Jeff Shero: Editor of underground paper *Rat Subterranean News*.

Frank "Big Black" Smith: Attica inmate leader.

Wesley Swearingen: FBI agent.

Pat Swinton: Melville Collective collaborator.

Tim: Josh's stepfather.

Vincent Tobia: BCI inspector.

NOTES

Preface

"Sam Melville was the only": Martin Sostre to Sharon Fischer, August 4, 1973, author's collection.

"the essential blueprint": Bryan Burrough, *Days of Rage*, (New York: Penguin, 2016).

Introduction: My Giant

a metaphor for the American factory: This theory, embraced by the labor movement, was put forward by C. L. R. James in his book *Mariners, Renegades & Castaways: The Story of Herman Melville and the World We Live In* (orig. publ. 1953; Hanover, NH: Dartmouth College, 2001).

Vietnam would go on: November 1, 1955–April 30, 1975, nineteen and a half years. Kennedy maxed out the number of "advisers" at fifteen thousand before his death in 1963. Johnson expanded it into a full war in August 1964, drafting over thirty-five thousand men a month at its peak. Nixon withdrew completely in April 1975.

1. A Weatherman Appears in My Living Room

the Sam Melville Group: The actual name was the Sam Melville/Jonathan Jackson Unit. Members renamed themselves the United Freedom Front, but they became more famously known as the Ohio Seven when they were brought to trial. Between 1975 and 1984 the UFF carried out at least twenty bombings and nine bank robberies in the United States, adopting the Melville MO of targeting corporate and government institutions with "safe" explosions. FBI records described them as the most successful of the leftist bombing groups, in that they remained active and unapprehended for almost a decade.

"The Vietnam War is only": Alpert, *Growing Up Underground*, 224.

2. The Columbia Gateway Drug

Dialogue and thoughts in this chapter are sourced mostly from "Eisner," interviews; Palmer and Krebs, interviews; my mother; and partially my imagination.

"I'm here for the meeting": Demmerle's dialogue is imagined. "Eisner," Krebs, Skodnick, and Friedman, interviews.

"We're gonna dismantle": "Eisner," Krebs, and Palmer, interviews.

Donations flowed: In reality, Sharon Krebs was still with her husband Allen in 1965 when they founded the Free University of New York (FUNY/Alternate U) together. However, Sharon had, according to multiple sources, begun an affair with Robin Palmer simultaneously.

"Sounds more like a masturbator": "Eisner," Krebs, and Palmer, interviews.

"Marriage. Family. Debt.": Melville, *Letters from Attica*; "Eisner," interviews.

"Remember Iran in '53?": Sloman, *Steal This Dream*.

"my fifth arrest": Robin Palmer often mentioned his extensive arrest record. Some in the New Left considered arrests a right of passage. FBI, Palmer file.

The demonstration made headlines: In February 1967, the first sit-in at Columbia took place in Dodge Hall. Eighteen members of Students for a Democratic Society (SDS) protested CIA recruitment on campus. Other protests erupted opposing the university's submission of student data to Selective Service boards. University president Grayson Kirk issued a ban on campus demonstrations starting September 25, 1967. Skodnick, interview; Varon, *Bringing the War Home*, 25.

King had hated: David J. Garrow, "When Martin Luther King Came Out Against Vietnam," *New York Times*, April 4, 2017; Varon, *Bringing the War Home*, 35, 115.

"We will free Columbia": This quote is from a famous missive written by Mark Rudd. Varon, *Bringing the War Home*, 26.

Nonviolent became National: Stokely Carmichael stepped down as chair in May of that year. H. Rap Brown (later known as Jamil Abdullah Al-Amin) replaced him. Brown renamed the group the Student *National* Coordinating Committee and supported violence. In his book *Die Nigger Die*, Brown described violent uprisings as "American as cherry pie."

Brown gave the go signal: Skodnick, interview.

"anyone over thirty!": Activist Jack Weinberg is credited with coining the phrase in 1964 during an interview. Demmerle's repeating it here is imagined but typical of what he and other provocateurs reportedly said at rallies. Other references: US Senate Select Committee, *Supplementary Detailed Staff Reports*; Lee and Shlain, "Season of the Witch," chapter 9 in *Acid Dreams*, 173; Swearingen, interview.

"I'll give it a couple of meetings": Cohen, interview. My father left several activist groups, disappointed with their lack of action.

It felt like rape: In one of our taped interviews, my mother remembered that when she asked Sam why he got so radical, he told her that the police binding him that day "felt like rape."

3. Hoover's "Black Problem"

Almost all Demmerle and Anderson dialogue in this chapter is inspired by FBI files I received through the Freedom of Information Act (FOIA), articles in the underground press, and my interviews with Swearingen and other FBI agents who were active on the case. Other sources include Sloman, *Steal This Dream*; US Senate Select Committee, *Supplementary Detailed Staff Reports*; and Lee and Shlain, "Season of the Witch," 173.

"Our Nation": Churchill and Vander Wall, *COINTELPRO Papers*, 177.

"These kids": Demmerle quoted himself in an interview in *Rat Subterranean News*, June 5–19, 1970.

FUNY was becoming: *Rat Subterranean News*, June 5–19, 1970; Hewitt, *Political Violence*; Lee and Shlain, "Season of the Witch," 173; Swearingen, interview; and my interviews with other agents. Also, FBI, Demmerle file, section 3, serial 1; US Senate Select Committee, *Supplementary Detailed Staff Reports*.

During his first year: David Bonner, "Remembering George Demmerle: Portrait of a Police Informer," *CounterPunch*, October 1–15, 2008, https://www.unz.com/PDF /PERIODICAL/Counterpunch-2008oct01/6-8/; Friedman, Skodnick, and Palmer, interviews.

"The helmet is my crown": Demmerle quotes himself in a *Rat Subterranean News* interview, June 5–19, 1970; Lee and Shlain, "Season of the Witch," 173.

"a fundraiser for Huey Newton": Dr. Huey Percy Newton (February 17, 1942–August 22, 1989) was a political activist and revolutionary who, along with Bobby Seale, founded the Black Panther Party in 1966. Newton served six months for assault with a deadly weapon. Shortly after his release, Newton was pulled over by an Oakland Police Department officer. Newton shot and killed the officer with the officer's gun as they wrestled.

"We get undercovers to pledge the money": Lee and Shlain, "Season of the Witch," 173; FBI, Demmerle file; Friedman, interview; *Rat Subterranean News*, June 5–19, 1970.

He cornered Demmerle: Sloman, *Steal This Dream*; Hoffman, *The Best of Abbie Hoffman*; Friedman, interview.

Hoffman had Crazy George follow him: Sloman, *Steal This Dream*.

"I'm not Prince Crazy for nothin'": Sloman, *Steal This Dream*.

"You are to provoke": Churchill and Vander Wall, COINTELPRO Papers; Hewitt, Political Violence; Lee and Shlain, "Season of the Witch," 173; Swearingen, interview.

As police overreacted: Palmer, interview.

Around the corner: FBI, Demmerle file; FBI, Melville file.

"The prison uniform": Rubin, We Are Everywhere.

"It will make a great target": Dialogue invented based on interviews with Syska coworkers and his boss, names withheld.

It meant Sam was dropping out: Interview with Syska boss.

4. From Wall Street to Bleecker Street

"15 years means": Melville, Letters from Attica, 106 (April 2, 1970).

"A recent issue of Time magazine": Melville, Letters from Attica, 141 (April 1, 1971).

an AT&T retail outlet: In 1983, the DynaTAC 8000x was the first commercially available handheld mobile phone.

"'What's the crime of bombing a bank'": My father's question is adapted from Bertolt Brecht's The Threepenny Opera.

5. "He Left You His Eyes"

This chapter's dialogue and thoughts are the product of conversations with my mother and "Eisner," interviews.

a cinder had hit him: This story of how Sam lost his sight in one eye is anecdotal and has never been independently verified, but it's the way Sam often retold the story. North Tonawanda was the site of a large freight depot built by the Erie Railroad (now the site of a railroad museum), and Tonawanda was a center of manufacturing, railroads being the main means of shipping. Railroads ran on coal well into the 1950s, so Sam's cinder story is likely true.

6. Rogue

He repeatedly told his brother: Jack Hoffman and Dan Simon, Run Run Run: The Lives of Abbie Hoffman (New York: Tarcher/Putnam, 1994), 278.

Colonel Oliver North's secret plan: The Iran-Contra scandal began as an operation to free the seven American hostages held in Lebanon by Hezbollah. A faction of pro-US Iranians promised to free the hostages in exchange for arms shipments. Lieutenant Colonel North fell on his sword, claiming he supplied the Iranians with weapons without the president's authority.

9. The Collegiate and the Collective

Some facts in this chapter were originally sourced from Alpert, *Growing Up Underground*, but through the years I've corroborated or disproven most them through interviews with those close to these events, specifically, Palmer, Krebs, Cohen, and Swinton. The dialogue and thoughts are imagined based on those sources and my instincts about my father.

"from the pig media": *Pig media* was a common New Left term for the mainstream press, including the *New York Times*. My father considered all sources other than underground presses to be pig media.

parried with her academic résumé: "Eisner," Palmer, Krebs, and Swinton, interviews. Some information about Alpert in this section came from talks with Bruce Kawin, who knew Sam and Jane during this period.

They saw each other regularly: Events inspired by Alpert, *Growing Up Underground*. All dialogue is imagined.

Sam and Diane had found: In Alpert, *Growing Up Underground*, 127, Jane claims that Diane and Sam "rented the apartment' and then Sam invited Jane to join them. However, FBI records state clearly that the lease was in Jane Alpert's name.

"Yes," Sam agreed: Alpert, *Growing Up Underground*; Alpert, Swinton, Palmer, Hughey, and two anonymous sources, interviews.

He pushed back at Jane: This remark is invented based on my father's dry sarcasm.

"When the pigs caught up to us": Palmer, interview.

"some creative ideas": Dialogue in this scene is invented for exposition purposes.

The women are fools: Jane's thoughts here are based on her writings of the time.

"Why is someone like you": Alpert, *Growing Up Underground*, 140; Melville, *Letters from Attica*; Alpert, Krebs, Swinton, Hughey, and Palmer, interviews.

11. Canadian Terrorists?

Some facts in this chapter were originally sourced from Alpert, *Growing Up Underground*, but through the years I've corroborated or disproven most them through interviews with collective members and FBI agents Swearingen, "Byers," and a redacted source, in addition to FBI, Melville file, sections 6, 8, 9, and 19; FBI, Demmerle file, section 2; and Southern District of New York Court Filings *State of New York v. Samuel Joseph Melville* (case no. 1741-70) and *US v. Melville*. The dialogue and thoughts are imagined based on those sources and my understanding of my father.

over fifty-two attacks: Other targets were Westmount City Hall, the headquarters of the Canadian Imperial Bank of Commerce in Montreal, and the Bordeaux Railway Bridge. William Fong, *J.W. McConnell: Financier, Philanthropist, Patriot* (Montreal:

McGill-Queen's University Press, 2008), 573; Louis Fournier, *FLQ: The Anatomy of an Underground Movement* (Toronto: NC Press, 1984).

capturing the FLQ's leaders: Alain Allard and Pierre Charette, twenty-two and twenty-four years old, respectively. Others arrested were André Normand, Roger Normand, Jean Goulet, Jean Cloutier, Louis-Philippe Aubert, and Bernard Mataigne. FBI, Melville file.

Today, BOSSI: Viola, "Terrorism."

full time to helping the fugitives: Cross-referenced FBI files of Palmer and Demmerle.

smoked a joint with Abbie Hoffman: Hoffman never forgot Sam Melville, and after Sam's death Abbie seemed almost haunted by it. Hoffman's own brother confirmed this, writing that Abbie "felt sure that in prison he would be assassinated and had repeatedly stated that if he ended up in Attica he'd be killed just like Sam Melville." (Hoffman and Simon, *Run Run Run*, 278.) While underground in 1974, Hoffman tried to sublet an apartment from Jack Siemiatychi, who later recalled, "He wouldn't give out details of where he'd been, but he made a reference to Sam Melville, who had been killed at Attica, and said, 'If they catch me, I'll end up like Sam.'" By December 1979 Hoffman was thinking of turning himself in and held a "war council" of six friends, including Chicago Eight codefendant Dave Dellinger and movement lawyer Michael Kennedy. Hoffman "repeatedly stated that if he ended up in Attica he'd be killed just like Sam Melville." Marty Jezer, *Abbie Hoffman: American Rebel* (New Brunswick, NJ: Rutgers University Press, 1991), 262–263.

stories from the "guests": Conversations with collective members; FBI, Melville file, sections 6, 8, 9, and 19.

"Canada already has our share": Sam told this story to collective members. Corroborated by *State of New York v. Samuel Joseph Melville*.

launched a small investigation: Thomas Dowling was the SA assigned to expand the Melville file.

almost two dozen members of the Black Panther Party: The Panther Twenty-One case would ultimately be the longest, and the costliest, trial in New York City history up to that point. The press, public, and even jurors had come to believe that the undercover detectives who infiltrated the Panther inner circle were more guilty of breaking laws than the Panthers themselves. Every defendant was cleared of all charges, and the NYPD was the subject of tremendous criticism. The landmark *Handschu* class action lawsuit emerged immediately after the case concluded; it resulted in the dramatic restraint on NYPD undercover spying operations.

Rutgers sociology professor: "Lester" is based on information sourced from FBI, Melville file, and FBI, Palmer file; however his persona here has been significantly altered.

"George Metesky was here": Conversations with collective members; Alpert, *Growing Up Underground*, 170–171. Abbie Hoffman also did this. See earlier note in this chapter about Hoffman's memory of Sam.

13. *Rat* and the Masturbators

Some facts in this chapter were originally from Alpert, *Growing Up Underground*. I've corroborated or disproven most them through interviews with collective members; FBI Melville file, sections 6, 8, 9, and 19; and interviews with FBI agents, Swearingen, "Byers," and another FBI source that has been redacted. The dialogue and thoughts are imagined.

"Hey, Princess Janie": The "princess" comments directed at Jane are invented to build her character. However, it is worth noting that others in the collective described her to me this way. The nickname became so pervasive that on the masthead of *Rat Subterranean News*, she was listed as "Princess Jane." Her listing on the masthead became a key lead for the FBI.

"There is no individual change": Taken almost verbatim from one of my father's prison letters. Melville, *Letters from Attica*, March 21, 1971.

"There are enough people in SDS": This comes from the same March 21, 1971, prison letter mentioned in the prior note, but I retailored the line and attributed it to Dave Hughey in his voice for narrative purposes.

"That's a myth": In *Growing Up Underground*, Alpert claims it was she who found Explo by looking up "Explosives" in the Yellow Pages. I got hold of a 1971 Yellow Pages and could not find it. Pat and Robin both also had different recollections. Robin disagreed vehemently with Jane and claimed that there are different types of dynamite and "only Sam knew what type of stuff we needed."

Jane pouted: Swinton, interview.

integrate Rat into the movement: Historian Abe Peck claimed *Rat*'s coverage of the Columbia Uprising made it the "*New York Times* of the underground press."

McCartney had secretly died: According to Shero, *Rat* was the originator of the famous rumor regarding the death of McCartney.

Jane disabled this suspicion: Shero, interview.

Pat tried to calm her: Swinton, interview.

Diane refused: "Eisner," Swinton, and Alpert, interviews; Alpert, *Growing Up Underground*

"I was calling to speak with Jocko": Alpert's depiction of this scene in *Growing Up Underground* triggered my memory of the same incident from when I was a child. I put together the missing pieces by talking to my mother. The version here is an amalgam.

"I thought Rasta meant": Dialogue here is invented to help build "Lester's" character.

"Have you thought about universities?": This conversation is alluded to in *Growing Up Underground* in a general way and confirmed by my 1990 interview with Robin Palmer and 1988 interview with Sharon Krebs.

anti-Castro radical faction, Acción Cubana: Acción Cubana DOJ/FBI doc., http://nsarchive.gwu.edu/NSAEBB/NSAEBB157/19760629.pdf.

John grew ever more uncomfortable: Alpert and Cohen, interviews.

Sharon's introduction sounded more: Alpert, *Growing Up Underground*, 196.

"You have never heard": This line, like much of the dialogue and thoughts in this section, is based somewhat on the version of events in Alpert, *Growing Up Underground*, but reimagined through my interviews with Palmer, Cohen, and Krebs and my instincts about my father.

"Panthers are crawling": Several FBI reports I reviewed discussed undercover assets within the Black Panther Party. Alpert also has her version of "Gil" expressing similar sentiments in *Growing Up Underground*.

he met Gil on the stoop: Imagined dialogue in this section is based on Swinton and Hughey, interviews; FBI, Melville file, regarding the bomb materials; and *United States v. Melville*, 306 F. Supp. 124 (SDNY 1969) and *State of New York v. Melville*.

As the hour progressed, Sam realized: Hughey, Cohen, and Swinton, interviews; Alpert, *Growing Up Underground*, 198–199.

"If you want to be sexual": Adapted from Alpert, *Growing Up Underground*.

"The revolution ain't tomorrow": Adapted from Alpert, *Growing Up Underground*, 179. My father repeated versions of this to several I spoke with.

14. The FBI's Bomb Expert

"Mister, um . . . Melville?": Dialogue adjusted for narrative purposes. It is a composite of conversations that took place over several months with three ex-FBI agents: Swearingen, "Byers," and a third agent who worked on the Melville case and spoke under the condition that I keep the agent anonymous.

"He was denied one": Swearingen, interview.

"a time of a management turmoil": Swearingen, interview.

"Jane's book is almost a complete fiction": Direct quote from Swearingen, interview.

15. *BOOM!*

Some facts here are sourced from Alpert, *Growing Up Underground*, but through the years I've corroborated or disproven most them through interviews with Palmer, Krebs, Alpert, Swinton, Cohen, Hughey, and Swearingen; Seedman and Hellman, *Chief!*; Sullivan, *The Bureau*; Villano, *Brick Agent*; FBI, Melville file; FBI, Demmerle file; FBI, Palmer file; and *US v. Melville* and *State of New York v. Melville*. The dialogue and thoughts are imagined based on the foregoing and my instincts about my father.

"a big difference": Shero, interview.

Jane's piece: It was placed on the desk of SA Thomas Dowling. Anderson is a composite of several agents, including Dowling.

two thousand agents: The number is based on an internal FBI memo, although the exact figure is hard to confirm. It was common in 1969 to have hundreds of agents sifting through files for weeks to do the work that today would be accomplished with one desktop computer in seconds.

a single typo in Rat: FBI, Melville file, section 8.

no George Demmerle: Demmerle stayed in San Francisco to be debriefed on the Oakland conference. His discussion with Robin Palmer was omitted from his report but confirmed by my interviews with Palmer. FBI, Demmerle file.

Demmerle also told Robin: Exactly when Demmerle learned of the Melville Collective is key to assessing the FBI's efficiency. Jane Alpert's *Growing Up Underground* alludes to Palmer spilling the beans to Demmerle about stealing dynamite from Explo at the Oakland caucus to get Seale's permission to go ahead with a bombing. But FBI agents claimed at hearings that they didn't connect the Explo heist to the Melville Collective until a month later. If the FBI knew about the theft of the explosives in August but allowed them to be used in eight terror bombings shortly afterward, that would have embarrassed Hoover and damaged his credibility with Congress. Given the facts, it is likely that the FBI removed all mention of Palmer in Demmerle's report on Oakland after the collective's arrest (there is none in the version I received via FOIA), and that at my father's preliminary hearing, the FBI coached Demmerle to claim he didn't take Palmer seriously enough to include the disclosure in his report. That made *Demmerle* appear incompetent rather than a division of the FBI.

it played a notorious role: Varon, *Bringing the War Home*, 119.

"United Fruit would get a headline": Alpert, *Growing Up Underground*, 200–201.

She was referring to Pyronics: Alpert, *Growing Up Underground* discusses this bombing, which was never officially attributed to the collective. Other collective members confirmed it, as did an FBI internal document dated September 29, 1969, found in FBI, Melville file. The memo linked Pyronics, United Fruit, and the Federal Building to the dynamite stolen from Explo and used by "Cuban groups."

"let's join this revolution": Invented dialog based on Swinton, interview; Alpert, *Growing Up Underground*, 179.

"Cuban Independence Day is January 1": In *Growing Up Underground*, Alpert criticizes my father for getting this fact wrong. Ironically, Jane gets the name and date of the holiday wrong as well (p. 202).

morning radio carried a report: I could not get the actual WBAI transcript, so this version is imagined. The factual basis for the broadcast came from Alpert, *Growing Up Underground*, 202; *Rat Subterranean News*, August 27–September 9, 1969; and the *East Village Other*.

Pat has United Fruit stickers: Hughey, interview; Alpert, *Growing Up Underground*.

"The Times is a shit paper": Dialogue invented but inspired by Alpert, *Growing Up Underground*.

Shero warned her: Shero, interview.

Swearingen filed a report: Swearingen, interview. Wesley Swearingen also worked on the noted case of the attempted railroad bridge bombing in Daisy, Kentucky, where the defendants were represented by prominent New York lawyers.

After Kennedy's assassination: Wesley Swearingen and other retired FBI agents have written books alleging an FBI conspiracy to cover up the mob's involvement in the Kennedy assassination—that Chicago crime boss Sam Giancana was instrumental and that it was no coincidence that Giancana was murdered days before he was to testify.

his counterpart in the Intelligence Division: FBI departments and their roles referred to here came from Swearingen, interview; and FBI files, and are corroborated by Seedman and Hellman, *Chief!*; Sullivan, *The Bureau*; and Villano, *Brick Agent*.

Black bag jobs: Since evidence gathered via black bag jobs was illegal, virtually nothing produced by the Security Division could be used in court.

Tomorrow, he would hold: Alpert, interview; Alpert, *Growing Up Underground*, 202.

"The revolution is today": All of Demmerle's dialogue is sourced from interviews he's given to the press and FBI, Demmerle file. His tone and style comes from Palmer, Krebs, and Alpert, interviews; and Alpert, *Growing Up Underground*.

He recalled Jane telling him this: Alpert admits in *Growing Up Underground* that she told Demmerle she was covering the Panther's National Conference for *Rat Subterranean News* when they were broth in Oakland.

George thinks Rat's infiltrated: Demmerle's belief that *Rat* is being infiltrated is invented for narrative purposes but composited from Demmerle's FBI reports and my conversations with Palmer, who was a witness to this conversation.

"You said that I needed": Alpert, *Growing Up Underground*. The dialog in this scene is loosely adapted from Alpert's memoir and fit to the chronology of this narrative.

"They're not going to listen": Alpert, *Growing Up Underground*; extrapolated loosely and dialogue adapted to be more in line with my instincts about my father's style.

At 11 PM, an explosion: Lawrence Van Gelder, "Blast Rips Bank in Financial Area," *New York Times*, August 21, 1969.

"I'd be a pretty bougie Betty": Swinton interview. Other events and dialog in this section come from Alpert, *Growing Up Underground*; Palmer, interview; and Swinton's recapitulation of these events in my discussions with her.

"The explosive device": "Wall Street Bombing," *Rat Subterranean News*, August 27– September 9, 1969.

Swearingen stood in Malone's office: Swearingen, interview; FBI, Melville file, section 9.

collective completed a list of targets: Swinton, interview.

Sam called a rooftop meeting: Alpert, *Growing Up Underground*, 209.

17. . . . And Jane

Excerpts had been reprinted: *Ramparts*, December 1971, 45.

"I was very much pressured": "Mother Right" by Jane Alpert, 1974, *Ms.* magazine can be found here: http://library.duke.edu/rubenstein/scriptorium/wlm/mother/.

"before the Symbionese Liberation Army took Patty Hearst": Patricia Campbell "Patty" Hearst (born February 20, 1954) is the granddaughter of American publishing mogul William Randolph Hearst. She became known for her 1974 kidnapping by the Symbionese Liberation Army, which offered her return in exchange for $2 million worth of food to be distributed to the poor in the Bay Area. The distribution did not go well, and the SLA refused to release Hearst. During her capture, Hearst became supportive of the SLA, taking part in their illegal activities, including a bank robbery. Hearst was convicted of armed robbery and given a maximum sentence of thirty-five years but served only twenty-two months before her sentence was commuted by President Jimmy Carter. She ultimately received a full pardon from President Bill Clinton in 2001. Both Hearst's autobiography, *Every Secret Thing*, and Alpert's memoir came out the same year, 1981. Both Hearst and Alpert wrote of dominance and manipulation, psychologically and sexually, by the radical left.

18. An Explosion in Foley Square

Some facts in this chapter were originally sourced from Alpert, *Growing Up Underground* and Seedman and Hellman, *Chief!*, but through the years I've corroborated or disproven some of their assertions through new information and interviews with collective members, Swearingen, and another FBI source who spoke to me anonymously. Other facts about FBI investigations were influenced by Villano, *Brick Agent*; Hewitt, *Political Violence*; Donner, *Protectors of Privilege*; Sullivan, *The Bureau*; and FBI, Melville file, sections 6, 8, 9, and 19. Dialogue is composited for accessibility and narrative exposition.

"Army was the clear target": FBI, Melville file; Swearingen, interview.

His boss was livid: Swearingen, interview.

"The timers": Swearingen, interview; Seedman also admits in his memoir, *Chief!*, that he had a problem getting a handle on the perpetrators because of the lack of physical evidence left behind at the scene of any bombing.

the FBI had refused to respond: FBI, Melville file; Swearingen, interview.

Swearingen begged Malone: Swearingen, interview.

Malone ordered him: One of the agents on whom "Joe Anderson" is based would say under oath that he had not known the name Melville at this point. However he is either lying or very forgetful, because he signed off on FLQ reports that linked Melville to them a month before. FBI, Melville file, section 239. If he was lying, he would have good reason. It would wax incompetent for the FBI if the collective committed four more bombings when Melville was already well known to them.

he called Police Chief Albert Seedman: Seedman and Hellman, *Chief!*

two FBI agents dispatched by Anderson: The agents were Thomas Dowling and his partner (name redacted). FBI, Melville file.

"Don't you get it, baby?": Alpert, *Growing Up Underground*. The dialogue is paraphrased and embellished for drama.

"Tonight we bombed": Swinton and Hughey, interviews; "Bang? Boom!," *Rat Subterranean News*, October 29, 1969; "Whitehall St. Center Shuts its Doors" and "Inductions Shifted to Brooklyn After Blast at Manhattan Center," *New York Times*, October 9, 1969; Alpert, *Growing Up Underground*, 218–219.

multiple devices were placed: On September 24, bombs were planted at the Madison Wisconsin Federal Office and the ROTC building at the University of Wisconsin. Alpert touches on the Midwest events in her memoir, *Growing Up Underground*. I cross-referenced her version with Melville's FBI reports I got through FOIA and connected the dots to the version herein.

Among them was a bomb: Hewitt, *Political Violence*. In *Growing Up Underground*, Alpert connects Sam to Rap Brown and the Milwaukee and Chicago bombings. I confirmed that there might be a connection through my conversations with Palmer and another source close to Brown who wishes to remain anonymous. FBI reports show that the FBI was close to connecting Melville to Brown and Milwaukee, but internal FBI memos claim that their illegally gathered evidence could not be used in court, and what little legal evidence it had gathered fell short of proof.

two agents parked outside: FBI, Melville file.

"That was dumb, Sam!": Alpert, *Growing Up Underground*; dialogue invented.

NYPD finally took the FBI's suggestion: Seedman and Hellman, *Chief!*; Alpert, *Growing Up Underground*, 215.

20. It Was a Great Night for the Revolution

Some facts in this chapter were originally sourced from Alpert, *Growing Up Underground*; and Seedman and Hellman, *Chief!* But through the years I've corroborated or disproven some of their assertions through interviews with collective members; Swearingen, interview; and other sources: FBI, Melville file; Villano, *Brick Agent*; Hewitt, *Political Violence*; Donner, *Protectors of Privilege*; and Sullivan, *The Bureau*. Dialogue in this chapter is sourced from my interviews with Palmer, Krebs, Alpert, Hughey, Swinton, Swearingen, and an anonymous FBI source, as well as my imagination.

When she revealed her plan to Lester: This dialogue is invented to demonstrate Jane's frustration with the situation.

"My hair hasn't been long enough to braid": I have no actual knowledge of how long Jane's hair was when she was thirteen.

Within an hour they had sex: Palmer, interview.

she confided in an outsider: I have only circumstantial evidence for this composite scene. Jane claims to consult with Morgan many times in *Growing Up Underground* and in other writings. I stitched this version together by inferences from Alpert, *Growing Up Underground*; Morgan, *Demon Lover*; YouTube videos of Morgan; and several of my interviewees who alleged a "controlling relationship" Morgan had over Alpert. Morgan's own words and actions in the press shortly after these events took place also contributed.

Calling from a Milwaukee phone booth: Jane summarized this conversation in her memoir; Alpert, *Growing Up Underground*, 222.

the FBI had figured out: How Jane knew the FBI had connected Sam to the failed Chicago Civic Center bombing remains a mystery. The Bureau didn't leak that detail to the public until after this conversation took place. She could have made a lucky guess or had an inside tie to the investigation, but the fact that FBI had connected the bombings was initially revealed in Arthur Greenspan and Mike Pearl, "The Bombings: Evidence Indicates It's One Man," *New York Post*, November 12, 1969.

Sam made calls to half a dozen militants: Palmer, interview.

"I talked with a hundred losers": Demmerle dialogue is invented but based on cross-referenced FBI files.

hung up, and called Anderson: Demmerle's testimony and his handler's reports, FBI, Demmerle file.

Puerto Rican nationals organized by Ivan Lopez: This group become known in the coming months as Movimiento Independentista Revolucionario en Armas (Armed Revolutionary Independence Movement), or MIRA. It was allegedly responsible for dozens of attacks in both Puerto Rico and the US starting in 1970. Its real-life organizer was Carlos Feliciano, on whom "Ivan Lopez" is partially based. The FBI connected Feliciano to at least one attack starting in 1970. Several of my father's prison letters (May 28, June 6, and June 18, 1970) mentioned his association with Feliciano, whom he encountered in the Tombs. Information on Carlos Feliciano and MIRA obtained from Viola, "Terrorism," and Viola's forthcoming book on political violence and police intelligence in New York City; and from "Police Investigate Puerto Rican Unit in Bombings Here," *New York Times*, May 19, 1970.

Sensing the biggest arrest of the year: Viola, "Terrorism." The reality was more complex than the account presented here, since "Anderson" is a fictitious amalgam of several agents working the Melville case. Sharing information with counterparts was uncommon at the time due to office compartmentalization and competitiveness. In today's FBI this would not be the case, due in part to the Patriot Act.

Jane was nursing a funk: Alpert, *Growing Up Underground*; Krebs and Palmer, interviews. Dialogue based on known facts.

Demmerle opened his apartment door: This section, based on what Demmerle told Anderson on November 9, 1969, comes from the sworn testimony of Demmerle's handler. Oddly, there is no corresponding report in Demmerle's file.

"About thirty others": I believe the number thirty is embellished by Anderson to make it sound like a far more intricate conspiracy than what he knew it to be, thus rationalizing why it took four months and over three hundred FBI agents to capture four disaffected subversives that they had under surveillance for several weeks.

"Decoy?": Demmerle testified that my father confessed to him in this meeting that the decoy was to lure away law enforcement so he could bomb the Federal Courthouse at 100 Centre Street, where the Panther Twenty-One trial was taking place. But this hardly seems likely, since law enforcement did not deploy a single unit to the courthouse, and in fact the building was successfully bombed the next day. This is just one of many holes in Demmerle's testimony and probably part of a version that he was coached to say by his handlers.

Monday, November 10: Swinton, interview; Alpert, *Growing Up Underground*; and *New York Times*, "Bombs Exploded in Three Buildings," November 11, 1969. (Some minor facts in the *New York Times* article differ from this text, as *Times* changed facts for security purposes. The version herein conforms to FBI, Melville file.)

ribbon recovered by the NYPD: Though Jane admits to typing eight copies and sending them to various wire services in *Growing Up Underground* (p. 224) and the FBI claims to have recovered a ribbon, I was not able to confirm that a ribbon was ever presented in court as evidence.

Jane, Pat, and David gathered: Alpert, *Growing Up Underground*, 226, 227. Dialogue invented based on agreed-upon facts.

"Have you heard?!": Shero and anonymous *Rat Subterranean News* staffer, interviews.

Swearingen stood in front of Cement Head: Swearingen, interview.

did not waste a second signing: FBI, Melville file, section 239.

Jane met David at her place: All dialogue in this section is imagined based on allegations in Alpert, *Growing Up Underground*, and based on a progression of other agreed-upon facts.

"You should be careful": A longer version of this interaction was originally printed in *Letters from Attica*, as was a reprint of Sam's interrogation transcript in his FBI file. It's tweaked here slightly for exposition.

Byers had no previous knowledge: Swearingen, interview.

We're not supposed to present: Swearingen, interview.

The agents handcuffed Sam: FBI, Melville file; "Byers" and Swearingen, interviews.

21. Rewards for the Wicked

Most facts in this chapter are agreed upon and sourced from the *New York Times*, *New York Post*, and *Daily News*; FBI, Melville file; Varon, *Bringing the War Home*; New York State Attorney General's Office court filings; Alpert, *Growing Up Underground*; and Swearingen, Krebs, and Shero, interviews.

When the NYPD broke into McCurdy: FBI, Melville file, McCurdy inventory.

As for others in the collective: Alpert, *Growing Up Underground*, 209.

She convinced Jeff Shero: Krebs, interview.

a takeover of Rat: Shero, interview; *Rat Subterranean News*.

"It would be racist for me": Alpert, *Growing Up Underground*, 233; Palmer, interview.

the last of its national "war council" meetings: Palmer, interview; Varon, *Bringing the War Home*, 115.

In this volatile climate: Varon, *Bringing the War Home*, 180, 184, 190; Swearingen, interview; *State of New York v. Melville*; *US v. Melville*.

the same day as the massacre: The infamous Kent State shooting involved National Guardsmen gunning down four unarmed students protesting US involvement in the Vietnam War. Pop star Neil Young wrote the song "Ohio" describing the event.

He pled guilty: FBI, Melville file; *State of New York v. Samuel Joseph Melville*; *US v. Melville*.

David ultimately pled: Fischer, interview.

considering firing his lawyer, withdrawing his plea: John Cohen, introduction to *Letters from Attica* by Sam Melville, 144 (May 7, 1971).

"If I end up in prison": Hoffman and Simon, *Run Run Run*, 278. While underground in 1974, Hoffman tried to sublet an apartment from Jack Siemiatychi, who later recalled, "He wouldn't give out details of where he'd been, but he made a reference to Sam Melville, who had been killed at Attica, and said, 'If they catch me, I'll end up like Sam.'" By December 1979 Hoffman was thinking of turning himself in and held a "war council" of six friends, including Chicago Eight codefendant Dave Dellinger and movement lawyer Michael Kennedy. Hoffman "repeatedly stated that if he ended up in Attica he'd be killed just like Sam Melville." Jezer, *Abbie Hoffman*, 262–263.

key players managed to find ways: Swearingen, interview.

Hoover himself got a nice gift: Churchill and Vander Wall, *COINTELPRO Papers*; Lee and Shlain, *Acid Dreams*; US Senate Select Committee, *Supplementary Detailed Staff Reports*.

Demmerle tried to reintegrate himself: FBI, Demmerle file; Bonner, "Remembering George Demmerle," https://www.unz.com/PDF/PERIODICAL/Counterpunch -2008oct01/6-8/.

rumors alleged a brief affair: Palmer and Krebs, interviews.

Morrow paid Jane $25,000: Anecdotal. This was a typical advance from Morrow for similar books at the time.

22. Fink's Bag-o-Marbles

Five Company was a cell block: Liman, *Attica*, 118, 129.

The odds were 62,978 to 1: This outcome, for seven or more blues to be randomly picked in a selection of 29 from a total population of 40 blues and 1,241 reds, is expected to happen only 0.0016 percent of the time, which is just 1 out of every 62,978 occurrences. The mathematical expected value is that only 1 blue will be picked (0.9055... rounded up).

23. The Attica Brothers

three of whom had not even gone: During the assault, Mancusi was in his office, Pfeil was at home, Oswald was outside the prison, and Monahan, the National Guard officer who instructed troopers, was outside the gates.

conflicting reports by the Bureau of Criminal Investigation: On occasional 1990s episodes of the TV show *Law & Order*, you may have heard cops referring to the BCI. Aside from scant references, it's remained under the public radar for almost eight decades. Its Wikipedia page was deleted around 2009. By 2015 almost all information about the organization had been removed from the Internet. For a time some info could be found at the website New York Troopers History, http://nytroopershistory.com /BCI-Bureau-Criminal-Investigation212.php, but the site has since been discontinued. It contained a résumé of BCI achievements; Attica was not mentioned.

passed up the command chain: Conversations with Fink and 1991 court testimony

24. Uprising

Some facts in this chapter were originally sourced from Liman, *Attica*; Rosenberg, *Doing Life*; Wicker, *A Time to Die*; Coons, *Attica Diary*; Oswald, *Attica: My Story*; Strollo, *Four Long Days*; Clark, *Brothers of Attica*; Melville, *Letters from Attica*; and articles in *Newsweek* and the *New York Times*. However, assertions in those sources have been refuted or supported in this text based on my interviews with Blyden, Rosenberg, Fink, Fischer, Palmer, Richard Abbott (state pathologist), and others who were in D Yard on September 9–13, 1971. All dialogue is invented for narrative purposes but based on the progression of agreed-upon events.

Jerry Rosenberg awoke: Rosenberg, *Doing Life*, 196.

as a "swell guy": Coons, *Attica Diary*.

Just one week before the uprising: Cohen, interview; Melville, *Letters from Attica*.

My father ripped a fist: This incident with Sam besting Boyle is Attica lore, backed up by Coons, *Attica Diary*; Liman, *Attica*, 107, 152; William B. Coons, "An Attica Graduate Tells His Story," *New York Times Magazine*, October 10, 1971; and conversations I had with Rosenberg. Placing Blyden as a witness to the event is my narrative device, but his presence is highly probable, as are the chess pieces. Chess was a popular game in Attica.

"Cunningham. We've been waiting": Liman, *Attica*, 175; Oswald, *Attica: My Story*, 63.

nineteen minutes into the uprising: Liman, *Attica*; Oswald, *Attica: My Story*, 64.

The Muslims stood out: Liman, *Attica*, 48, 49, 107.

Clark shouted like a drill sergeant: Wicker, *A Time to Die*, 92

Clark snapped back: "We need these pigs! Ain't no use going to the chair over some White devil that ain't worth your spit!" is paraphrased from Clark, *Brothers of Attica*, 53. All other dialogue and the basis for this scene is paraphrased from Liman, *Attica*; and Al-Jundi, Rosenberg, and Blyden, interviews.

"I'm already in this shithole": Rosenberg shared this bit of humor with me a month before his death, but I believe it's also noted in Liman, *Attica*, in investigative testimony by hostages.

"Look around, man": The basis for this exchange comes from Clark, *Brothers of Attica*, 51–53, but the dialogue is original.

"We can't have no Koran-quoting motherfuckers": This dialogue is imagined; however, the basis for it comes from Fink, interview. In my last conversation with her about

a year before her death, she said, "You want to know the truth about what Attica was about? It was about *gangs*." Liman, *Attica*, 198; Oswald, *Attica: My Story*, 219.

Black assembled a regiment: Other Purple Bands were Eric Thompson (a.k.a. Jomo Omowale), William Maynard (who was in the Tombs with Sam), and Bernard Stroble (a.k.a. Shango). Fischer, interview; Liman, *Attica*, 198; Clark, *Brothers of Attica*, 58, 59, 60.

attempt to identify as "the ringleaders": Charges and sentences come from Oswald, *Attica: My Story*, appendix; however, these are not reliable. Getting sentencing stats from the New York penal system involved a great deal of red tape and privacy issues at the time of this writing. I relied on Oswald's book, combined with interviews with family and associates.

There were several others: Peter Butler and Skip Broome, Caucasian, unaffiliated; Frank Lott, thirty-eight, life for murder, Muslim; Flip Crowley, twenty-nine, nine years for drug possession, Muslim; Jomo (Eric Thompson) Omowale, thirty-one, twenty years for murder, Panther, Sunni Muslim; Bernard (Shango) Stroble, thirty-four, twenty years for murder, Muslim.

leaders began to work together: Rosenberg, interview; Liman, *Attica*; Oswald, *Attica: My Story*, 218–219.

Russell Oswald had finished walking: Oswald, *Attica: My Story*, 74–76; *Activity Report to Rockefeller*, April 1971.

"Muslims don't even believe": Rosenberg, interview.

His first recommendation to Oswald: Dialogue is paraphrased from Ed Koch, *All the Best: Letters from a Feisty Mayor* (New York: Simon & Schuster, 1990) and supported by comments in Oswald, *Attica: My Story*; and an interview I conducted with a former Koch aid.

it might have been forgotten: Historian Heather Ann Thompson claimed in her Pulitzer Prize–winning treatise *Blood in the Water* (New York: Pantheon, 2016), chapter 1, footnote 51, that Sam's letter was the spark of the uprising.

"Poder hermano!": Melville, *Letters from Attica*, 168.

"U r beautiful brothers!": Melville, *Letters from Attica*, 171.

Thursday, September 9: Liman, *Attica*, 176; Oswald, *Attica: My Story*, 53, 64.

26. Trouble at the Factory

Facts in this chapter were originally sourced from Liman, *Attica*; Rosenberg, *Doing Life*; Wicker, *A Time to Die*; Coons, *Attica Diary*; Oswald, *Attica: My Story*; Strollo, *Four Long Days*; Clark, *Brothers of Attica*; Melville, *Letters from Attica*. Many assertions in those books have been refuted or confirmed based on my interviews with Blyden, Rosenberg, Fink, Fischer, Palmer, Richard Abbott (state pathologist), and Paul Cambria, Tobia's law partner and friend. All dialogue is invented unless otherwise noted.

"Ed needs you at Attica": This scene and all dialogue of Tobia's is invented for narrative purposes from a reverse engineering of a logical progression of events based on established facts in previously mentioned sources.

joined his BCI unit and reported to Stillwell: Liman, *Attica*; Palmer, interview.

"Oswald is telling us": Oswald, *Attica: My Story* 88, 321.

Friday, September 10: Liman, *Attica*, 215.

Robin was anxious for intel: Palmer, interview.

"This is far worse than Auburn": Paraphrased from Oswald's comments to the press.

a small acoustic band: Rosenberg, *Doing Life*, 200.

"When the world sees this": When Blyden spoke with me in 1991, he used almost this exact phrase to describe the situation.

their TV image: Newsreel footage.

mounting accusations of his treachery: In his book *Attica: My Story* (pp. 86–87, 106), Oswald states that Sam Melville was "not to be seen at the table." But in news footage, my father can be seen standing right behind Barkley and directly in front of Oswald. My guess is that Oswald made the knowingly false claim so he could imply that Sam was fortifying defenses while negotiations were still at a workable point.

"More chefs in the kitchen": Clark, *Brothers of Attica*, 101–105.

"It's official now": This exchange between my father and Don Noble is inspired by 1991 interviews with Al-Jundi, Fischer, Rosenberg, and Fink.

27. "Their Throats Were Slashed"

"We are men": Barkley, taken from newsreel footage; supported by Rosenberg, *Doing Life*, 199.

"Dec. 21, 1991—Brother Herbert X. Blyden": The original note is in the author's collection.

28. Kunstler and the Observers

high-profile prisoner sympathizers: Liman, *Attica*.

"Tomorrow, there will be more of us": Not a direct quote, but similar wording was reported in Attica memoirs, (including Oswald, *Attica: My Story*, 243) and *Newsweek* coverage of the event.

"Bill, today I look up": Imagined response based on my father's letters and the general attitude of many in the yard.

"I hope we meet again.": Kunstler publicly claimed a scene like this took place. I embellished it to emphasize Sam's thoughts about the Observers and their agenda based on my interviews with Al-Jundi and Palmer and my instincts about my father.

29. Raiding Fink's Bunker

"What is it you're trying to learn": My initial taped interview with Akil Al-Jundi took place in 1989 in a Manhattan restaurant. This scene took place in December 1991 and was a follow-up.

30. September 13, 9:05 AM

Some facts in this chapter were originally sourced from Liman, *Attica*; Rosenberg, *Doing Life*; Wicker, *A Time to Die*; Coons, *Attica Diary*; Oswald, *Attica: My Story*; Strollo, *Four Long Days*; Clark, *Brothers of Attica*; Melville, *Letters from Attica*; and articles in *Newsweek* and the *New York Times*. However, assertions in those sources have been refuted or supported in this text based on my interviews with Blyden, Rosenberg, Fink, Fischer, Palmer, Richard Abbott (state pathologist), and others who were in D Yard on September 9–13, 1971. All dialogue is invented for narrative purposes but based on the progression of agreed-upon events.

The plan to retake the prison: Strollo, *Four Long Days*, 102.

"Two assault teams. Rubber bullets": Rubber bullets were first in use about a year before Attica, deployed by the British Ministry of Defence against the IRA.

Sam agreed: This exchange was extrapolated from my interviews with Rosenberg, Al-Jundi, Blyden, and Palmer, and statements in Clark's book *Brothers of Attica*; and Liman, *Attica*, 346.

roll a fifty-five-gallon oil drum: Palmer, interview; Liman, *Attica*, 346.

Sam cracked open the oil barrel: Palmer, interview.

nodded but started to hand out ladles: Several inmates testified that they didn't know what was in the bottles, but they knew that they wouldn't explode.

As Seale was being processed: This exchange among the Spokespersons, although imagined here, has been alluded to through Liman, *Attica*, and confirmed through testimony in civil trials. This is Rosenberg's version, which I learned during my interviews with him.

It was not merely one death: Stewart Dan was the reporter. Kenneth Hess, Barry Jay Schwartz, and Michael "Crazy Micky" Privitera were executed by inmates. Fischer, interview.

in his defining moment Seale addressed: This is speculation by me and the press, but it rings true based on my conversations with several who were close to the events, including Rosenberg and Al-Jundi.

"Amnesty, amnesty!": Wicker, *Time to Die*; Oswald, *Attica: My Story*, 114.

As the remaining Observers passed him: There is some dispute as to which Observer Sam gave this note. Jones was my best guess given my resources.

"Power to the people!": This is a shortened version. The complete version can be found in the introduction to the new edition of Melville, *Letters from Attica* (Chicago: Chicago Review Press, 2022). See also Oswald, *Attica: My Story*, 113.

sang the song he'd written for me: Although this scene is obviously poetic license, the unicorn song is real. His words give so much insight into his character that I felt it deserved a place here.

Blyden gathered in the tunnel: Clark, *Brothers of Attica*. This exchange among the Spokespersons has been confirmed through testimony in civil trials. This is Rosenberg's version, which I learned during my interviews with him, capped by the "We mean business" quote from *Brothers of Attica*. However, it should be noted that Clark glosses over this meeting of the key Spokespersons in *Brothers*, mentioning only vague conversation with some on pp. 118–120. Since the book was published in 1973, his attorneys might have been concerned about still-lingering charges.

"We are MEN!": Wicker, *A Time to Die*, 90.

"We do not want to rule": Rosenberg, *Doing Life*, 199. This statement has been time-shifted for dramatic continuity. It was actually made by Barkley on September 10 or 11, not September 13 as depicted here.

Clark and Noble suggested: Try as I did, no one I interviewed seemed to want to take responsibility for the idea of decentralizing of the hostages, nor would anyone say at whose direction the idea was executed. I choose for this depiction Clark, because he had the military background to fathom the idea, and Noble, because he was the most outspoken Purple Band. However, I have little doubt that my father, due to his radical guerrilla résumé and the fact that he was the ad hoc general in charge of defense, was also consulted.

At the front gate, 470 troopers: Liman, *Attica*, 344–362; Oswald, *Attica: My Story*, 81.

The helicopter appeared: Liman, *Attica*, 352.

"Holy shit, they're here": Palmer, interview.

33. Beautiful Things

When I interviewed Tobia's good friend: Paul Cambria, interview.

"Sam Melville was the only": Sostre to Sharon Fischer, August 4, 1973. A copy is in the author's collection.

SOURCES AND
INTERVIEW SUBJECTS

Attica Experts/Witnesses

Richard Abbott
Akil Al-Jundi
Herbert Blyden
Michael Deutsch
Elizabeth Fink
Sharon Fischer
Joe Heath
Jerry Rosenberg
Ellen Yacknin

Radicals and Radical Lawyers/Experts

Karima Al-Amin
Jane Alpert
David Bonner
John Cohen
Lew Friedman
Barbara Hanshoe
Tom Hayden
David Hughey
Liz Gains
Bill Krane
Sharon Krebs
William Kunstler

Robin Palmer
Mark Rudd
Jeffrey Shero
Pat Swinton
Jeremy Varon
Cathy Wilkerson

Sam's Friends

Ollie David
"Diane Eisner" (two separate sources who make up the composite character
    by this name)
Herb Gerstein
Ruth Melville
Phil Narolanski
Sharon Rosenberg
Mort Silverman
Roy Skodnick
Barbara Spielberg

FBI/Law Enforcement

"Henry Byers" (pseudonym for the agent who was my father's interrogator)
Paul Cambria
Wesley Swearingen (includes both extensive taped and e-mail interviews and
    redacted chapters from his memoir *FBI Secrets* about his work on the
    Melville case)

SELECTED
BIBLIOGRAPHY

Alpert, Jane. *Growing Up Underground.* 1st ed. New York: Morrow, 1981.

Bell, Malcolm. *The Attica Turkey Shoot: Carnage, Cover-Up, and the Pursuit of Justice.* New York: Skyhorse, 2017.

Churchill, Ward, and Jim Vander Wall. *The COINTELPRO Papers: Documents for the FBI's Secret Wars Against Dissent in the United States.* Boston: South End Press, 1990.

Clark, Richard X. *Brothers of Attica.* New York: Putnam, 1974.

Coons, William R. *Attica Diary.* New York: Stein and Day, 1972.

Donner, Frank. *Protectors of Privilege: Red Squads and Police Repression in Urban America.* Berkeley: University of California Press, 1992.

Federal Bureau of Investigation. George Demmerle file. FOIPA no. 1319364-0.

———. Richard "Robin" Palmer file. File no. 59162622.

———. Samuel Joseph Melville file. FOIPA no. 1315776-0. File no. 52-91969.

Hewitt, Christopher. *Political Violence and Terrorism in America: A Chronology.* Santa Barbara, CA: Praeger, 2005.

Hoffman, Abbie. *The Best of Abbie Hoffman: Selections from "Revolution for the Hell of It," "Woodstock Nation," "Steal This Book," and "New Writings."* New York: Da Capo Press, 1994.

Jones, Thai. *A Radical Line: From the Labor Movement to the Weather Underground, One Family's Century of Conscience.* Washington, DC: Free Press, 2004.

Lee, Martin A., and Bruce Shlain. *Acid Dreams: The Complete Social History of LSD; The CIA, the Sixties, and Beyond.* New York: Grove Press, 1994.

Liman, Arthur. *Attica: The Official Report of the New York State Special Commission on Attica.* New York: Praeger, 1972. A summary of the McKay report.

Melville, Samuel. *Letters from Attica.* 1st ed. New York: William Morrow, 1972.

Morgan, Robin. *The Demon Lover: The Roots of Terrorism.* New York: Simon & Schuster, 2000.

Oswald, Russell G. *Attica: My Story*. New York: Doubleday, 1972.

Rosenberg, Jerry. *Doing Life*. New York: St. Martin's/Marek, 1982.

Rubin, Jerry. *We Are Everywhere*. New York: HarperCollins, 1971.

Schott, Joseph L. *No Left Turns: The FBI in Peace & War*. Santa Barbara, CA: Praeger, 1975.

Seedman, Albert A., and Peter Hellman. *Chief!: Classic Cases from the Files of the Chief of Detectives*. New York: Arthur Fields Books, 1974.

Sloman, Larry. *Steal This Dream: Abbie Hoffman and the Countercultural Revolution in America*. New York: Doubleday, 1998.

Strollo, Anthony R. *Four Long Days: Return to Attica, September 9–13, 1971*. Hurley, NY: American Life Associates, 1994.

Sullivan, William C. *The Bureau: My Thirty Years in Hoover's FBI*. New York: Norton, 1979.

Swearingen, M. Wesley. *FBI Secrets: An Agent's Exposé*. Boston: South End Press, 1995.

US Senate Select Committee to Study Governmental Operations with Respect to Intelligence Activities. *Final Report*. Book 3, *Supplementary Detailed Staff Reports on Intelligence Activities and the Rights of Americans*. Washington, DC: US Government Printing Office, 1976.

Varon, Jeremy Peter. *Bringing the War Home: The Weather Underground, the Red Army Faction, and Revolutionary Violence in the Sixties and Seventies*. Berkeley: University of California Press, 2004.

Villano, Anthony. *Brick Agent: Inside the Mafia for the FBI*. New York: Quadrangle, 1977.

Viola, David. "Terrorism and the Response to Terrorism in New York City During the Long Sixties." PhD diss., CUNY, 2017.

Wicker, Tom. *A Time to Die: The Attica Prison Revolt*. New York: Quadrangle, 1975.